Where the Aunts Are

Where the Aunts Are
Family, Feminism, and Kinship in Popular Culture

Patricia J. Sotirin
&
Laura L. Ellingson

BAYLOR UNIVERSITY PRESS

Cover design by Matt Roeser

The images from *The Andy Griffith Show*, *Raising Helen*, *Bewitched*, and *Auntie Mame* are courtesy of Photofest.
"I Ain't Yr Mama" is used by permission of the artist Opal Palmer Adisa.

Library of Congress Cataloging-in-Publication Data

Sotirin, Patricia J.
  Where the aunts are : family, feminism, and kinship in popular culture / Patricia J. Sotirin and Laura L. Ellingson.
 254 p. cm.
  Includes bibliographical references and index.
  ISBN 978-1-60258-330-6 (hbk. : alk. paper)
1. Aunts. 2. Families in mass media. 3. Women in mass media. 4. Women in popular culture. I. Ellingson, Laura L. II. Title.
  HQ759.94.S68 2013
  306.87—dc23
                                2012028959

Printed in the United States of America on acid-free paper with a minimum of 30% post-consumer waste recycled content.

For my father
　　—PJS

For Glenn
　　—LLE

CONTENTS

ACKNOWLEDGMENTS

The authors extend their heartfelt thanks—as always—to our feminist colleagues in the Organization for the Study of Communication, Language, and Gender (http://www.osclg.org) for their tremendous encouragement and inspiration throughout this project. To the Ethnogs and the FemNogs, we say: Rock on (and thanks)!

The first author wishes to thank Jennifer Slack, Vicky Bergvall, and Diane Shoos for their unflagging enthusiasm and helpful comments. Thanks as well to my students and colleagues in the Department of Humanities and the editorial staff of *Women & Language*. I am deeply grateful for longtime friendships: Barbara, Cathy, Susan, Linda, and Suzanne. My own aunts and uncles continue to inspire my work on aunts: Tess, Stacia, Pat, and Stan, and most especially my Uncle Sam. For the honor of being their aunt, thanks to my nieces and nephews: Kale (and Lee), Neko, Andrea, Paige, John, and my great-nephew Malakai. For love, generosity, and time away, I am truly grateful to my siblings: Barbie, Paula, Chris (and Scott), and Rob (and Jill). My most heartfelt gratitude in this and all my endeavors is due my children: Elena (and Kelly), Tara (Eli and Alan), Tavis, and Zakris. My work as always is dedicated to my father, Paul; he and Lorraine are my most staunch supporters. Finally, I wish to remember with love my late mother; she would have enjoyed this book.

The second author offers her thanks to Amy Shachter, Don Dodson, and Diane Jonte-Pace in the SCU Provost's Office, and Dean Atom Yee for their financial support of my research. Warm thanks to the members of the SCU Women's and Gender Studies Program, the Communication Department, and the Women's Faculty Group for their freely shared insights, support, and chocolate! Hugs to my many scholar-friends in the field of communication, particularly those whose creativity and brilliance inspire me to do my best work (in addition to my coauthor, of course!): Patrice Buzzanell, Carolyn Ellis, Lainey Jenks, and Lynn Harter.

My deepest appreciation to my family, my parents Jane and Larry, Jim, Brigitte, Zachory, Jamie, Mark, Diane, Miette, Eric, Elizabeth, Sam, Nina, Dennis, Becca, Barbara, Janice, Paul, Alan, Steve, Marissa, Matt, and especially my chosen-sister Genni. For her empathy and fabulous text messages, I thank Beloved Auntie Joan. I couldn't work without the support and friendship of my feisty and fabulous early morning crew—Kim, Sarah, Pauline, Connie, Gail, Alison, Robin, Casey, and, yes—Pat and Barbara, too!! Matt, Mary, Lisa, and Tully were also a great source of encouragement and a lot of fun, as were Westley, Buttercup, and Murray.

I offer tremendous gratitude to my partner Glenn Ellingson, a man of great patience, brilliance, and love. In our case, "I couldn't have done it without you" isn't simply a cliché; it's the truth.

In closing, we are both very grateful to have worked with wonderful people in publishing this book. Our thanks to Kristian Borofka for diligently compiling bibliographic materials despite sometimes minimal cues and to Elisabeth Wolfe for her careful indexing. It has been our pleasure to work with the team at Baylor University Press, especially Jordan Rowan Fannin, editorial assistant and copy editor extraordinaire, Jenny Hunt, associate production manager and good-natured problem solver, and Carrie Watterson, for amazing line editing. As always, we end on a note of sincere thanks to our tall and handsome editor Carey Newman for his wisdom and patience. He has remained undaunted and encouraging throughout our adventures in aunting.

WHAT'S UP WITH AUNTS?

The aunt is a familiar, often well-loved, and sometimes notorious character in popular narratives about family, femininity, and kinship: maternal Aunt Bee from *The Andy Griffith Show*, matriarchal Aunt Vivian from *The Fresh Prince of Bel-Air*, malevolent Aunt Petunia in the Harry Potter books and movies, breakfast icon Aunt Jemima, eccentric Auntie Mame, and the magical aunts who instruct *Sabrina, the Teenage Witch*, to name a few. Well-loved aunts are not always well behaved, and, while their small transgressions do not make them feminist revolutionaries, we believe that these intriguing female characters deserve critical attention. Accordingly, this book is a feminist "aunting" foray against the force of conventional ideologies about femininity, mothering, family, and domestic life in popular media narratives. We will examine how popular aunt characters afford us both critical insights into the limits of prevailing cultural norms and hopeful re-visions of gendered justice in everyday life.

After all, we live in a postfeminist culture, a culture where many people believe we have achieved equality and self-determination for all women, regardless of race, class, or sexuality. Yet we labor under impossible ideals of perfect motherhood, the cultural pathologization of single womanhood, intersecting oppressions based in sex, race,

1

class, and other social and material differences, and social and legal discrimination against families that cannot enact the nuclear family norm. Our popular culture landscape is dominated by neotraditional gender ideologies that call women back to inequitable roles and ambitions in the name of individual empowerment, romantic love, and the inevitability of maternal urges. These ideologies are especially visible in the ubiquitous domestic narratives available across popular entertainment media, including television, film, websites, popular fiction books, and even marketing images.

In many of these narratives, aunts play secondary but vital roles seemingly as complicit characters in the conventional stories of family life. Seen from one angle, aunts in recent mainstream popular culture are conservative characters. However, from a critical feminist perspective, these same figures are surprisingly unconventional and progressive—they surreptitiously transgress the cultural norms with which they seemingly comply. In other words, aunts prove to be "double agents" in popular narratives about family, femininity, and culture because, while they conform, they also subtly call into question social and cultural conventions and ideologies.

This "double agent" status requires a feminist "re-visioning."[1] Our analysis focuses on aunt characters in mainstream media because these figures imaginatively "embody" the aunt in stereotypic, readily recognizable, and broadly familiar performances that offer a visible and accessible focus for feminist critique. But we are critical of the ways their narrative performances reproduce what have been called "postfeminist" discourses of femininity, choice, individualism, and the end of feminism. Nonetheless, we have faith in popular culture aunts as perceptive guides to alternative ways of understanding and doing gendered lives: these figures inspire us to recognize multiple possibilities for feminine identity and domestic life. Given ongoing public discussions over glass ceilings and wage inequities, violence against women, changing family configurations,[2] women's reproductive rights, alternative arrangements and sexualities in marriage and parenting,[3] and the fate of feminism,[4] it is timely to offer a hopeful, progressive, and concrete feminist re-vision of women's possibilities in the guise of a familiar family figure: the aunt. The figure of the aunt in popular culture provides us with productive sites—even political rallying points—for advancing social justice.

Here's why: the aunt may exceed or transgress normative feminine roles—an aunt character can be more maternal than the mother or a living enactment of everything the mother forbids; she may be a witch, hysteric, seductress, or eccentric. Each of these figures offers a readily apparent narrative of feminine identity and empowerment and a model of extended family relationships set within specific historical and cultural contexts. Each is embroiled in the tensions, contradictions, and struggles that riddle lived experiences of identity, family, domesticity, and community. Each is engaged in the question motivating the narratives characterizing "women's culture": How do we overcome everyday trials and personal disappointments (in life under patriarchy) to realize a good life (complete with husband, children, and home)?[5] For the most part, the narratives offer widely accepted, familiar, and readily consumable answers. We acknowledge that there is pleasure in the very conventionality of such narratives. But we think that there are loose ends inviting us to see things differently. Many of these loose ends seem to fray around the figure of the aunt.

A few caveats are in order before we begin. First, we highlight aunt characters that have enjoyed broad popularity in recent mainstream, commercial, media-saturated U.S. culture. Please be forewarned that our selection of aunt characters is not meant to be exhaustive. If we have left out your favorite aunt character, we invite you to add her. We also do not mean to distill from this sample the features of an ideal aunt archetype. As we will show, it is the variability in cultural scripts for aunts and aunting that make this character ripe for feminist revision. Finally, we do not claim to speak for fans of the texts we critique nor do we wish to imply that popular media consumers in general endorse or share our interpretations.[6] While we are ourselves fans of many of these texts, we admittedly offer a far-from-mainstream perspective. At the same time, we hope that our interpretations invite readers to recast popular aunt figures as points of juncture where divergent cultural meanings and practices concerning women, kinship, and feminism are played out, albeit not always overtly or by explicit intention.

The alternative renderings of aunts we offer are creative and hopeful and reflect a commitment to feminist critique and intervention. Yet any such commitments must address the contemporary postfeminist perception that feminism in itself is no longer necessary and even detrimental to the status and ongoing progress of women.[7] In some ways, the aunt figures we discuss contribute to the ongoing popular rejection of feminism as a political, intellectual, and sociocultural force. Accordingly, the alternative readings we offer are in themselves feminist forays into cultural politics.

WHAT'S THE MATTER WITH POSTFEMINISM?

Postfeminism is not one ideological perspective or discourse but a web of dominant cultural themes and logics, normative forces, and institutionalized practices regulating and reproduced in the meaningful conduct of gendered lives.[8] The pervasive but diffuse nature of postfeminism constitutes "a powerful and versatile cultural presence."[9] Further, postfeminism is *post*-feminist, not only implying a chronological progression in which feminism has been eclipsed but a shift in popular consciousness that moves against and beyond feminist perspectives. Although there is no definitive description of postfeminism, the term is used to describe texts and activities "that appear to advance feminist interests despite their concurrent participation in and perpetuation of oppressive structures."[10] Hence, in the dominant popular perception, feminism is to blame for crises of identity, intimacy, family, and sexuality, and a myriad of social issues.

At the same time, postfeminism rehabilitates aspects of women's experiences critiqued by feminism into elements of women's empowerment and possibilities; for example, the commercialization of "girl power" undermines feminist arguments about the complexities of girls' lives by celebrating empowerment through consumption, urging girls to reclaim traditional norms of femininity, and advocating neotraditional ambitions like heterosexual romance and marriage.[11] Not surprisingly, feminists have described in detail how postfeminism depoliticizes feminist agendas and agencies.[12] Further, along with dissipating the collective social force of feminism, postfeminist appeals often affirm the privileging of white, heterosexual, and elitist perspectives and assumptions.[13] For example, the kind of sexual empowerment enjoyed by the four women characters in the popular television and movie franchise *Sex and the City* incorporates privileges of race, class, and heteronormativity. The neotraditional, depoliticizing, and essentialist tendencies of postfeminist cultural themes and logics seriously confound, weaken, and even dismantle feminist challenges to social discrimination and oppression. It is in this context that we draw attention to the quiet transgressions of popular aunts.

HERE COME THE AUNTS

The aunt's history as a character in popular culture is a fairly short one.[14] While almost everyone can tell a story about their aunt or a story about their own experience as an aunt, there is surprisingly little evidence of aunts in popular narratives until the eighteenth century.[15] A close examination of novels from that time reveals the pervasiveness of strong aunts mothering orphaned children, especially girls.[16] This aunting character appeared thanks to the increasing prevalence of an ideology of maternalism even as mothers' rights were being dismissed legally, economically, and socially. While motherhood became sentimentalized as a woman's crowning achievement, mothering as woman's primary role became increasingly restrictive, equated with private life and domesticity, and mothers' claims to property and children were dismissed in favor of male heirs and guardians. In literary fiction of the time, this contrary maternal idealization/disempowerment was represented in a popular narrative theme about orphaned children. Enter the powerful, wise, but unconventional aunt who became the orphans' caretaker. These aunts added a "female energy to the text" and served as "placeholders in the novel for a kind of maternal power."[17] By the second half of the eighteenth century, this aunt character was a standard plot device arguably because there was a need to retain but constrict a strong female character in keeping with the cultural and political revisions of women's power and place.[18]

It was in the eighteenth and nineteenth centuries that aunthood emerged with a literary flourish and many of the stereotypes we continue to hold were introduced over the course of the next two hundred years: spinster aunts, maternal aunts, hapless aunts, eccentric aunts, loving and beloved aunts, "bad, sad, and mad" aunts.[19] It has been said that the "Victorian era was the aunt's finest hour" not only because these characters proliferated in popular genres but also because they were drawn both as gender pioneers in a restrictive era and as reminders of childhood who were treated with sentimentalized affection.[20]

The maternal aunt is well represented in American narratives written in the late nineteenth and early twentieth centuries: Mark Twain's Tom Sawyer and his Aunt Polly, Rebecca of Sunnybrook Farm and her stern aunts Miranda and Jane, Dorothy Gale and her Auntie Em in *The Wizard of Oz* (all of which were also made into films). As family historians have documented, the American experience of immigration and westward migration entailed a heavy demand on family resources such as extended kin, maternal substitutes, and unconventional women—roles often filled by aunts. Yet by the turn of and throughout the twentieth century, popular aunts in print, theater, and children's fare were frequently portrayed less as kin enabling family life and more as farcical twists in the family tree: aunts were cast as dotty, ludicrously pretentious, pompous, absurdly prim and unmarried, or stingy and old. In part, larger changes may have framed the aunt's disparagement. Between 1900 and 1950 a shift occurred in the governance of familial relations. An instrumental focus on resources for survival was supplanted by a psychological focus on inner life and selves, accompanied by the entrenchment of a conception of the nuclear family as a haven.[21] Given such cultural reimaginings of the family, the aunt's role became less critical as a family resource or a helpmate. At the same time, the disciplining force of farcical portrayals, set in the context of the struggles over women's rights and roles at the turn of the twentieth century, suggests the denigration of a powerful female presence.

We are drawn to the contrary characterizations of the aunt as a popular culture figure over the past few hundred years. The aunt has been portrayed as both powerful and weak, wise and dotty, lustful and prim, socially liberated and constricted. This rich legacy carries over to aunts in popular culture today.

Fast Forward to Today's Aunts and Aunting

"Now, at the beginning of a new millennium, the great age of the aunt is over," intoned one observer recently.[22] We beg to differ. The turn of the twenty-first century has seen a renewed interest in the aunt. Several celebrations of the cultural, familial, and personal significance of aunts have appeared in trade publications.[23] One popular tribute, *Aunties: Our Older, Cooler, Wiser Friends*,[24] asserts that aunts are unheralded cultural resources whose contributions to childrearing, family support, self-development, and kinship are invaluable. In *Aunties: Thirty-Five Writers Celebrate Their Other Mothers*, aunts are depicted as nurturing, independent, eccentric, exemplary, and strong.[25] Several websites ostensibly created by and promoting aunts have emerged, such as savvyauntie.com and crazyauntpurl.com. The website savvyauntie.com proclaims itself as "the first community for cool aunts, great aunts, godmothers, and all women who love kids."[26] The video trailer for the corresponding book features young children proclaiming their love for their aunties.[27] All evidence points to aunts as "cool."[28]

Moving beyond popular celebrations, recent scholarship attests to the significance of aunting in contemporary extended kin practices.[29] One book-length study finds that among the most important contributions of aunts and uncles is their emotional and often material investment in generativity, that is, the cross-generational continuity of family traditions, identities, and beliefs.[30] Another study examines the burdens and rewards of undertaking custodial care of nieces and nephews by black aunts.[31]

Our own research argues for the importance of the cultural, social, and interpersonal practices performed by those who act as aunts, whether in biological/legal families or in voluntary or chosen kin relationships.[32] In *Aunting: Cultural Practices That Sustain Family and Community Life*, we frame aunting as something that people *do* rather than something that people *are*, that is, a fixed role.[33] Further, we found tremendous variety in aunting practices, which included substantial caregiving or minor and sporadic visits; material, spiritual, and emotional support; friendship, direct mentoring, or unintended role modeling; generativity; and a sense of kin connection, even with little face-to-face interaction in some cases. Based on our analyses, we suggest that aunting offers a repertoire of cultural practices characterized by relational flexibility and responsive variations that has broad applications for intergenerational relationships whether in the family, education, or the workplace.[34] We hold that aunting is especially significant given the challenges of family life today, including the decline in real income, the lack of affordable child care, elder care, and health care, and mobility and migration patterns. Aunting appears to contribute in significant and acknowledged ways to the resilience and adaptability of families and communities.

The contemporary significance of aunting is informed by changing (and often embattled) conceptions of kinship and family over the late twentieth and early twenty-first centuries. Specifically, the idea that kinship relationships are based on family lineage, whether by blood or marriage, has been challenged by those who argue that kinship is a cultural construction that can take many forms.[35] Similarly, scholars argue for more inclusive conceptions of the family even as popular debates over the dominance of the nuclear family have become more vociferous. We find in such emergent reconfigurations an invitation to rethink the aunt figure in popular cultural imagination.

Rerunning the Aunt

The popular aunts we discuss are not bound to any particular popular medium—we consider aunts in popular books (*Travels with My Aunt*), films (*Raising Helen*), on the Internet (Savvy Auntie), and on television (*The Andy Griffith Show*). This mix of mediated texts acknowledges that the contemporary media consumer experiences popular culture in a synergistic environment that is not focused on one medium but that creates an " 'echo chamber' of repetition and reinforcement."[36] For example, postfeminist themes and logics echo across the range of media texts that include popular aunt figures. For this reason, it is important to take note of the proliferation and convergence of popular media forms.

Many of the aunt narratives that we examine originated in books that have been adapted for film or television.[37] Books remain an important popular medium, despite the profusion of visual media. The popularity of e-books and devices such as the Kindle, Nook, and iPad provide consumers access to free downloads of classic novels, as well as an ever-expanding pool of millions of published books. Moreover, some evidence points to consumer choices being shaped by the relative anonymity provided by e-readers; that is, no one can tell whether you are reading a bodice-ripper or an international thriller rather than a Pulitzer Prize winner or the latest professional treatise.[38] Choices are also being shaped by social media that enable (and require) authors to converse with their audiences.[39] Meanwhile popular books, typically fiction but also nonfiction (e.g., *Marley and Me*), frequently become movies or even cross over into television, particular on premium channels, such as HBO's adaptation of the Sookie Stackhouse book series into the popular TV series *True Blood*. Such crossovers may have increased, rather than decreased, sales of books, as audiences discover ways in which the stories connect and diverge across media and online fan forums debate such details, further circulating these narratives across popular culture media.

Along with print formats, most of the popular aunts we consider can be accessed through rebroadcasts: as syndicated reruns on television, online, or as movie rebroadcasts. Rebroadcasting enables viewers to indulge their idiosyncratic preferences across channels and media. A viewer accessing rebroadcasted material might see a classic movie like *The Wizard of Oz*, a television series rerun from *The Andy Griffith Show*, an episode from a current TV series such as *Tyler Perry's House of Payne*, or the most recent Harry Potter movie. Further, movies and television shows can be viewed digitally on a variety of platforms—not only the channels devoted to reruns like TV Land, Me-TV, and Nick at Nite or to syndicated programming like The CW[40] but also the heritage websites devoted to past television fare like tvland.com, iloveoldtvshows.com, and hulu.com. In addition, both television series and movies can be rented through services like Netflix or watched on demand through cable or satellite services, purchased in boxed sets or single DVDs, or viewed online on channel or program websites.[41] Thanks to rebroadcasting in its various forms, the aunt characters in past programs and movies remain vivid in the contemporary cultural imagination, always available thanks to the televisual "regime of mediated repetition."[42]

However, our concern is not with rebroadcasting per se but with the way this synergy shapes popular nostalgia and contributes to the appeal of visions of domestic life and gendered relations that idealize, dehistoricize, and caricature lived relations or that denigrate or repress alternative possibilities.[43] We focus particularly on ways that such visions can affirm neotraditional postfeminist gender ideologies. Along with feminist cultural theorists and media critics, we worry that, for young women especially, the postfeminist promise of "having it all" (career, family, economic stability, physical well-being) is informed by a "mixture of nostalgic longing and progressive faith in a brighter future" that is often contrary to feminist sensibilities and political commitments.[44]

INTERPRETING POPULAR AUNTS

We take as a starting point for our own practices of critical feminist interpretation the commitment to a situated point of view that takes up a text "first of all as a clue to how we live, how we have been living, how we have been led to imagine ourselves, how our language has trapped as well as liberated us, and how we can begin to see—and therefore live—afresh."[45] We adapt this call for feminist re-visioning as a basis for critically exploring the complex linkages and resonances among diverse elements—meanings, values, practices, institutions, material conditions—that frame popular aunts as simultaneously regressive and transgressive.[46] This means that our interpretations focus on three areas of concern: first, the implications of postfeminist discourses for women's lived choices; second, the intersection of postfeminism and dominant cultural discourses of family, kinship, and gendered identities; and, third, the distinctions among postfeminist appeals and a feminist agenda of social justice and gender constructionism.

The poststructuralist feminist approach we employ is not monolithic, and we weave together two methodological strands: one emphasizes the critique of dominant cultural ideologies, particularly those of gender and sexuality, while the other adopts an ironic feminist perspective. One strategy of critique is to challenge dichotomies, that is, to show the normative force implicit in such gendered binaries as male/female, masculine/feminine, rational/emotional, order/clutter, where one side is valued over the other.[47] The goal is to contest the taken-for-granted appeal of these constructions and to show that they offer only one of many possible ways to understand gendered selves and ways of relating. Thus, feminist poststructuralist analysis opens up a "discursive space" so as to enable a diversity of ways of thinking, being, and acting.

Feminist irony draws on a poststructuralist commitment to the discursive struggle over meaning.[48] Irony is best known as a humorous juxtaposition of literal and intended meanings or an exaggerated disjuncture between what is expected and what actually unfolds. Ironies challenge the claims about experience and subjectivity in dominant ideologies by highlighting inconsistencies and contradictions and by positioning those who laugh (or grin wryly) as complicit in such textual subversions. Ironies abound in postfeminist prescriptions, and we call attention to these ironies as a strategy for challenging their commonsensical appeal and normative force.

Finally, we do not tap audience interpretations per se. Instead, we parse texts for the subjects whose experiences they describe. In poststructuralism, no single audience can authenticate the interpretation of a social text, because interpretation is open, situated, and partisan. Thus, it is critical to note our own situated identities as white, heterosexual, and middle-class academics. In addition, our differences matter: one of us is a single mother, the other chose not to be a mother. And our embodied experiences situate us differently: for one of us, issues of ableism are part of daily experience, while, for the other, it is issues of ageism. So our views do not come from "nowhere" but make sense in the context of our experiences and identities. In this regard, we recognize ourselves, our lives and situations, as those to whom these texts speak. There is a sense of irony in this recognition that serves our feminist critique well because it affords us a "doubleness of perspective" in that we find ourselves caught between incompatible subject positions.[49] Our analyses depend on such a doubleness thanks to the tensions between our own insinuation within these texts as middle-class white women immersed in and responsive to postfeminist culture and our critical sensibilities as feminist scholars. Throughout our discussion of these strategies, we tap our own ambivalence as subjects of postfeminist discourses. Uncomfortably ambivalent positions are useful because they open spaces for provisional identities and affiliations, for remaining on the move among possible interpretations, and for attending to the specificities and differences within any*thing*—ideas, identities, material objects—that we may take as solid, coherent, and straightforward.[50]

THE PROMISE OF AUNTS

Our focus in this book is not on popular media per se but on how transgressive aspects of aunts in mainstream popular culture can energize feminist agendas for social change. Aunts may seem to be minor figures in popular domestic narratives, too peripheral to justify the feminist ambitions of this project. Yet we argue for taking popular aunts seriously. In critiquing mainstream representations, we draw attention to what is at stake in accepting the implicit analogies that link the aunt to cultural ideals of mothering and the family and failing to engage the conservative politics that often accompany such associations. We see three ways in which aunts offer transgressive and progressive counterpoints to postfeminist appeals.

First, aunts transgress the myth of the loving, self-sacrificing mother and the ideal of the natural, nuclear family and afford an alternative relational perspective on how families can be enacted and valued. Performances of aunting in mainstream popular culture transgress normative constraints to articulate progressive visions of families of choice, a reinvention of feminine kinship, and a revaluation of caring and caregiving, both economically and culturally. Thus, the presence of aunts in popular imagination forces a crack in hegemonic conceptualizations of family relations. We urge feminists to exploit and enlarge these fissures by embracing the aunt as a rallying point for affirming nonnuclear relationships as valid modes of family life.

Second, because aunting is not as explicitly defined or disciplined as mothering in contemporary culture, popular culture performances of aunts offer more critical latitude for questioning the appeals of postfeminist discourses. After all, postfeminist logics make women's choices and actions (stay single or get married, have children or remain child free, work or stay home, etc.) central to resolving difficult social problems such as economic disparities, work and family balance, and educational stratifications.[51] Aunts in popular culture embody post-feminist choices and solutions to the pernicious frustrations, dissatis-factions, disadvantages, discriminations, and oppressions in women's lives. The transgressions we identify recontextualize and repoliticize the issues involved.

Finally, the transgressions in mainstream popular performances of aunts invite critical recognition that cultural images have political significance. The contradictions of this figure implicate larger socio-cultural tensions and debates. Even as secondary characters, popular aunts invoke pernicious assumptions about women's essential mater-nality, racialized hierarchies and stigmas, institutionalized sanctions against gender deviance, and the coercion of heteronormativity. By considering the assumptions that make any particular popular aunt fig-ure sensible and familiar, we confront the politics of taken-for-granted understandings and practices. In this sense, the aunts who circulate through popular culture become much less benign and yet much more significant as sites for feminist critique and re-vision.

Aunts may be minor characters in popular domestic narratives, but these figures can be read as transgressing normative sanctions about who women are, how domesticity works, and what counts as family. We have found popular aunts to be the basis for rich counternarra-tives that decry taken-for-granted gender disparities and offer feminist re-visions of the issues complicating everyday life.

(Not) Like a Mother

Black and White Maternal Aunts

"My aunt is like a mother to me." In this chapter, we explore this commonplace analogy between the aunt and the mother. Both real-world descriptions and popular culture depictions promote this analogy between the aunt and the mother. The aunt as maternal caretaker with primary responsibility for her nieces and nephews is a familiar figure on the popular culture scene. Consider Auntie Em in *The Wizard of Oz*, Dorothy's maternal caretaker and her anchor to home throughout her Oz adventures. Or Aunt Bee of the television series *The Andy Griffith Show*, the maternal caretaker for Andy and his TV son in the fictional town of Mayberry.

Yet an underlying opposition troubles this connection between aunting and mothering: the aunt is like a mother *but not a mother*.[1] In popular culture narratives, this inherent opposition—"not a mother"— is often overpowered by a "maternalist" ideology centered around the conviction that women are maternal by nature. From this view, it is little wonder that the aunt is like a mother; after all, the aunt is compelled by her nature as a woman to be motherly with her nieces and nephews. Ideals of mothering, the mother-child relationship, and even family stability come to apply to aunting and aunts as well as to mothering and mothers. Yet once we begin to question these associations and explore how the aunt is *not* like a mother, useful differences emerge that give us much broader, more inclusive, and sometimes troubling conceptions of mothering, kinship, family, domesticity, femininity, and community. Importantly, these differences counter the emphasis in postfeminism on women's choices to either "have it all" (career, family, and intimacy) or find ultimate fulfillment in heterosexual intimacy and motherhood.

Our explication begins with an archetypal figure of the maternal aunt: Aunt Bee on the classic sitcom *The Andy Griffith Show*[2] because she was one of the first television sitcom aunts to gain a lasting hold on public memory.[3] This figure links aunting explicitly to the white, middle-class, and historically recent cultural ideal of the mother as the selfless and loving center of the family.[4] We then set the ideal maternal aunt within the racialized discourses that have shaped contemporary popular narratives. We contend that the maternal aunts of black domestic situation comedies enact a postfeminist construction of pernicious stereotypes of the black lady (respectable, middle class), the matriarch, and the strong black woman and reinforce the hegemonic value of nuclear family stability.[5] Our point throughout is that the popular maternal aunt—whether black or white—is "like a mother" in ways that re-enforce dominant and often oppressive gendered, classed, and racialized visions of intimacy, family, and kinship. However, each of these characters transgresses in small but powerful ways the cultural ideals of mothering and mothers, transgressions that productively link popular maternal aunts to feminist visions for progressive change.

AUNT BEE: THE SELFLESS, LOVING, MATERNAL AUNT

The Andy Griffith series debuted in 1960 and aired for eight seasons, making it one of the most popular family sitcoms of the sixties.[6] Since then, the show's popularity in reruns and on the Internet[7] cast it as part of our American television heritage, the cultural (re)production of shared memories, histories, and meanings that constitute what is commonly taken to be the American experience,[8] in this case, the nostalgia for small-town "traditional" family life centered around the nuclear family and anchored in selfless maternal care.

The links between the aunt as mother, the nuclear family, and cultural nostalgia for a sanitized version of American small-town life are starkly evident across the episodes of *The Andy Griffith Show* that centrally feature Aunt Bee (about 55 out of 249 original shows). Aunt Bee mothers both her widowed nephew, Sheriff Andy Taylor, and his son, Opie, in the absence of a wife and mother. Aunt Bee was introduced into the Griffith bachelor household in the premiere episode "The New Housekeeper."[9] The plot centers on Opie's resistance to her and his eventual acceptance based on his realization of *her* need to care for him and his father and their need for maternal love and housekeeping order. Given that the show casts her as the maternal center of the Taylor family, she affirms the promise of the nuclear family as a source of nurture, resilience, and strength, offering cultural reassurance that the bosom of the family is larger than the biological mother (a reassurance physically embodied in the plump, matronly dowdiness of actress Frances Bavier).

Figure 1.1: The maternal aunt exemplar: Aunt Bee at the breakfast table with her nephew Andy and his son Opie (from The Andy Griffith Show, *1960–1968). Shown are Ron Howard as Opie Taylor, Andy Griffith as Andy Taylor, and Frances Bavier as Aunt Bee.*

This reassuring image of the patriarchal nuclear family is enhanced by the sitcom's depiction of Mayberry as a small, unsullied Southern town where family remains at the center of social and community life, an image deeply rooted in popular imagination. Mayberry's formulaic depiction of small-town life plays out a cultural fantasy not only of the rural pastoral but of the desirability of this uniquely American way of life, inviting a recommitment to the "imagined community" of the American nation-state.[10] As the mother figure in this scenario, Aunt Bee soothes cultural anxieties over loss, absence, and instability—of the mother, of the home, of community, and of intimacy. The aunt as mother is in the home, the home is in the heart of America, and all is well.[11]

Transgressing the Maternal Ideal

In spite of the assurances of the maternal aunt figure, Aunt Bee transgresses this depiction of idealized American family life in subtle ways that invite us to critically examine this representation of the maternal aunt and her place in the family. First, her presence unsettles the insularity and stability of the nuclear family. By standing in for the deceased mother, Aunt Bee marks an absence in the familial triangle, creating a dynamic imbalance that unsettles assumptions even as it affirms the value of the mother and the ideal family. In addition, Aunt Bee belies the cultural promise of feminine fulfillment in marriage, home, and family. Several episodes revolve around Aunt Bee's need to be needed, her ongoing insecurity about her place in Andy's home and affections, and the patriarchal relationship between Andy as provider/protector and Aunt Bee as domestic/dependent.[12] For example, in the episode "Andy and Opie, Housekeepers," Andy and Opie deliberately mess up their home so that Aunt Bee will feel needed when she returns from a trip.[13] In "The Bed Jacket," Andy fails to realize that Aunt Bee had her heart set on an atypically extravagant birthday gift and gives her something functional. She cries in disappointment upon opening the gift. Andy ends up selling his favorite fishing pole to buy the gift she had hoped for.[14] The point is that Aunt Bee exhibits considerable anxiety over her place in the male Taylors' home and hearts.

We are not implying that Aunt Bee is secretly a subversive figure; certainly this character can easily be understood in terms of the dominant narratives of feminine dependency, masculine agency, patriarchal domesticity, and heteronormativity and hence effectively recuperated. After all, Aunt Bee appears to deny some central feminist tenets in her unreflective acceptance of an older woman's asexual, caretaking role: that the personal is political, that domesticity can be oppressive, and that maternality is an ambivalent experience. At the same time, however, her ongoing anxieties about her place as a homemaker, her relationships as a caregiver, and her own desires as a woman call attention to the emotional costs and the gendered inequities of caretaking that continue, despite progressive efforts over the past several decades to restructure familial relations.[15] It is Aunt Bee's vulnerabilities and dissatisfactions that invite our feminist visions of economic restructuring and families of choice inspired by the figure of the aunt.

We set Bee's anxieties in the context of the exploitation of women's caring labor. Aunt Bee's "spinster aunt" arrangement with her nephew—exchanging care for (white, middle-class) economic and emotional security—casts her as a "prisoner of love" whose emotional investment in caring labor binds her to the domestic sphere and reframes her contributions as maternal love and as an innate maternal need to be a caregiver.[16] Yet the maternal aunt, like other care providers who take on emotional commitments along with their caretaking responsibilities, is disadvantaged in both intimate relationships and economic realities. Loving care is both highly prized and poorly compensated.

Against the cultural ideal of self-sacrificing care, Aunt Bee's uneasiness and vulnerability resonate with the exploitation of caring labor in contemporary U.S. society. Feminists argue that it is time to redistribute the responsibilities for care more equally across stratifications of gender, class, and race and to encourage familial relations and public policies that provide reasonable economic as well as social rewards for quality care.[17] Indeed, there are calls for a "caring labor" movement encompassing workers, providers, consumers, and policy makers in order to rectify the gap between the value of and compensation for caring labor.[18] Rearticulating Aunt Bee's spinster bargain to a feminist critique of the economics of care might cast Bee as a political rallying point for such a revaluation of caring labor.

In addition, while the Taylor family appears quite conventional—even a paragon of natural (heterosexual, middle-class, Christian) family values—it is not.[19] Aunt Bee and Andy as parenting partners fulfill neither the procreative imperative of the nuclear family nor the sexual monogamy required in conservative, Christian family mandates. This exclusionary and restrictive vision of the family enjoys both mythic status and political currency in American cultural politics.[20] Conservative doctrine holds that the heterosexual marriage with (biological) children is the nuclear core of the family and the primal and sovereign political and economic basis of American life, dedicated to procreation, the accumulation of private property, autonomous parental control, and an innately gendered division of roles and capacities (women as first and foremost "wives, homemakers, and mothers" and men as "husbands, homebuilders, and fathers").[21] Such a doctrine demands that the natural, nuclear family be the structuring principle of kinship and communities as well as national economic and political programs and policies.

Counter to this doctrinal view of the nuclear family, the Taylors enact an asexual, nonprocreative model of family life based on extended kin relations and emotional commitments of choice rather than on institutionalized sexual and marital relations. In the course of the series, Aunt Bee dates a number of eligible men while Andy has a steady girlfriend. These dating relationships transgress the emotional self-sufficiency and sexual monogamy of the natural family ideal and in effect model a more open family arrangement, one the Taylors seem to prefer. In one episode, "Wedding Bells for Aunt Bee," Bee invents a fiancé so that Andy will feel free to marry.[22] Instead, he forgoes the opportunity to enter into a potentially procreative marriage in favor of the alternative family arrangement and mutual commitments he shares with Bee. In episodes such as this and across the series more generally, an asexual parenting partnership between Bee and Andy is foregrounded, implicitly extolling voluntary families of choice.

Our point is that the quiet transgressions of Aunt Bee's partnership with Andy are sympathetic to feminist calls for a more self-reflexive, inclusive, nonessentialized and progressive understanding of family and social life,[23] an understanding that promotes diverse, responsive, and creative models of kin and care. Feminists have offered cogent arguments for the normalization of gay and lesbian families, warning against the intolerance, prejudice, and disrespect of conservative mandates and public policies that denigrate and disadvantage unconventional family arrangements and relationships because such repressive models of family life diminish the creativity and diversity of social life overall.[24] Joined to this concern, the maternal aunt offers a rallying point for recognizing and reclaiming nonnuclear familial relationships, extended kin-care arrangements, and same-sex and nonprocreative parenting partnerships as valid social forms.

MATERNAL BLACK AUNTS: POSTFEMINIST AND POSTRACIAL MATRIARCHAL LADIES[25]

While we have argued for transgressions that link Aunt Bee to significant feminist concerns about and alternative models of kin and family, there is a critical "present absence" in her television portrait: race.[26] Race is both present and absent in the unmarked whiteness of Mayberry's characters and in the invisibility of black characters, black culture, or the history of black and white relations in the South.[27] This absence sets the ideal maternal aunt figure within the racialized discursive formation that has shaped the popular narratives of family and kinship occupying commercial television situation comedies in the U.S. over the past fifty years. Aunt Bee's whiteness is part of the complex of femininity, domesticity, home, and hospitality that makes up a collective fantasy of Southern life, invisibly but deeply etched by racial segregation and stratification.[28] An equally potent "postracial" fantasy about race relations, black family life, and black womanhood is evident in the character of the black maternal aunt appearing in the black sitcoms that proliferated from the 1970s to the 2000s.[29] These sitcoms combined (albeit uneasily) the legacy of the civil rights demand for difference, equity, and authenticity with an assimilationist ideology and the commodification or marketing of blackness in popular culture.

Race on television underwent a dramatic shift in the early 1970s when *Andy Griffith* and several popular spin-offs known as hillbilly sitcoms were cancelled despite their ongoing popularity.[30] These shows were replaced by a new spate of programs responding to prevailing perceptions that prime time television lacked both quality and relevance coupled with a desire to appeal to a young urban viewing population.[31] These included *All in the Family* (1971–1979), *Good Times* (1974–1979), *The Jeffersons* (1975–1985), and *Sanford and Son* (1972–1977), each developed by producer Norman Lear's Tandem/TAT Productions, which became synonymous with sitcoms focused on issues of social relevance situated at the juncture of race and domesticity.[32]

The logic of representation in these shows held 1970s "relevance television" to a politics of authenticity—"keeping it real"—often reduced to an essentialist argument over whether a representation of raced experience was "black enough."[33] Authenticity is a political claim, asserting both the cultural value of blackness as a sign of difference and the difference between blackness and hegemonic whiteness. Critics and fans alike participated in arguments over what could be taken as signs of authentic blackness—dreadlocks? vernacular speech? ghetto origins?—and signs of "selling out"—"white" speech? middle-class tastes? living in the burbs? The value of blackness gained cultural currency, leading to what has been called the commodification of blackness, that is, divorcing signs of blackness from the contexts (social, political, historical) of their production in order to circulate and profit from them within the cultural economy.[34]

These contestations over blackness were evident in television programming during the last decades of the twentieth century. The stereotypic representations of black difference in the 1970s "ghetto" sitcoms were dramatically countered by the highly successful *Cosby Show* (1984–1992) featuring a black middle-class family living a culturally normative, enviably harmonious, stable, and economically secure life. *The Cosby Show* enjoyed a transracial popularity that proved the market viability of black sitcoms.[35] Critics have argued that *Cosby* was based in "enlightened racism" promoting an assimilationist ideology.[36] At the same time, aspects of black culture and aesthetics began to gain prominence in popular culture, particularly in the music industry with the popularity of rap and hip-hop. During the 1990s, commercial television aggressively marketed blackness as a consumable sign, whether of (hip, urban, cool) lifestyle, identity, history, or material products.[37] A proliferation of black sitcoms accompanied this strategy, most of which featured stereotypic black characters, many drawing on racist caricatures. This leads us to explore the specific ways that postfeminist and postracial sensibilities are evident in the domestic comedies featuring black maternal aunts.

We highlight four sitcoms featuring maternal aunts in order to explore how this figure brings together postracial and postfeminist elements, the legacies of black slavery and black class status, and attendant images of black womanhood. These shows originally aired between 1990 and 2011: *The Fresh Prince of Bel-Air* (1990–1996), *The Jamie Foxx Show* (1996–2001), *The Bernie Mac Show* (2001–2006), and *Tyler Perry's House of Payne* (2006–2012). All involve ensemble casts depicting family life centered around male comedians—Will Smith, Jamie Foxx, Bernie Mac, and Tyler Perry[38]—and all of these shows were created and produced by black production teams.[39] All depict a pluralist, multiracial vision of social life marked by harmony and opportunity.[40] Across these shows, allusions to black culture— rap, hip-hop, jazz, blues, African-inspired dress, Southern food, black entertainers making celebrity appearances, and the like—assert representational claims to "keeping it real" while deferring the political, economic, and social inequities that inform both the history and contemporary conditions of African American life.[41]

Both of the shows produced in the 1990s, *The Fresh Prince of Bel-Air* and *The Jamie Foxx Show*, focus on exaggerated representations of young, virile black men who leave a ghetto upbringing and move in with a higher-class aunt and uncle, bringing with them identifying markers of black authenticity, namely, ghetto savvy, popular black musical forms like hip-hop and rap, and "cool" black masculinity combined with traditional stereotypes like black buck magnetism, coon jive, and buffoonery. The other two shows, produced in the 2000s, *Bernie Mac* and *House of Payne*, are "dramedies" mixing exaggerated, crassly racialized comedic "neominstrel" elements with dramatic elements ostensibly dealing with contemporary African American issues, notably drug addiction, criminality, unemployment, and family tensions.[42] For example, in *Bernie Mac*, Bernie and Aunt

Wanda take in his drug-addicted sister's three children. In *House of Payne*, an extended family deals with a young mother's drug addiction, a son's chronic unemployment, and a troubled foster child.

Each of these shows in its own way advanced the dominant "postracial" sensibility of the millennial decade that civil rights racial antagonisms have been "taken into account." Illustratively, Bernie Mac asserts his racial differences from his Encino neighbors as black cultural performances, not as social challenges, while the Paynes deal with "black" issues without overtly addressing racial inequities and institutionalized discrimination.[43] In these sitcoms, the characters' ongoing troubles are presented as personal issues that inevitably require family love and Christian faith but not social action. There is little representation of cross-racial tensions or explicit engagement with the politics of race.[44] Instead, race is the subject of cultural allusions and "black history lessons."[45] All four shows mute the politics of these issues with updated black stereotypes and narratives, enacting "keeping it real" as a depoliticized claim to racial authenticity with transracial market appeal.[46] Not only do these shows participate in the commodification of blackness in the post-*Cosby* sitcom era; they also adopt the "enlightened sexism" of postfeminist discourses—the acceptance of a retrograde sexism under the auspices of irony and a sense that feminism went too far in pushing against women's oppressions.[47]

Importantly, all four shows feature a maternal aunt figure whose characterization complicates the simple analogy "the aunt is like a mother" with difficult cultural associations of black womanhood and mothering. These sitcom aunt figures demonstrate the tenacity of racial stereotypes repackaged in postracial and postfeminist sensibilities. Yet we contend that the black maternal aunt also points to complexities beyond raced and gendered stereotypes and oppressive legacies. Cast as the family's moral, cultural, and spiritual anchor, she nonetheless remains an ambivalent figure who transgresses the sitcom narrative's ready assurances that issues affecting the black family and community can be resolved in a thirty-minute episode.

At first glance, the maternal aunt character seems too narratively subordinate to carry the significance we attribute to her. In all four shows, she is merely a supporting character in the cast and in the series' narratives. Nonetheless, she is without exception the center of a nuclear family and extended family relations, a partner in a solid marital relationship, and a primary source of moral, social, and material support for her family, particularly her (celebrity) nephew. These attractive middle-aged women are strong willed, assertive, well dressed, and career oriented. Aunt Vivian Banks in *Fresh Prince* is a college professor married to and the equal of her husband, a judge. Aunt Helen King in *The Jamie Foxx Show* owns and manages the King's Towers hotel and manages her gambling husband and errant nephew Jamie as well. Aunt Wanda in *The Bernie Mac Show* is an exceptionally attractive AT&T executive married to a stand-up comedian who is the one at home with the kids. Aunt Ella Payne in *House of Payne* is a staunch Christian who asserts matriarchal discipline over her buffoonish husband Curtis and her ever-expanding extended family. These maternal aunt characters are depicted in terms drawn from postfeminist discourses: they are successful as mothers (always first) and in their careers, they are not afraid to express their (hetero)sexuality within the limits of middle-class norms of decorum, and they enjoy a materially comfortable consumerist lifestyle.

These postfeminist depictions of the maternal aunt facilitate the recuperation of two stereotypes of black womanhood: the black matriarch and the black lady. We admit that the success with which the black sitcom aunt refigures the denigrating associations of these stereotypes is partial and ambivalent, always a matter of how attributes of class, race, and sexuality are configured within particular narratives. These sitcom portrayals are accountable to cultural associations, particularly the negative legacies of these stereotypes that are deeply embedded in cultural memory. For example, while negative legacies of black motherhood abound—the mammy, the crack mother, the mad black woman[48]—the notoriety of the matriarch was fixed in the U.S. mainstream cultural imagination thanks to the infamous 1965 Moynihan Report, a federal analysis of the black family that blamed urban lower-class black mothers for instituting the female-headed, dysfunctional, and impoverished black ghetto family and emasculating black men.[49] Even those in the black community who admire the matriarch cast this figure as intimidating or "fierce."[50] Thus, the black maternal sitcom aunt draws on tenacious and problematic cultural and social legacies as a black matriarch.

At the same time, the negative images of the black matriarch are overshadowed by another contrasting image linked to race respectability, social status, and class sensibilities: the black lady. The black lady image is just as deeply embedded in cultural imagination as the "moral icon" of the race, embodying and upholding African American respectability.[51] The black lady image was refigured in the context of the postracial sensibilities of the 1990s, as middle-class status shifted from a sign of race betrayal to an acceptable representation of black mobility and status ambitions.[52]

The Cosby Show's Clair Huxtable epitomized this postfeminist, postracial refiguration: the mother of four children, a successful lawyer, the sexually attractive wife and partner of a professional black man, this characterization countered the stereotype of the emasculating black matriarch while reinforcing the moral and class status of the black lady and the strong black woman (a stereotypic image in itself).[53] Though not a maternal aunt herself, the character of Clair Huxtable established a paradigmatic postfeminist model for the black maternal aunt.[54] In focus groups with black viewers, Means Coleman (2000) learned that women viewers found the Clair Huxtable character to be a positive role model even as these viewers recognized and often resented the demeaning stereotypes portrayed in most black sitcoms.[55] Little wonder that Aunt Vivian Banks in *The Fresh Prince of Bel Air*, a show that appeared just after the *Cosby Show* ended, was seen as a similarly admirable maternal character modeled on Clair Huxtable.[56]

Admittedly, the aunt characters we are discussing remain narratively underdeveloped, often cast in terms of clichés rather than complexities (although one might argue that this is in part due to the nature of the sitcom genre itself).[57] They are rarely shown outside the home, tying them to domestic life despite their careerism.[58] Further, while their husbands and nephews grant them deference, these maternal aunts are rarely the narrative focus of these shows, suggesting once more that they are neither equal to nor independent of the men around them. Finally, all of these maternal aunts walk the very thin line of black ladyhood, held to norms of middle-class respectability that permit "black sassiness" only within narrow standards of feminine civility and sexuality.[59] In short, while the sitcom maternal aunt as a strong matriarchal black lady presents a positive image of black womanhood, she remains entrapped in racially inflected domestic, class, familial, and heterosexual conventions that paradoxically deny the empowerment that postfeminist black womanhood appears to enact.

Those episodes of *Fresh Prince* that spotlight the Aunt Vivian character demonstrate how this positive characterization of the contemporary strong black lady is cast within a depoliticized narrative of racial assimilation and a tempered performance of the middle-aged black woman's sexuality and sassiness. In the series, Will "Fresh Prince" Smith moves into the Bel-Air, California, mansion of his well-to-do uncle Philip Banks, a judge, and aunt Vivian, a university history professor, and their three children, to escape from what his mother, Aunt Vivian's sister Vy, fears will be a destiny of crime and poverty in their West Philadelphia ghetto neighborhood. The sitcom focuses on Will's charm, virility, and street savvy in contrast to his male cousin Carlton Banks, a stuffed shirt whose blackness has been diminished by class affectations, and his female cousin Hilary Banks, a sexy sophisticate, or, as producer Quincy Jones put it, "a classic Black American Princess."[60]

In the episode "Love at First Fight,"[61] Vivian recalls her own struggles against self-doubt and poor decisions, attesting to her strength of character and independent spirit. The episode affirms mainstream neoliberal cultural values of talent, hard work, determination, and individual achievement as the basis for overcoming racially based disadvantages. Exhorting Will's girlfriend to make the most of her opportunities, Vivian admits that she had to make an effort to "fit in" to an ivory tower culture, overtly advocating the goal of assimilation. In "The Big Four-Oh,"[62] we learn that Vivian's early career ambition was to be a professional dancer when, in defiance of her fortieth birthday, she left her professorial position to audition for a dance role, was offered a lead, and turned it down in order to be with her family. The moral of the story is that, despite talent and ambition, a woman's true fulfillment lies in marriage and children. In addition, her fear of aging positions Vivian as a woman whose cultural value is determined by appearance and youthfulness despite her intelligence, talent, and successful academic career. It is as a matriarchal figure that Vivian negotiates the racialized demands of ladyhood and the sexism of a youth-dominated culture. At the same time, her performance of strong black womanhood remains subject to the anxieties of postfeminist femininity.

The fate of the Aunt Vivian character on *Fresh Prince* illustrates the contrary tensions of sexual and social empowerment and subordination that affects this paradoxical representation of the black maternal aunt. While the Aunt Vivian character was cast as a central character with her own narrative development during the first three seasons, the narrative arc of the Aunt Vivian character altered course abruptly with the beginning of the show's fourth season when the actress playing Aunt Vivian was dismissed for creative differences.[63] She was replaced by a lighter-skinned actress without acknowledgment in the show's narrative except when one of Will's friends observed, "Mrs. Banks, since you had that baby, there's something different about you." In a comic reaction making use of the "fourth wall" and the option for self-reflexivity in television comedy, Will turned to the camera and cringed, stepping out of character to share the audience's recognition of the switch in actresses.[64]

Through the remaining three seasons, the Aunt Vivian character was more focused on her place in her family and less overtly career oriented. She remained a foil and support for Will and enacted stereotypic feminine behaviors in mundane marital disputes, including various episodes in which she expressed jealousy over a past girlfriend, anger over her husband's white lies, and a middle-aged woman's anxieties over aging and life transitions. With the change in actresses, the narrative arc of the Aunt Vivian character shifted from that of a prominent character in her own right to that of a helpmate with less prominence in the storyline in comparison with the other characters and the male star in the show. Although Aunt Vivian is a positive image of the black matriarchal figure, her disposability (literally) and narrative subordination undermines depictions of the middle-aged black woman's equality and empowerment.

In contrast to Aunt Vivian and the other black sitcom aunts, the enactment of class status, careerism, and conventional shapeliness seem absent from the characterization of Ella Payne, the matriarchal character on *House of Payne*, a recent black sitcom featuring a maternal aunt.[65] The dark-skinned, overweight matriarch Ella exerts wisdom, discipline, and gospel faith over a multigenerational extended family, including her son and nephew and their wives and children, a foster son, and assorted close friends.[66] This characterization of the contemporary matriarch emphasizes her maternal nature and Christian gospel spirituality, ostensibly in an appeal to working-class African American viewers.[67] While Christian faith is often offered as a character supplement in the other black maternal aunt performances, Ella Payne's faith and charity are central to her character. Throughout the series, Ella exhorts the other characters to have faith in Jesus and often calls them together in prayer. For example, in the double episode "We've Come This Far by Faith," the younger members of the family engage in an acrimonious confrontation in a hospital waiting room until Ella angrily stops them and insists that they join hands in prayer for the recovery of Calvin's infant son.[68] In "Payneful Visit," her best friend Claretha despairs of dying after a diagnosis of leukemia, and Ella exhorts her to believe in Jesus ("God doesn't give us burdens we can't bear") despite Claretha's angry denouncements.[69]

Casting the black aunt as the voice of a very powerful black spiritual tradition grants considerable authority to the matriarchal figure while, at the same time, rendering her subject to the authority of a higher power and casting her as the mouthpiece for traditions of black religiosity. Spirituality and Christian theology are significant forces in black culture and history that have shaped black communal life as well as black women's resilience. Yet the theological perspective Ella voices is ambiguous, tapping into a tradition of collective hope and struggle and of bearing up under suffering while extolling faith in prosperity and individual salvation.[70] While black scholars have argued for the liberatory potential of a black spiritual ethics that promotes community compassion and solidarity, Ella's faith is often expressed in platitudes about bearing individual burdens and praying together as a family.[71] Even though she expresses the power of black spirituality, this maternal aunt domesticates this power and refocuses this energy on the family.

In summary, while these black maternal aunts resist stereotypic attributes of the black matriarch, they remain defined by motherhood and marriage, affirming postfeminist conceptions of women's maternality. At the same time, these aunts take on the expectations that a "black lady" will uphold black respectability and class aspirations although these expectations are reframed within a postfeminist perspective that exhorts them to be successful in their own right. Further, all of these aunts anchor both sexuality and maternality in a stable heterosexual marriage and a nuclear family. This representation of black family life assures white and black viewers that the black family is self-contained, resilient, stable, ultimately harmonious, and a loving haven, images that accord with mainstream (white) family values, thus reinforcing the hegemony of the nuclear family unit and incorporating blackness into the dominant social order.[72]

In short, the black maternal aunt combines postfeminist and postracial attributes with elements of tenacious stereotypes: fierce family care, maternal wisdom, Christian commitments, class proprieties, tempered sexuality, sassy black woman attitude, and careerism. In the tradition of Clair Huxtable, these maternal black sitcom aunts conflate positive and negative images of black womanhood—progressive and neotraditional, sexual and chaste, empowered and subordinated, maternal and careerist, beneficiary of feminist and civil rights movements yet still subject to the intense intersections of class, race, and gender oppressions and legacies of denigration. We turn now to a discussion of whether these contrary images of the black maternal aunt invite transgressive feminist alternatives.

Transgressing Denigrating Images and Postfeminist Promises

We have argued that black sitcom representations of the maternal aunt can be seen as a complex juncture not only for a subset of historically tenacious stereotypes of black women but also for social perceptions of race, gender, family life, and age as well as cultural assumptions about lifestyle, values, and practices of reproduction and care. Despite this complexity, representations of the sitcom aunt fail to transgress conservative, stereotypic images of middle-class black womanhood. Across the four sitcoms, the black maternal aunt is represented through a commodifiable image of blackness that flirts with the persistent appeal of negative stereotypes about sexuality—the black woman's sexual proclivities, for example—and the positive class and lifestyle appeal of the black lady, wrapping these together as attributes of the strong black married woman. Further, this image fits with post-feminist appeals to women's sexual empowerment, careerism, and the primacy of marriage and maternalism. This compound yet reductive representational strategy seems to offer little basis for transgression nor much hope for feminist re-vision.

However, the positive stereotypes and political quietude of this strategy inspire us to reflect on its representational work. More than any other of the standard characters in a family sitcom, the black maternal aunt most readily enacts hegemonic limits on and models of race, sexuality, and mothering. So contradictions become critical possibilities for bringing other discussions and assumptions to bear that entertain transgressive re-visions of the black maternal aunt. Consider the oppositions that position the black maternal aunt as sexual yet maternal: white/black, male/female, old/young. First, given the history of the black family sitcom, we can trace an implicit contrast with the paradigm of the white spinster maternal aunt exemplified by Aunt Bee. Unlike Aunt Bee's asexual relationship with the patriarchal figure of her nephew or the silliness of her matronly heterosexual attractions, the black maternal aunts are depicted as heterosexually attractive and desirable. Not only do their own husbands profess sexual desire but various other men—past boyfriends and acquaintances—affirm the sexual allure of a black woman's presence.[73] Yet this contrast affirms the (white) cultural suspicion of black sexuality that troubles the black aunt's representation of both class and motherhood.

This suspicion is affirmed in another definitive contrast: all of the sitcom aunts are depicted in terms of male/female and husband/wife relations. Sexual tension and domestic conflict are mainstays of the sitcom genre, so this is not surprising. Yet apart from genre expectations, a conventional marriage is critical to the representation of the maternal aunt's sexuality. By containing her desire within a monogamous marriage, the sitcom narratives defer yet acknowledge the myths, biases, and fears of the black woman's sexuality. In addition, black couples in these sitcoms uphold traditional gender asymmetries despite lip service to a more egalitarian model of love and marriage.[74] Further, the loving stability of these marital depictions highlights the desirability of marriage and idealizes black relationships.[75] In a variety of ways, these heteronormative representations are modes of hegemonic containment and incorporation that call attention to the need for more imaginative and promising models of gender dynamics in popular portrayals of the middle-class black marriage.

All of the black maternal aunts are depicted through a third contrast: every one of the four sitcoms pairs the black aunt with a sexualized, usually younger, female character.[76] This contrast casts the black aunt as a yardstick of social and moral propriety. As one scholar aptly put it, "The performance of middle-class black womanhood is tied to impossible standards of respectability."[77] For example, Vivian Banks stands in contrast to her Black American Princess daughter and the racial prejudices of her sister Vy. Wanda McCullough stands in contrast to Bernie's sisters, one of whom gave up her children and the other of whom is too immature to have children. Aunt Ella Payne asserts wisdom and faith against the erratic behavior of all the other women characters on the show—her son's and nephew's girlfriends/wives, especially her nephew's wife, Janine, the crack addict. These constructions emphasize the black aunt's tempered sexuality and imply a mainstream conception of the "good" (chaste, demure, monogamous) bourgeois lady of the house. Yet this contrast between the maternal aunt and a younger black woman reduces their differences to age and lifestyle and subjects both to the conservative social and sexual expectations governing the black lady.[78] Thus, despite their differences, these representations uphold the prevailing stereotypes of (middle-class) black women's sexuality. Taken together, these contrasts reproduce a repressive representation of black women's sexuality and deny contextualizing politics of race, class, and history. Yet in condensing differing relations of power and experience, these black maternal aunt figures invite critical reflections on the identities, relations, and possibilities they enact. From a feminist perspective, we urge representational strategies that expand rather than constrict popular images of black women's lives and explore rather than flatten intersecting relations of privilege, difference, and oppression.[79]

The maternal aunt performances also transgress postracial assurances that race relations are no longer about structured discrimination and inequities but amount to multicultural differences. Accordingly, explicit performances of racial and gender stereotypes are not to be taken seriously but as ironic exaggerations of difference.[80] All four shows frequently portray both husbands and nephews as irresponsible and inept, obsessed with proving their manliness through heterosexual conquest, and dependent on the maternal aunts to bail them out of interpersonal, social, and financial blunders. This depiction of strong black women and irresponsible black men courts stereotypic cultural perceptions of emasculating black matriarchs.[81] Yet such depictions are comic because, after all, the untenability of these representations is supposed to be self-evident in a racially enlightened society. However, for us, these caricatures transgress postracial irony.

Fourth, the maternal aunt poses yet transgresses reassurances that black family life accords with normative ideals of the nurturing, self-sacrificing mother in an affection-based, self-governing family. These images explicitly discipline black families to a normative model that simply does not accord with lived realities: for example, in 2009 the number of black children who lived with their mother as the sole parent was 54 percent. However, as we argued in the case of Aunt Bee, the familial arrangements depicted in these black sitcoms complicate rather than replicate the nuclear family ideal and depict a more fluid, multigenerational practice of familial kinship care.[82] While Aunt Bee is taken in by her nephew Andy to form an insulated nuclear family unit with him and his son Opie, the black maternal aunts are not taken in by relatives but take in their nephews and nieces along with their wives, girlfriends, children, and friends. For example, Will Smith is taken in by his rich aunt and uncle. Helen and Junior King take in their nephew Jamie King. Bernie Mac and Wanda take in his drug-addicted sister's three children. Ella and Curtis Payne take in their nephew C.J. and his two children after his drug-addicted wife burns down their home, provide a home for one of the children when the nephew's family moves out, take in a foster son, and provide a home for various friends. These are informal care arrangements that resonate with traditions of black maternal kin networks, with the significant role of aunting as a familial resource, and with the value of kinship care in lieu of foster care.[83] Given that black children remain the largest demographic group in the child welfare system, depictions of family life that include kinship care both resonate with common experience and sustain the significance of kin networks and communal caregiving and caretaking.[84] These are not models of choice or voluntary families; rather, these alternative arrangements offer models of familial life that draw a much wider family circle.[85]

Finally, there is an absent presence in the portrayal of black sitcom aunts: black women's friendships, communities, and critical sensibilities.[86] While all of the sitcoms include episodes that highlight women's friendships, these relationships are downplayed in three of the four shows. Only *House of Payne* allows the maternal aunt any close women friends who have ongoing roles in the show.[87] Otherwise, the aunts relate to other women mainly through their familial roles, as a mother to her daughters or daughters-in-law, as a sister, or as a mother figure to her nephew's girlfriends. The absence of women's relationships with women reasserts the significance of women's nuclear family roles, affirms motherhood as the most powerful option for women, and reproduces a conservative heterosexism. In addition, isolating the aunt from the larger black community serves to keep the sitcom focused on individual (often personality-based) problems and private family life.

Significantly, the aunt's isolation and individualism reinforces a powerful stereotype of black womanhood: the strong black woman.[88] This construction extols "'a seemingly irrepressible spirit unbroken by a legacy of oppression, poverty, and rejection'" as a defining virtue of black womanhood.[89] According to one black feminist scholar, "A strong black woman typically learns from women kin to combine 'attitude, altitude, image, and faith' so as to develop 'a self-concept that [can] withstand the all-too-common experiences of male rejection, economic deprivation, crushing family responsibilities, and countless forms of discrimination.' "[90] Yet this powerful image is double edged. For while black women's resilience and strength are rightly celebrated, being strong can mean remaining stoic in the face of injustices and oppressions and repressing vulnerabilities and suffering.[91] This is a stereotype that fits the sitcom format well. So, while Vivian Banks might express self-doubt as she nears forty years of age or Ella Payne might cry after failing her college test thanks to the incessant and trivial demands of her family, the end of the episode finds them in control again, strong, resolute, resilient, and uncritical of the structured inequities and intersecting oppressions that have configured their immediate difficulties.

Hence, the black maternal aunts we discuss here are visible but barely vocal. While they enact individual empowerment, confident sexuality, and racial pride, they do not speak to the interlaced disadvantages and discriminations that remain woven into the fabric of everyday life in the contemporary United States. Further, the absence of women's friendships in these sitcoms not only fails to adequately engage this important aspect of black women's culture and communality but resonates with the reported schisms across the black community, particularly around class mobility and privilege, and the tensions among women in the black middle class who must compete for black men, economic opportunities, and social status.[92] Finally, as black feminist scholars have pointed out, the lack of adequately complex images of black women and the emphasis on individual rather than collective strength and struggle has detrimental implications for us all. Without richer images of black women, their relationships, and lives, we are encouraged to make do with reductive conceptions not only of women but of social and cultural relations that lead us to unwittingly accept stratified injustices and mundane denigrations as taken-for-granted societal conditions.[93]

BLACK AND WHITE MATERNAL AUNTS

We began this chapter by critiquing the iconic appeal of Aunt Bee, calling into question the links among femininity, domesticity, family, and nation that constitute Bee as a paradigmatic maternal aunt figure.

We have shown that the psychosocial promises of security and happiness articulated in this iconic image are riddled by anxieties, insecurities, and disaffections.

In addition, the absence of racial identities and tensions in narratives of Aunt Bee inspired an in-depth exploration of the black maternal sitcom aunt. This figure is drawn on a tension between the racial loyalties demanded of a respectable "black lady" and the legacy of (white) cultural suspicions invoked by the black matriarch. This tension reflects the historic mix of misogyny and racism grounded in the legacy of American slavery and underwrites the suppression or exaggeration of black women's sexuality in popular culture representations.[94] We have called into question the links among race, femininity, family, sexuality, and social order, arguing that the black maternal aunt enacts images of black womanhood and family that are bound to both postracial and postfeminist discourses.

Yet there are transgressive possibilities in a close reading of the maternal black aunt that move against prevailing images of black women's sexuality, black marriages and families, and stereotypes like the matriarch, the black lady, and the strong black woman. We admit that sitcom representations of maternal aunts, whether black or white, remain in thrall to conventional mainstream cultural values and social perceptions. Yet these figures are more richly drawn than one might expect, and in the tensions and nuances of their characterizations we find possibilities for feminist critique and re-vision.

"Othered" Aunting

RACE, CLASS, AND INSTITUTIONALIZED MISOGYNY

The legacy of the mammy aunt in the United States is troubling and persistent.[1] Although thought of as part of the history of the pre–Civil War American South, the black mammy figure maintains a tenacious hold on current cultural imagination, deeply influencing contemporary views of women's roles as they intersect with race and class. For example, it is not uncommon to see black mammy figurines in Southern souvenir shops. Their familiarity is a reminder of the all-too-ready assumption that African American women are "naturally" fit for servitude. Strolling the streets of New Orleans in the autumn of 2011, the authors saw several ceramic mammies, as well as postcards featuring vintage advertisements with mammies. Intending to read them critically as cultural texts, Laura brought them to the checkout counter. "They are suitable for framing," the shopkeeper explained brightly, to Laura's dismay.

Moreover, such unthinking invocations of the mammy are not isolated in Southern locales. On its website, the Historical Society of the Town of Greenwich, Connecticut, documents Civil War era history and features a photograph from their collection that portrays an African American woman identified only as "Aunt Nanny, a Greenwich woman who worked for the Bush Family."[2] This is but one example of lingering associations not only between black women and the mammy role but between the black mammy and the title and role of aunt. This woman was a domestic employee for the Bush family, yet her individual identity is completely erased by history, leaving her named only for the function she served for the white family—child care and housework. Her title of aunt is not a signal of inclusion within the family unit but of a proprietary claim on her services. The mammy aunt's sublimation to her servant role is left unmarked by the Historical Society, which fails to note that the woman had a name and an identity prior to (and presumably after) serving the Bush family. Historical accounts such as these contribute to a normalization of elitism and historical dismissal: poor women's names are not worthy of preservation, while the names of affluent white families are carefully recorded. In the process, the persistent tie between servanthood and aunting is implicitly documented.

The black and white family sitcoms discussed in the previous chapter remind us that gender identity necessarily intersects with race, socioeconomic class, sexual orientation, and other positionalities.[3] While all aunts embody and resist assorted stereotypes of femininity, culture inscribes on the bodies of aunts of color the legacies of racism, none more so than the mammy or servant aunt. The familiar American image of the mammy sets the benevolent maternal aunt in a historical-political context of slavery and genocide. The "mammy" or "auntie" is a nonwhite domestic servant whose popular image refigures maternal benevolence and domestic order as a fiction of the faithful, obedient, smiling house slave—often referred to as Aunt Sally—who embraces her domestic responsibilities and loves the family that exploits her.[4] Popular representations of the mammy aunt are almost universally of heavyset women whose large bosoms symbolize their roles as nurturers for more powerful others; their bodies literally provided sustenance for others, first through breast milk and then later through the preparation of food. Reality was a sharp contrast to these images, however, as slave mammies generally were malnourished and consequently quite thin, as we can tell from historical photographs of real slave women who functioned as wet nurses, child-care providers, and household slaves.[5]

While bestowing the aunt title upon a woman unrelated by blood or marriage is often a positive mark of affection and reciprocal obligation among perceived peers, part of the legacy of bestowing "aunt" status on a woman is deeply troubling. The title "aunt" traditionally signified the elevation of the mammy above other servants (who were addressed by first name) while withholding the authority and legitimacy afforded by being addressed formally as "mister" or "mistress."[6] Southern whites adopted the terms "aunt" and "uncle" to refer to slaves in a specifically nonreciprocal show of power and authority, even if coupled with some affection.[7] Hence, the identification of a black woman as a mammy articulates maternality and domesticity with white privilege and black enslavement. The title can also reflect a socioeconomic boundary, linking the woman's position to the family while marking her as essentially outside of the family unit. Servants—slaves or economically disadvantaged women, particularly immigrants and minorities—historically have been designated "aunt."[8] In this chapter, we draw upon black feminist and womanist theories and perspectives to engage the historical role of slave women as mammies and the persistent representation of mammy aunts in popular culture, including in contemporary society with its postfeminist and postracial patina. We then acknowledge the resilience of black women in the face of oppression, highlighted by the reappropriation of Aunt Jemima as a figure of protest against injustice and as a means of communicating persistent, troubling racial inequalities, particularly as these discourses intersect with sexism. Poetry, painting, and other artwork powerfully assert the complex intersections of racism, classism, and sexism in the mammy aunt image for black women and men and for contemporary cultural politics.

Black Feminism, Womanism, and Media Representations of Black Women

Gender cannot be understood in a vacuum; that aspect of identity always intersects with other factors such as age, race, (dis)ability, sexuality, and socioeconomic class. The term "intersectionality" describes overlapping and intersecting oppressions.[9] Black feminists attend particularly to the political realities of interlocking oppressions.[10] An allied perspective that recognizes multiple oppressions while also highlighting strength and resiliency rooted in intersectional identities is called womanism.[11] Womanism advances self-love specifically as a woman, empowerment, appreciation for other women and women's culture, and close relationships with women, focusing on celebrating femaleness but not to the exclusion of men.[12] We have sought to inform our interpretations of intersectionality by learning from the theoretical work of womanist and black feminist scholars and are mindful that as we position ourselves as cultural critics of aunting across differences, we are inescapably tied to our white privilege and educational privilege.[13]

Black feminist and womanist perspectives on popular culture illuminate the complexities of the mammy aunt as a burdensome— and potentially subversive—image for black women. As we argued in the previous chapter, images of black women in media are very limited and rely heavily on negative stereotypes. Standard portrayals of black women cast them as sexually promiscuous (Jezebel), as matriarchs (Mammy), or as angry, strident, and domineering (Sapphire); caricatures include "welfare queen" and pregnant teen, and more recently, the Oprah entrepreneur.[14] These representations are neither complimentary nor nuanced.[15] Ultimately, the stereotypical images of black women offered by an industry operated by people who include few women and fewer women of color bolster current hierarchies: "these images prevail because they reinforce hegemonic definitions of blackness. More insidiously, because these stereotypes establish black female subservience as desirable and normative, they validate the continued economic subjugation of African American women."[16] The relations among class, race, and gender matter in stratifying hierarchical relations of domination and oppression. As we argued in the previous chapter, middle-class black women struggle against these stereotypes in particular ways, while in this chapter we are concerned with the denigrations associated with working-class status, poverty, and subservience. We examine the servitude of the mammy aunt as a particular cultural, social, and political construction that upholds the dichotomies between white women's and black women's cultural legacies and frames black women's claims to femininity and cultural space, as well as the relation of both to domesticity.

Comforting Racism: Mammy Aunts in Fiction and Film

Mammy aunts are common in North American fiction; the classic exemplar is Harriet Beecher Stowe's *Uncle Tom's Cabin*, the novel that spawned a number of theatrical performances and contributed to intense public debate over slavery. Although far more fantasy than reality, this book left an indelible stamp on race relations in the U.S., providing enduring cultural icons condensing race, age, and female-ness, such as the innocent, almost angelic white girl Little Eva, the dancing black girl Topsy, and the mammy Aunt Chloe—all of whom became staple characters in minstrel shows. In *Uncle Tom's Cabin*, Aunt Chloe, Uncle Tom's wife, serves as the cook for the couple's white owners the Shelbys, nurturing the master and his family. Even when her beloved husband is sold to pay off debts for the Shelbys, Aunt Chloe does not turn against the white family who owns her. She is por-trayed as simply and inevitably maternal, embracing servitude, serving her own children after the Shelbys, and continuing to do so regardless of horrific events. As she prepares to bid farewell to her husband, Aunt Chloe nurtures by cooking breakfast:

> The simple morning meal now smoked on the table, for Mrs. Shelby had excused Aunt Chloe's attendance at the great house that morn-ing. The poor soul had expended all her little energies on this farewell feast—had killed and dressed her choicest chicken, and prepared her corn-cake with scrupulous exactness, just to her hus-band's taste, and brought out certain mysterious jars on the mantel-piece, some preserves that were never produced except on extreme occasions.[17]

Domestic labor is all she can think to do to honor her departing hus-band, to prepare him for his arduous journey ahead. Yet while she decries the selling of her husband, Aunt Chloe does not dispute the rightness of her disempowerment. Mrs. Shelby is portrayed as power-less to stop her cruel husband from selling Tom, yet it is Aunt Chloe who comforts her mistress as they cry together. "And in those tears they all shed together, the high and the lowly, melted away all the heart-burnings and anger of the oppressed," the reader is told. Though their tears are shed from very different positions of subordination, this passage erases the black woman's anger and reconciles her to her subjugation. The passage diminishes the black woman's grief, loss, and injustice and assuages the white woman's shame and culpability.[18] Even when losing her husband, Aunt Chloe does not turn against her mistress; Chloe continues to relieve Mrs. Shelby of domestic work, capably wielding the burdens of her own family's household and that of her mistress in good cheer. The inevitability and naturalness of this mammy aunt's servitude to her white mistress is reinforced by her uninterrupted performance of domestic duty in the face of personal tragedy and institutionalized injustice.

Likewise, classic movies such as *Imitation of Life* and *Gone with the Wind* portray the willingly subservient mammy aunt.[19] For example, *Imitation of Life* is the story of a black matriarch whose light-skinned daughter abandons her to pass as white. This matriarchal figure fulfills the stereotype of the long-suffering, self-sacrificing black mammy, including the visual imagery of a mammy's body—large breasts, heavy, and dark skinned.[20] In *Gone with the Wind*, Scarlett's slave Mammy (played by Oscar-winning actor Hattie McDaniel) devotes herself to the white family that owns her, representing the role that traditional mammies "often play as the moral guardians of their white female charges."[21] The domestic subjugation of the traditional mammy is complemented by the racial, social, and cultural privileges conferred on those who own another human being.[22] The continued popularity, periodic rebroadcasting, and release in 2009 of a digitally remastered seventieth anniversary collector's edition DVD of *Gone with the Wind*,[23] alongside continued sales of Margaret Mitchell's novel on which it was based and a sequel novel authorized by Mitchell's heirs,[24] attests to the continued economic force of white nostalgic longing for a past that promotes racial hierarchy as normative.[25]

Owning a Little Piece of Mammy: Black Collectibles

The appeal of owning a subservient other remains strong, and we turn to a tangible remnant of the mammy as property. The sustained popular practice of collecting vintage mammy figurines, signs, and household goods betrays the ongoing cultural relevance of the mammy. Between 1880 and the late 1950s, tens of thousands of "black collectibles" offering derogatory and degrading images of African Americans were produced, mostly in the form of household goods, reinforcing existing stereotypes.[26] These vintage offerings included napkin holders, salt and pepper shakers, sugar bowl and creamer sets, syrup jugs, cookie jars, toothpick holders, flour canisters, and numerous other examples of kitchen kitsch. In addition to vintage signs and advertisements printed with images of the mammy aunt, far more disturbing are the objects that literally instrumentalize the classic mammy aunt's body; that is, the pitcher or salt shaker is shaped like a mammy's body and one pours syrup from her upraised arm or shakes salt from her head. Of central importance is that black collectibles were made by and for white producers and consumers; many were originally given away as premiums to people who purchased household foods and cleaning products. Yet they are still popular commodities even in a postracial society that denies lingering inequalities.[27] The brisk trade in mammy vintage collectibles (often labeled Aunt Sally, Aunt Jemima, or just auntie) evidences the continued popularity of these items with today's consumer.[28] On a single day in 2011, a simple online search located 1032 auctions and fixed-price items available for purchase (with many auction lots featuring more than one item) on the eBay online auction site, and of course collectibles are available in antique shops and vintage stores.[29]

The appeal of these products may lie in their materialization of cultural nostalgia. The use of the "fictive kin" title of aunt for slaves on whom some power-laden affection was bestowed is integral to the meaning of the racist items today. Indeed, "it is the power to evoke emotion that induces the viewer consciously and unconsciously to accept the stereotypes that the objects themselves portray."[30] We may try to respond to racist kitsch as though it were divested of meaning, but this is impossible; "In its failed effort to move unobtrusively among the objects of our everyday encounter, racist kitsch unwittingly reveals itself to be profoundly laden with meaning."[31] During the New Orleans visit described in the opening of this chapter, we were stopped in our tracks by a three-foot-tall mammy figurine holding a tray in the front of a souvenir shop. The figurine mesmerized us. Despite a sign in the shop window warning, "No pictures allowed," we took a picture—for documentation? Voyeurism? Naïveté? White guilt? The presence of this figurine shocked us, yet we had to have a visual souvenir. Even with "oppositional" curating of racist objects, framed in museums as evidence of legacies of racism, the objects do visual violence to audiences who cannot look away.[32]

While the racist aspects of these collectibles are of critical importance, gender often ends up sidelined in the discussion. And yet the mammy aunt is inherently situated at a complex intersection of race, class, and gender oppressions. The reduction of the mammy to souvenir kitsch obscures the historical exploitation of black women's physical and emotional labor and celebrates her place as a servant in the white home while erasing her place in the black family: "being without family, she is always available for work."[33] As embodied in collectibles, the mammy aunt is bound physically and economically to the domestic sphere and specifically to white domestic service. Her servitude creates the white home as "private haven" that enables the white family to move within the public sphere more easily; indeed her labor—even if symbolic—helps to liberate affluent women from domestic service. From the shelf or table where they are displayed or used for serving food, mammy aunts symbolize nurturance without power or freedom. Yet the mammy's wide grin portrays her as happy with her lot in life. It is not a far stretch to say that owning a mammy figurine is a not-too-subtle symbol of owning the legacy of servitude that the object obviously embodies; her perpetually smiling face has become a sign of false assurance that what's past is past and there is no cause for unease in continued ownership.

Still on the Box: Aunt Jemima as Iconic Marketing Image

The complications of raced and gendered legacies and contemporary appeals embodied in the commodified mammy aunt figure are readily apparent in the most famous and long-lived mammy image: Aunt Jemima, fictional figurehead for a line of pancake mixes and breakfast syrups, now manufactured by the Quaker Oats Company. The image of Aunt Jemima was created in 1893 to sell self-rising pancake flour, one of the first convenience products marketed to both ease the burden of housewives and to promote a lifestyle based upon the regular consumption of convenience items.[34] Such a lifestyle demonstrated a family's economic power and its ability to have the mother/wife of the family conform to feminine ideals instead of perform hard labor. Although white housewives might aspire to be like the Betty Crocker featured on some boxes, the Aunt Jemima products instead "offered the opportunity to *have* Aunt Jemima, securing a type of femininity, whiteness, and class uplift" through the purchase of a product bearing the picture of a black woman.[35]

Aunt Jemima was originally portrayed by African American women who adopted the role as paid actors to sell the product by appealing to middle-class American nostalgia for the antebellum South. Jemima became a stock character in early movies such as *The Birth of a Nation*. She was initially depicted as a traditional Southern cook—a plump, jolly and very black woman dressed in a nondescript gingham apron with a red bandana around her nappy hair. The text of a 1954 ad appearing in *Ladies Home Journal* portrays Aunt Jemima in the context of Southern slavery: "Aunt Jemima Pancakes—Legend of Riverboat Paddlewheelers: Passengers on the river boats would point out the Colonel Higbee plantation. Aunt Jemima, cook there for many years, made it famous. Her pancakes, light and tender, had a matchless flavor."[36] While the ad does not state that Colonel Higbee owned Aunt Jemima, his title of colonel, labeling the home a plantation, naming her as "aunt," and depicting her in a classic slave head rag and stereotypical mammy appearance implies it quite clearly. Moreover, the romantic legend of old-time riverboats is further meant to appeal to white people's nostalgia for the antebellum South. A more direct appeal to the modern housewife is reflected in an ad from 1960 that features a drawing of a white man and two kids in their pajamas on the staircase of a home with the text "Hooray! It's Aunt Jemima Day! Even if you got up half an hour early and made your own pancakes from scratch, you'd still be hard-pressed to match Aunt Jemima for taste and tenderness. Why? The exclusive Aunt Jemima blend of flours gives you extra flavor and lightness."[37] The "you" being addressed is the unpictured, idealized housewife who is encouraged to use Aunt Jemima's labor-saving product to produce wonderful pancakes for her family. The visual appearance of Aunt Jemima changed during the course of the civil rights movement in the U.S. By the 1970s, Aunt Jemima had morphed into a trim, meticulously attired medium-dark woman with a fashionable, straightened hairdo. However, common to all of the Aunt Jemima images was a wide white-toothed smile perpetuating white belief in the benefits of servitude and oppression for black domestics.

Today the Aunt Jemima "brand tradition" offers the promise of nourishing good health to the current generation of affluent consumers. The company's current website claims, "The Aunt Jemima® brand of pancake mixes and syrups has been around for over 100 years and has earned the reputation of quality, warmth, nourishment, and trust. The Aunt Jemima® brand is used by millions of loving moms and dads who take pride in preparing hot, nutritious breakfasts for their families."[38] Aunt Jemima's labor continues to benefit an idealized image of families—this time the nuclear family of the suburbs rather than the antebellum plantation. Jemima as a brand image is equated with "quality, warmth, nourishment, and trust." The brand promise is directed to parents, retaining Aunt Jemima's mammy legacy of creating home as a haven and providing sustenance for their children's bodies and hearts.

Of course, the postfeminist consumer generally does not consciously think about the mammy aunt as a producer of domestic labor for them, any more than she or he is likely to believe that the sexy model comes with the car purchase or that the new brand of wax will really make her want to dance around her clean kitchen in an evening gown. However, the lack of conscious reflection does not change the emotional and symbolic associations of the mammy aunt as that of someone who produces food for one's family to consume and who cheerfully and indulgently cleans up afterward. To be sure, Aunt Jemima would have been replaced by another figure if she had stopped being an effective icon. And while it seems obvious that her effectiveness stems from pleasurable associations with home and family, it is also her associations with raced and gendered hierarchies of privilege and subordination that make her such a useful icon. Ownership, servitude, and power over another are the other side of Aunt Jemima's appeal. We may think her historical legacies as a slave or bound domestic servant are irrelevant, but the ability to identify with this icon signifies that "her historical baggage is exactly what makes her effective."[39] Yet this baggage is denied by popular belief in gender and racial equality, enabling Aunt Jemima's continued prominent place in today's supermarkets to continue unproblematized.

What are the possibilities for feminist interpretation of an image inescapably burdened with the shameful history of racism? By allowing us to reflect upon the way her legacy of enslavement is taken for granted and the troubling associations of her current appeal, the mammy aunt may provide a spark for much-needed conversations about race relations and persistent inequities. Indeed, we find that the mammy figure transgresses the unreflective acceptance of her cultural bondage in a number of noteworthy projects explicitly aimed at redressing her silenced history of subjugation. These include projects of historical recovery as well as creative works of protest.

TELLING IT DIFFERENTLY

Speaking Aloud: Telling Omitted Histories

One way in which the mammy aunt has been refigured in a potentially transgressive manner is in projects that recover untold histories of African Americans. Black filmmaker John Singleton sought to tell one of the many stories omitted by official U.S. histories of race relations in the early twentieth-century South. His historic Hollywood epic *Rosewood* portrayed (in fictionalized form) a real incident in which mob violence resulted in the destruction of an African American town in Florida in the 1920s and the murder of many of its citizens.[40] The story illustrates how invoking racist stereotypes can easily escalate into violence.

In the story, Aunt Sarah, a black woman who is well known and respected within her African American community, does washing and ironing for a white woman, Fanny Taylor, whose racist lies about her adulterous affair are the spark that ignites racial hatred into dramatic violence. Fanny is portrayed not as a gentlewoman but as a lower-class, coarse woman who routinely cheats on her husband. Yet Fanny presumably has sufficient economic means to hire Aunt Sarah to do her laundry for her. Aunt Sarah knows of Fanny's adultery and witnesses her lover beating her and then fleeing. When Fanny blames an unidentified black man for her beating, the town's white men form a posse and go on a killing and burning spree. When asked for her account of what happened, Aunt Sarah sees no point in telling the truth, and says instead, "Black is just another word for guilty." Later, when the violence escalates, she desperately tries to help her family and neighbors by reminding the white mob, "I was midwife to more than half of you!" As she is about to explain what she saw, Aunt Sarah is shot and killed, silencing her forever. Eventually a white man stands up to the mob and quells the violence.

On one hand, this film is firmly about history; it focuses on past events and offers a dramatic narrative that illustrates the evils of racism. Director John Singleton offers a powerful social critique; the movie is a painful reminder of the heavy toll of racism. The recreated historical events rely on a clear narrative of good versus evil and of the redemption found by a white man who stands up against racist violence to try to save some of the black citizens. The narrative relies on the classic trope of white fears over black male rape of pure white womanhood, but without interrogating the gender dynamics inherent in the conflict. Instead, binaries prevail; Fanny is unquestionably bad and Aunt Sarah is good, adultery is bad and fidelity is good, independence is masculine and midwifery and domestic work are feminine.

In reclaiming this forgotten bit of history, the director privileges a close examination of race while largely ignoring the nuances of gender as they intersect with it, despite the centrality of gender and sexuality to the main plotline. In this sense, the film rejects the postracial fallacy of color blindness. However, the film not only fails to question how racism influences and is influenced by sexism but actually affirms sexist stereotyping. In the epic storyline, gender is relevant only inasmuch as the stereotypical fear of black male sexual violence despoiling the purity of white womanhood is invoked as a plot device. Singleton's accomplishment is rightly applauded:

by reclaiming the history of Rosewood, the movie speaks aloud the shameful, terrorist history of racist violence in the U.S. and creates the visual spectacle of this terrorism with cinematic skill. However, it is the transgressive potential of Aunt Sarah's character that we find most significant about this film.

Revisiting the movie's narrative, we find Aunt Sarah as the locus of gender, race, and class tensions in Rosewood. Yet reading this movie as an indictment of racism obscures Aunt Sarah's significance as a mammy aunt even as her significance to the unfolding racist violence is dramatically emphasized.[41] She is the town's "mammy aunt," performing as midwife and housemaid to more than half the inhabitants. And she is murdered as soon as she steps out of her domestic, nurturing role and speaks up in opposition to a public force. Fanny upsets the social order by having sex with a lover when her husband is out of the house and then invoking the tried-and-true threat of black male sexuality to cover her sins. Yet she escapes unpunished, while Aunt Sarah becomes the scapegoat because she refuses to be invisible and silent. Aunt Sarah's murder constitutes a powerful lesson on where black women belong—in domestic servitude, where they labor and witness but never tell. When Aunt Sarah speaks, she asserts an identity specifically as a gendered subject not merely a domestic object. She speaks as a black female witness to white gender violence. And she speaks on the authority of her feminine role as black midwife to the white community. Aunt Sarah symbolizes not only the contradictory logic of racist violence but also the ways in which racism and sexism intersect literally within the bodies of women of color. When she is shot, her dead body prompts the white male hero to intercede in the mob violence and lead many of the black community members to a safe hiding place.

We might argue that Aunt Sarah's act of self-sacrifice empowers her; she is a postfeminist heroine, a woman who asserts what she knows to be the truth. Yet this reading fails to appreciate that it is Aunt Sarah's role as witness that is her most crucial significance. The kin relation that Aunt Sarah claims across racial lines in Rosewood positions her as a knowing witness to their lives. She brought both black and white into the world—she is like a mother but not a mother.

Like a mother, she is witness to their sins and harbors their guilt over the everyday brutality of racial hatred and sexual betrayal. And when she speaks, we know she will testify to the intersectionalities of gender, race, sexuality, and violence. Women like Aunt Sarah have been erased from the historic script of race relations, yet the movie casts her testimony as both intimate and truthful. Moreover, her voice resonates with current news accounts that feature the intersection of gender with ethnic warfare, where rape is used as a war tactic, and of political assaults on reproductive freedom that directly affect women's bodies. The character of Aunt Sarah refigures the mammy aunt as a transgressive voice, disrupting received scripts and testifying to the intersectional violence of race and gender relations.

Rebellious Mammy: Images of Art and Protest

We turn now not to subtle transgressions but to wide fissures deliberately carved in dominant ideologies by civil rights activist artists. This departs from our attempt to read against the grain of culture; here we feature profoundly meaningful representations that speak directly back to historical legacies of the oppressive mammy aunt image. We suggest that the character of Aunt Jemima can function as subversive when reclaimed or reappropriated by African American artists who transform her through their artistic visions. Through theater performance, painting, film, and other artwork, the Aunt Jemima character becomes angry, militant, discontent, powerful, and able to speak for herself; she is transformed. This adds to the transgressive possibilities of the aunt to go beyond the claims of a postracial, postgender world. The figure of Aunt Jemima becomes subversive in three ways: first, she speaks up about historical realities and legacies that are denied; second, she challenges stereotypes and how they distort understanding of real black women's lives; and third, she functions as an example of a strong black woman speaking out loud as a counterpoint to the silencing of black women's realities. We examine how these three subversions are articulated by black visual artists, poets, playwrights, and bloggers.

Despite—and because of—the racist legacy of Aunt Jemima as a brand name and her status as the most well-known mammy aunt,

she has also persisted as a reclaimed image of protest in art by African American artists, particularly women, speaking back to the legacy.[42] This explicit reclaiming of the mammy aunt, particularly Aunt
Jemima, in artistic works of the civil rights movement and of the ongoing resistance to racism offers explicit, assertive, often aggressive, frequently confrontational transgressions of the societal status quo. Much
of this art was generated during the civil rights and women's liberation movements of the late 1960s and 1970s, at the height of the black
power movement and the rise of more radical feminisms as the second
wave crested. We applaud these powerful and radical re-visionings of
Aunt Jemima, and the work that continues the conversation about the
intersection of popular culture with identity, oppression, and social
power. We see these as important aspects of the social and historical
context in which audiences encounter and make sense of more subtly
transgressive mammy aunt figures. In addition, they ask unflinching
questions about intersections of race, class, gender, and sexuality.

Perhaps the most well-known example of Aunt Jemima protest art
is the work of Betye Saar, an artist who works in assemblage, or bringing together found three-dimensional objects to create an art installation. In 1972 her mixed media piece *The Liberation of Aunt Jemima*
expressed her engagement with the black arts movement call to challenge racial stereotypes.[43] In it, she incorporated three different versions of Aunt Jemima "to question and turn around such images" of
the mammy aunt. In the piece, the largest Aunt Jemima holds a broom,
a rifle, and a pistol, combining her traditional smiling subservience
with the potential for violent resistance. In 1998, Saar offered another
mixed-media installation in which she returned to these themes. She
titled this series *Women + Warriors: The Return of Aunt Jemima*. It
featured vintage collectibles of black slave women, text from advertisements and other documents, and images on vintage washboards.
The contrast of the cheerful slogans and messages with the hard labor
signified by the washboards and images of slave women toiling renders the mammy aunts' supposedly happy subservience deeply problematic. Another artist, Joe Overstreet, created a painting that also
confronts both gender and racial stereotypes of Aunt Jemima from
his perspective as an African American man. Overstreet's *The New*

Jemima depicts Aunt Jemima with a rifle and a syrup bottle refashioned as a grenade, displaying a militancy similar to Saar's and attesting to the painful legacy of the mammy image for black men as well as black women.

African American poets also have invoked Aunt Jemima in their creative representations. The tradition of black protest poetry is rooted in the oral tradition of slave songs and the writings of W.E.B. Du Bois and other early influential African American writers. The Harlem Renaissance and the civil rights protests of the 1960s both formed rich contexts for authoring poems that spoke about the black experience of suffering and injustice, as well as pride and resilience.[44] This legacy of creating poetry to express protest includes historical and contemporary attention to the troubling capitalist icon of Aunt Jemima. As with Saar's artwork, Aunt Jemima remains a touchstone or reference point for articulating African American women's identities at the intersection of race, class, and gender. We highlight the poems of two contemporary African American women authors to demonstrate the subversive refiguration of the mammy aunt and the persistence of this image in the psyche of women who resist being cast into that oppressive role.[45]

Contemporary African American writer and activist Opal Palmer Adisa wrote a poem that speaks back to the mammy aunt's iconic brand image. Adisa superimposed her voice onto a vintage print advertisement for Aunt Jemima's pancake mix, forming a multimedia text, "I Ain't Yr Mama." Adisa refers to both the classic slave mammy image of Aunt Jemima and the newer version that currently appears on the product line.

> I am so sick and tired of carrying Aunt Jemima
>   around with me.
> Seems like she done got plastic surgery like Michael Jackson
> She be lighter with thin lips you can't hardly kiss
> Got to put lipstick on to see them
> And her hair is all pressed and lays flat on her head—dead like
> And they want you to believe that's me
> That ain't me

Figure 2.1: "I Ain't Yr Mama." Aunt Jemima Protest Art by writer and activist Opal Palmer Adisa (2004).

And I sure as hell ain't going to make you no pancakes
Or get you no syrup to sweet them
I ain't yr mama
. . .
I's myself
My very own self
big black plain and beautiful
for those with eyes to see the real me.[46]

Adisa carefully differentiates herself from the expectations that she selflessly nurture white folks or anyone else, for that matter. Instead, she is her "very own self" who resists the racist legacy of the aunt mammy. While she thoroughly refutes the icon, however, she affirms its persistence as the iconic referent against which she must struggle to build a self of her own.

African American poet Lucille Clifton, Pulitzer Prize finalist for her poetry, wrote her poem "slave cabin, sotterly plantation, maryland, 1989" as protest against the portrayal of slave life at a historically preserved plantation she visited.[47] The poem focuses on an item on display at a plantation, "aunt nanny's bench," and the woman for whom the bench is named.[48] The slave woman's name references only her utility to the family who owns her and for whom she labors arduously.[49] This evocative poem invites readers to imagine a slave woman whose nurturing of others exhausts her but who hums to reassure herself that she has a name apart from that conferred upon her to describe her forced labor. By imagining Aunt Nanny as engaging in the subtle but crucial resistance of humming her name, Clifton speaks back to the legacy of slave aunts, especially their enforced nurturing of the very people who exploited them. Through her poem, Clifton registers outrage, sadness, and pain and yet also insists that the slave woman knew what her name really was, affirming the resilience of the mammy aunt in the face of tremendous oppression. Clifton's eloquent objection notwithstanding, relics of mammy aunts continue to be showcased in museums accompanied by narratives that largely reflect the point of view of the slave owners rather than the slaves.[50] These relics and narratives resonate thematically throughout popular culture—novels, movies, advertisements, collectibles. Thus, the oppressive legacy of the mammy aunt is institutionalized as part of the received history of race in the United States. The tradition of protest art refiguring Aunt Jemima and the mammy aunt figure counters the persistence of this image of cheerful oppression.

Theater is another powerful medium of protest. Glenda Dickerson and Breena Clarke wrote *Re/membering Aunt Jemima: A Menstrual Show*, which adapted conventions of minstrel shows to tell a decidedly feminine-focused historical construction of the intersection of racism and sexism for black women in U.S. history.[51] Clarke explains:

we see Aunt Jemima as an icon rooted in the ancient African tradition of household orisha . . . who fearlessly guards the peace of our
homes as she presides over our bread-baking and clothes-making.
Aunt Jemima is not a joke to us. On the contrary, we attempt to
show that African people used to revere the qualities for which
she is now denigrated. Aunt Jemima has big lips; she is fat; she
wears bright colors; she is smiling. We have been taught to fear all
these qualities. Voluptuous lips are ugly only when measured by
European standards; the same with steatopygous buttocks. We hate
her headrag, but forget that it makes sense for a person who does
her kind of work to cover her head. It was somebody else's culture
which told us we look stupid in bright colors. . . . We think she
smiles without cause and that this is somehow shameful. But how
do we know why she smiles? The smile of Aunt Jemima is no less
enigmatic than the smile of Mona Lisa.[52]

In their show, Dickerson and Clarke use conventions of a minstrel
show but reclaim a black woman's perspective; for example, they
transform what is denigrated about Aunt Jemima's body into signs of
beauty. The show is primarily about women, hence the "menstrual"
show, pointing out the way that minstrel traditions are doubly racist
and sexist.[53] The show "attempts to unpack the stereotypes of black
women"[54] by including numerous daughters of Aunt Jemima, by different fathers, representing different historical periods, with a mix
of fictional characters drawn from literature, films, and historical
accounts. The later daughters who struggle with feminist ideals in the
face of intersections of racism and sexism confront a "difficulty [that]
comes not from attempting to assert a black feminist perspective, but
from the necessary task of rescuing it from its vilification."[55] In this
work, the playwrights have reclaimed the history of black women by
voicing Aunt Jemima's experience in their own terms to render more
complex the story of real women whose lives cannot be reduced to the
Aunt Jemima icon.[56]

A final way in which Aunt Jemima has been questioned and transformed is on the Internet. For example, in the online world of social
commentary, Professor Tracey Salisbury's blog demonstrates the

continued resonance of the mammy aunt for protest rhetoric. Her blog Aunt Jemima's Revenge[57] sports the tag line "The Master's Tools Will Never Dismantle The Master's House" from African American poet Audre Lorde.[58] Salisbury describes her blog in this way: "One bad sista's view of the worlds of politics, sports, books, popular culture, education, feminism, black folks, movies, hip hop, travel, and whatever else strikes my fancy." The website's banner also features pictures from Saar's series *The Liberation of Aunt Jemima*, further demonstrating the power of this icon as a rallying point for protest and resistance at the intersection of racism, sexism, and classism. This blog, highlighting an African American feminist perspective, speaks back to the white and male privileges that remain central to the use of the Internet. The performance of race in cyberspace is not somehow absent because material bodies are not readily accessible. Rather "opportunities for (self-)representation get funneled through the systems developed by programmers whose racial value systems are embedded in the worlds they have constructed."[59] Salisburg's racialized body speaks powerfully through the online medium, enacting an activist's revenge on the systems that continue to make Aunt Jemima recognizable.

A PERSISTENT FIGURE

The mammy aunt retains significant cultural currency today, attesting to the ongoing legacy of social inequality and racism. We have pointed to one subtle transgression in the form of the Aunt Sarah character in the *Rosewood* epic film and the assertive, even aggressive, transgressions and transformations in African American protest artwork. The continued unreflexive mainstream acceptance of the mammy aunt's presence troubles us, and rightly so. Aunt Jemima is integral to the received account of U.S. slavery, and her legacy informs contemporary negative images of black women. The politicized images of Aunt Jemima and the mammy aunts set these figures against themselves: as figures who speak or remain silent, who fight injustice or acquiesce, who nurture or who pass the burdens of caregiving. We are aware that these are not dichotomous possibilities but strategic options that are more or less responsive to circumstances of subjugation, oppression, and injustice. Moreover, race relations embody far more complex intersections of multiple races, ethnicities, and genders beyond the black and white aunts we examined here and in chapter 1. Even though the troubling racist legacy of Aunt Jemima and the mammy aunts may not consciously shape the cultural meanings of most of the aunt figures in popular culture, we hold this figure to be critical to our overall understanding of aunts.

Like a (Bad) Mother

Neotraditional and Malevolent Aunts

Aunt figures are surprisingly prevalent in contemporary popular culture aimed at women—the so-called chick genres of film, television, and popular fiction, typically involving romantic heterosexual and maternal fantasies. We contend that a bad-to-good mothering narrative is evident across the mediated representations of postfeminist aunts in these genres, in which a career-obsessed young woman finds herself mothering her nieces and nephews. This she does badly at first, but eventually her maternal instincts triumph, and she proves to be a good mother. In the process of her transformation, she typically finds heterosexual love with a man who is clearly husband material. This variation on the girl-meets-boy romance casts women's life aspirations in terms of a postfeminist discourse of empowerment through marriage and motherhood at the expense of career ambition. We call this aunt the neotraditional maternal aunt because this figure most clearly enacts the injunctions inherent to postfeminist cultural messages that children, family, and a good man are key to women's fulfillment.

Another maternal aunt figure in contemporary popular media draws on a legacy of childhood anxieties over the bad mother. We call this figure the malevolent maternal aunt. Unsurprisingly, these narratives feature the resilient child as a hero figure triumphing against the cruelties of a malicious caretaker. By turning our attention to the aunts who play supporting roles in this heroic narrative, we find that malicious aunts uphold the postfeminist emphasis on motherhood by inverting it. They also embody a backlash argument against feminism: their malevolence contradicts women's essential need for children and caretaking, showing us the perversions that can potentially follow feminism's campaign against the biological and cultural mandates for mothering. We argue that both bad-to-good and malevolent aunt figures hold transgressive potential. Specifically, both of these maternal aunt figures call into question the postfeminist celebration of a "maternal instinct" and provoke reflections on home and family as the "happy ending" of the maternal romance. Both of these aunt figures force us to reconsider the analogy "my aunt is like a mother." They remind us about the cultural baggage that accompanies the identity of the mother, the practices of mothering, and the institution of motherhood. In the end, these aunt figures offer us both more and less than the contemporary romances in which they participate.

MOTHERHOOD AS THE ULTIMATE CAREER ASPIRATION: NEOTRADITIONAL MATERNAL AUNTS

The tension of the aunt as like a mother / not a mother comes to the fore as we consider recent film depictions of the neotraditional maternal aunt: *Mostly Martha*,[1] *No Reservations*,[2] *Raising Helen*,[3] and a Hallmark made-for-television movie, *Three Weeks, Three Kids*.[4] Across these films, initially independent and career-oriented women are depicted as discovering themselves in mothering, consumption, and (hetero)sexuality. All four films begin with an emancipated, professional, middle-class white woman, the figure who most represents the benefits and limits of liberal feminism. In her neotraditional guise, this "liberated" woman "has it all" yet suffers from a primordial lack that stunts her emotional life and social relationships: the childless woman is incomplete. After an unexpected turn of events—usually a sister's death but sometimes merely a change in the sister's vacation plans—these women are unexpectedly confronted with custodial responsibility for their niece(s) and/or nephew(s). All four films depict the woman who is married to her career as emotionally incomplete and (often unknowingly) alienated from her "true" self. In addition, all four films depict an inexorable relational development between aunt and children from initial resistance to love and mutual dependence. Each film introduces a heterosexual love interest, a man/husband/father character who fulfills both the woman's need for love and the normative nuclear family arrangement. In the end, the aunt who began as a career woman gives up her career for a more fulfilling role as a mother.

The film *Mostly Martha* exemplifies the neotraditional maternal aunt. The plot focuses on Martha Klein, an obsessive-compulsive master chef working in an haute cuisine restaurant. She is depicted as emotionally inaccessible though superbly competent and confident as a professional. Unable to relate to people, she "cools off" at work in a walk-in cooler. The movie opens with Martha on the therapist's couch, describing with thinly veiled sexual imagery an elaborate recipe for baking doves (the bird of love). She is clearly sexually repressed and sensually closed except through her cooking. Her only human connection is with her sister, who dies in a car accident on a trip to visit Martha, throwing Martha and her nine-year-old niece Lina together. At work, Martha is confronted by Mario, a new sous chef, an Italian who is as openly sensual and relationally responsive as she is closed and alienated. Through the power of a child's dependence along with her heterosexual attraction to the Italian chef, Martha realizes her maternal needs and her capabilities for love, and, through these realizations, she recovers her own *joie de vivre*. In a narrative twist, Martha gives Lina up to her biological father when he finally appears. Unsurprisingly, she regrets this move. After Lina's Italian father takes her to Italy, Martha and Mario give up their positions in the restaurant to follow Lina. As Mario and Martha travel from Germany to Italy, Martha is literally transformed from a bad mother who gave her child away to a good mother who gives up her own career to be with her child. Despite her rocky relationships with both the child and the man, Martha begins to flower as a woman and a sensual being. Once in Italy, Martha and Mario reunite with Lina, marry, and open their own restaurant.

Scholars have applauded *Mostly Martha* for reasons other than its depiction of the maternal aunt. For example, the film has been extolled for the way it depicts multicultural assimilation while preserving German nationalism[5] and as representative of cinematic shifts in the

German film industry after Germany's incorporation into the European Union.[6] In one analysis, *Mostly Martha* advances multiculturalism in the guise of a "repressed Germanic girl meets sensual Italian boy" story, a plotline that advances a scenario about multicultural Europe as a place where national identities remain identifiable even as intercultural engagements (or romance) strengthen both parties.[7] This interpretation of the film casts it as a narrative of nation, immigration, and multiculturalism. Yet this analysis ignores the emphasis in the film on motherhood and domesticity embodied in the maternal aunt. This is surprising since the film highlights Martha's relation to food as an erotic substitution; Martha's professional perfectionism is an obvious diversion of her sensuality into her culinary creations.

Other scholars have labeled *Mostly Martha* a "food film," in which the sensuality of cooking, eating, and food itself serves as a primary leitmotif. As a chef, Martha is obsessed with perfecting her artistry but to the detriment of her own sensual relationship to food, love, and life. During the course of the film, it is through the sensuality of food, cooking together, and sharing meals that she opens to her own needs and passions. The message seems quite clear: as a career chef, Martha was emotionally and sensually closed, driving her crazy (literally); as a lover and a mother, Martha's life is fulfilled, she finds completeness and happiness, she is able to love and be loved.

The centrality of maternal need is evident in a key scene in which Martha awakens in the middle of the night to the sound of her dead sister's voice and finds that Lina is watching a home video of herself and her mother.[8] In the scene, Martha stands behind Lina as both watch the video, positioning Martha as a spectator of the "authentic" mother-daughter bond that she does not share with Lina. We see Martha confronted by the analogy of aunting: she is like a mother but not a mother. The film depicts this as an agonizing moment of maternal lack and inadequacy.[9] But this scene also demonstrates the antifeminist stance of *Mostly Martha*. Martha's self-alienation and deep dissatisfactions are the result of her careerism and her professional success. And the context is feminism's campaign to open opportunities for women in the public sphere.[10] In this sense, *Mostly Martha* is a postfeminist cautionary tale. Martha's pathologies are a kind of fallout from the success of feminism in pushing women to have it all, because such an ambition risks neglecting and even losing the most essential aspect of the female self, the need for motherhood.[11]

In *No Reservations*, the American version of *Mostly Martha*, the multiculturalist and nationalistic themes are gone, and there is only the story of a repressed woman, Kate, whose essential sensuality and self-fulfillment are realized through heterosexual love (opposites attract) and the need of and for a child. The film was a modest success in its U.S. release and did slightly better in its worldwide showing. Its bland, predictable storyline, bereft of the cultural-political dimensions of *Mostly Martha*, relies on the postfeminist appeal of the maternal aunt figure: the crisis of self that career women like Martha and Kate experience can only be resolved through romance, domesticity, family, and, especially, motherhood. The implicit invitation is to read every woman's story into this message. Indeed, such "chick flick" fare is constructed upon an implicit argument that women's frustrations are not due to economic inequities, institutionalized discrimination, or historically entrenched gender subordination but to the essential lack a woman suffers without a man and a child.[12] More importantly, such films offer a utopian view of heteronormative romance and family life centered on women's deep fulfillment through maternity and love that invests "women's culture" with a sense of shared pleasure and hope, as we will discuss shortly.

Perhaps the paradigmatic example of this formula is the 2004 film *Raising Helen*, in which the lead character throws over a rewarding career to care for her dead sister's three children, finding love with a Lutheran pastor at the same time. The appeal of *Raising Helen* is that women really can have it all as long as what they *really* want is marriage and family. Like the women in *Mostly Martha* and *No Reservations*, Helen is too obsessed with work (an enviable position in the fashion industry) to realize her own loneliness and lack of fulfillment. When her sister and brother-in-law die unexpectedly, a letter from her sister assigns Helen responsibility for the three children rather than another sister, Jenny, whose sole focus is motherhood and family.

The contrast calls attention to Helen's seeming lack of fitness for the role of mother. She does not want to care for the kids and is quite

*Figure 3.1: The neotraditional aunt: Helen Harris and her nieces and nephew
(from the 2004 film* Raising Helen, *directed by Garry Marshall). Shown are Hayden
Panettiere as niece Audrey Davis, Abigail Breslin as niece Sarah Davis, Kate
Hudson as Aunt Helen Harris, and Spencer Breslin as nephew Henry Davis.*

ignorant of what they need, whereas Jenny has been caring for children (including her little sister Helen) all her life. Helen initially cares
for the kids as an aunt: she plays the fun aunt, the indulgent aunt, and
the cool aunt rather than exercising the maturity, responsibility, and
discipline that a good mother might. An unlikely love interest is the
principal of the children's elementary school, Dan Parker, a Lutheran
pastor who stands in contrast to the urbane men in Helen's fashion
industry world. Dan is grounded physically, socially, emotionally, and
spiritually—he is clearly both husband and father material, and, in
good chick flick fashion, he is, in his words, "a sexy man of God,"
embodying forbidden desire and the lure of fulfillment.

In a climatic scene in the movie, Helen cannot control her teenaged niece, and she and Jenny must track the girl down to a sleazy
motel where the school bad boy is about to rob her of her virginity.
Jenny threatens the boy with a baseball bat while Helen cowers outside

the room. The camera juxtaposes the two women—Jenny, the "good" mother, fearless and frightening in the face of a threat to her child; Helen, the "bad" mother, unable to control her child or her own emotions, as much a child as the child, literally hiding rather than confronting her motherly responsibilities. Helen, the "bad" mother, gives up her children to Jenny, who packs them into her minivan and leaves Helen alone on the curb. Eventually, Helen realizes her misery and need for the children; Jenny is convinced that Helen has become a "good" mother when Helen confronts her teenaged niece about a fake identification card. The final shot of the movie is an ideal nuclear family tableau: Helen and Dan, with the youngest child on his shoulders, a picture of a happy family outing at the zoo.

Not only is the movie premised on the traditional assumption that a woman without a man and a child is ultimately unfulfilled, but there is a postfeminist assumption as well that a woman's fitness as a mother will ultimately be appealing to a (postfeminist) man.[13] Whether single or not, a woman's ability to mother remains a sign of her worth and value as a mate. In this sense, the narrative expounded in *Raising Helen, No Reservations*, and *Mostly Martha* is not a female fantasy after all but a cultural assurance that women can have it all—children and a man, possibly in that order.[14] In addition, all of these films promote a neotraditional view of gender relations in the labor market, subordinating the woman's career ambitions to her maternal needs. Even when she has multiple children to care for, pursuing a career or even earning a living wage should not be a woman's chief concerns. Compromising her value in the labor market is compensated by her increased value in the marriage market, ensuring that a man with a career will earn enough to sustain the family (of course, none of the men in these films abandons his career ambitions).

In *Three Weeks, Three Kids*, the cultural dream of family and children is again played out as a talented, young, single graphic designer is suddenly saddled with custodial responsibility for her sister's children after their grandmother reneges on an agreement to stay with them while their parents take a second honeymoon. As in the other films, the young aunt undergoes a metamorphosis, turning from a carefree spirit unwilling to make a commitment (to either an attractive job offer or her boyfriend) into a mature woman embracing her desires for commitment (the job, a man, and her love for children). The twist in this version is that it only takes three weeks for this aunt to realize her ultimate destiny—in that time, she not only makes the mistakes that catalyze her shift from carefree aunt to responsible mother but she also dumps her equally commitment-phobic boyfriend and takes up with the handsome newcomer across the street, who is stable, handy, cooks, and loves children. Without belaboring the point, this film promotes an implicit claim that despite the choices feminism has secured for women—whether to work or have a family, whether to play around or commit to a husband—women who deny their desire for family and a lifelong heterosexual relationship are inevitably dissatisfied and unstable. The neotraditional maternal aunt offers a useful embodiment of this truism because this figure starts out, by definition, as an aunt and "not a mother." By acting "as if" she is a mother, these single childless aunts realize their essential desires through a self-transformative journey from "bad" to "good" mother.

Altogether, these films reiterate an essentialist cultural narrative of "retreatism" that mandates women's retreat from careers and urban life into the home and the small town.[15] The "happy ending" of all of four films we have considered involves a retreat from the professional world and incorporates the aunt into the heterosexual, nuclear family.[16] In *Mostly Martha*, Martha retreats from the urban, professional life of a master chef to marriage and a family restaurant in the idyllic Italian countryside. In *No Reservations*, Kate retreats from the urban, professional life of a master chef to a neighborhood bistro that she runs with her lover and her niece. In *Raising Helen*, Helen retreats from the fast-paced professional world of high fashion publicity to become a stay-at-home mother with her pastor boyfriend. In *Three Weeks, Three Kids*, Jennifer retreats from a carefree, high-spirited lifestyle without commitments to a commitment at work, a serious relationship, and, without doubt, to the goal of a family like her sister's.

At the same time, the emphasis in these films is that these women *voluntarily chose* to retreat to the private, domestic, intimate sphere, opting out of the career track.[17] This choice is critical: while mothering and family are the culturally preferred choices, all of these movies make clear that women have choices. The neotraditional postfeminist message seems to be that women can choose among many options, but the most fulfilling option, the option that returns a woman to her essential self, is to opt out of public life, professional careers, and urban living, retreating to a separate sphere of private, intimate, domestic life.

TRANSGRESSING THE BAD-TO-GOOD MOTHERING NARRATIVE

The transgressions of the neotraditional maternal aunts in these films have significant implications for cultural conceptions of family, marriage, motherhood, and sexuality. We offer four socially progressive transgressions. First, in these films, a young career woman is the focus of a narrative about recovering the authentic female self by choosing family over career. The films cast this young woman as an aunt in order to emphasize her volition—these women are not pregnant, married, or economically desperate. Indeed, they are contributing consumer citizens. From our perspective, it is clear that these films are about the perennial problem of the single, emancipated woman. At stake is the normative social order based on the persistence of patriarchy, which requires women to take their place as wives and mothers.[18] Such films pathologize the single woman and contribute to the pressure on young women to define their lives in terms of marriage and children.[19] What is exposed through these narratives is a postfeminist paradox: women have choices, but only the right choices will do. And the right choice is never career over family. As these films make clear, debates over work/family balance may be as much about disciplining women's choices as resolving an imbalance.[20] These aunts make evident that women are not truly free to choose in a society that seemingly offers choices and yet disciplines women for not making the "right" choice.

Second, like Andy Griffith's Aunt Bee (chapter 1), these narratives seem to promote yet also undermine the heterosexual nuclear family ideal. The aunt-headed families are not based in procreation; rather, the maternal aunts constitute a family on the basis of existing kin. While these films all settle the maternal aunt in what promises to be a procreative heterosexual union, it is the aunt by herself who creates a family, an act of creation that radically undermines the need for heterosexual reproduction. The inadvertently transgressive vision in these films is that families can be constituted on the basis of choice. Indeed, such families need not be procreative or heterosexual, opening the conception of family to many more alternatives.[21]

Third, neotraditional maternal aunt characters appear in a genre of romance narrative known as "chick flicks" that is often denigrated for formulaic and sexist representations of women's lives. However, there is considerable feminist analysis that argues for a more positive framing.[22] While we have argued that the neotraditional aunt is in cahoots with conservative models of women's nature and gender roles, we admit that such a sweeping critique does not account for the pleasure or popularity of such characters or the romance narratives they populate. Chick flicks or romantic comedies ("romcoms"), romance novels, soap operas, and other media constituting a "women's culture" transgress their own conservative conventions through the intensity of women's desire for the promises offered by these narratives. That is, chick flicks and other women-focused popular media affirm women's desire for the "good life in love" and present "utopian" resolutions of the unresolvable tensions among women's desires and the institutions that discipline them (marriage, family, education, labor, the market, the state).[23] These mediated narratives lay out a story that is reassuringly familiar and maps women's emotional lives onto a recognizable (white, heteronormative) scenario.[24] The twist in the "bad-to-good mothering" narrative is that the aunt's denial of her maternal essence is the reason for her self-alienation, so she has to get children first before getting the man. Nonetheless, postfeminist maternal aunts conform to the paradigmatic narrative.

Although the shallow sentimentalism of these movies is obvious, the narrative itself embodies a mode of "complaint" that stands witness to the personal humiliations and mundane suffering of women's lives.[25] Admittedly, there is a sense of optimism and reassurance as well that reconciles women to their "natural" place in society. Women's genres that feature this narrative and the romance, sentimentality, melodrama, and irony that are its aesthetic style serve to contain, condense, and homogenize women's experiences across significant differences in race, class, age, weight, and the like. Further, on the one hand, the conservative denial of gender politics in these genres of inti-mate complaint undermines the viability of women's culture as a basis for realizing a feminist political agenda. And yet, on the other hand, the transgressive force that the bad-to-good maternal aunt marshals in these "chick flicks" brings together the *collective* witnessing of those small injustices that go unnoticed but still hurt; the *communally* shared pleasures of the texts; and the *shared* hope, if not of overcom-ing gendered relations of power and the institutions that sustain them, then at least the hope of women surviving, even thriving, under such conditions. Shared recognition, pleasure, and hope among women are relational resources that feminism cannot afford to neglect or dismiss.

Finally, these maternal aunts transgress the implicit but normative elements of postfeminist privilege—whiteness, (upper) middle-class aspirations, social and economic capital—that inform their portrayals of "good" and "bad" mothering. Whereas "good" mothering means "opting out" of a career, "bad" mothering is synonymous with inepti-tude. Martha does not know how to comfort her suddenly motherless niece, while Helen does not know how to discipline her three charges. These images of "good" and "bad" mothers are race and class specific; as we discussed in chapter 2, middle-class black mothers are subject to much different images (mammy, black lady, strong black woman), and, when lower-class black mothers are depicted as "bad," the images are much more damaging than ineptness.

Further, the postfeminist "retreatism" with which each film ends its maternal narrative involves downward mobility for middle-class women, an ending that is often an economically unsustainable fairy tale. This is perhaps most dramatically evidenced in statistics about the current U.S. recession. While men's unemployment rates increased and women's rates decreased between 2007 and 2011, women occu-pied more vulnerable job positions (service, public sector, low wage, part time). Even those professional women who were able to "opt out" of the workforce to care for their families appear to be opting back in, according to recent studies by the Center for Work-Life Policy.[26] Hence, the "happy ending" in these narratives fails to address both race and class stratifications and the gendered politics of the ongo-ing economic crisis.[27] At the same time, the underlying postfeminist charge that feminism has pushed women into the workplace against their nature obscures and depoliticizes persistent inequities and material conditions that are oversimplified or ignored in these films. For these reasons, we hold that, from our critical feminist perspective, the neotraditional maternal aunt transgresses her "happy ending" because reflecting on this paradigmatic narrative raises questions about unacknowledged privilege, race and class inequities, and the economics of "retreatism."

The neotraditional aunt starts out as a "bad" mother but ends up as a "good" mother. But the image of the bad mother is entrenched in the cultural imagination. We turn now to several aunts in popular culture who embody cultural fears of bad mothering. These aunts do not transform from "bad" to "good" mothering in the course of a narrative; they remain malevolent throughout. The malevolent aunts pervert maternalism and family values and inspire us to confront prevailing normative assumptions about maternal care, the ethics of intimate relationships, and the nature of home.

NOT LIKE A MOTHER, NOT LIKE A HOME: LIVING WITH MALEVOLENT AUNTS

The cultural anxieties that aunting as mothering both inspires and assuages are given exaggerated expression in the figure of the malevolent aunt. These custodial aunts fulfill their responsibilities for taking care of their nieces and/or nephews in ways that are negligent, harmful, or exploitive. We have argued that the neotraditional maternal aunts in films like *Raising Helen* and *Mostly Martha* progressed from "bad" mothering to "good" mothers through a process of self-transformation and an embrace of their essential desire for family. The malevolent aunts we examine now make no such transformation. These are aunts who mother badly without redress.

For example, in the wildly successful children's fantasy series by J. K. Rowling about apprentice wizard Harry Potter, Harry, the protagonist, lives with a malevolent custodial aunt.[28] In all the books in this popular series, Aunt Petunia suffers Harry's presence in her home with resentment, cruelty, and grudging provision.[29] Although she never turns him out, she subjects him to ongoing humiliation and degradation, metaphorically conveyed in the early books by his bedroom being a closet under the stairs. Likewise, in *James and the Giant Peach*, an award-winning children's book by Roald Dahl and an animated movie version with the same title,[30] Aunt Sponge and Aunt Spiker make their orphaned nephew James' life miserable until he finally escapes them by rolling away inside a giant peach. In both depictions, the custodial aunt is not loving and selflessly devoted but disdainful and mean.

These malevolent aunts treat their nephews with a personalized cruelty that violates deeply entrenched Western norms of child care, nurture, and family relations as loving and benevolent. As custodial caretakers, aunts like Aunt Petunia, Aunt Spiker, and Aunt Sponge affirm by perverting the cultural value and romantic illusions of maternal care. These figures embody the aberrant mother, "the most dreaded of all the monstrous-feminine symbols," because she desecrates "maternal instincts [that] are supposed to be innate."[31] The link between aunting and mothering casts the malice of the aunt as both immoral and unnatural, a distortion of the feminine mothering imperative.

Yet this aunt's malicious ill treatment of her nieces and nephews circumvents any simple dichotomy between the good and the monstrous mother. Unlike Aunt Bee or Aunt Martha or Aunt Helen, these aunts do not mother their nephews but enact aunting as personalized malice, complicating the simple analogy of aunting as mothering.[32] These aunting narratives may be thought of as postfeminist tales of warning: such corrosions and abdications of mothering are what happens when women can choose whether to fulfill or ignore their essential maternal natures.[33] In the Harry Potter series, Aunt Petunia chooses her own son over Harry (complicated by sibling jealousy and her own rejection of magic). Aunts Sponge and Spiker choose consumer pleasures and their own comfort over any maternal feelings for nephew James.

Yet when we reconsider these aunts from a feminist perspective, we find that, rather than condemning their bad mothering, our attention is drawn to the norms of mother care and home that ground such condemnations, reflections that transgress our initial censure and cast these malevolent aunts as catalysts for more ethical and responsive relationships.

RUNNING AWAY FROM THE (DIS)COMFORTS OF HOME: TRANSGRESSING MALEVOLENCE

To suggest that maternal malevolence might have a socially productive dimension runs counter to commonplace norms. Yet we contend that the mothering relationships depicted in these performances generatively transgress their own transgressions of mothering and caregiving. First, these aunts enact a way of relating that facilitates their nephews' crucial development of autonomy, and, second, they illustrate the potential of aunting as an *alternative to* rather than a *substitute for* mothering.

The personalized hostility of these aunts realizes a form of relational intimacy that refuses to objectify or instrumentalize the other.[34] Too often, intimate relations are realized in ways that deny the singularity of the other. That is, when I love you because you are my niece or nephew, I reduce the singularity of you to the qualities of the aunt/ niece or aunt/nephew relationship. In contrast, Harry's Aunt Petunia despises Harry because he is Harry, not because she dislikes him as a nephew or because he has been left on her doorstep. While we prefer benevolence, malevolence also can be the basis for a personalized intimacy.

In the context of such personalized ill-will, both Harry and James exercise the introspective, imaginative, and volitional skills that realize self-definition and autonomy.[35] Harry Potter comes to reflect on and eventually to act on the differences between his magical life at Hogwarts, a resident school for witchcraft and wizardry, and the injustices he suffers in his aunt's home. Likewise, James' aunts, through their exploitation and negligence, provoke his imaginative travels via the magic peach. We do not claim that popular narratives cast these cartoonishly cruel aunts as *intentionally* nurturing autonomy in their nephews or nieces. On the contrary, this form of maternal aunting transgresses cultural expectations that caretakers will protect children from danger and attend to their needs with care and affection. Nonetheless, these transgressions catalyze the development of skills that prepare Harry and James for adventure, freedom, and self-determination.[36]

When intimate relationships are abusive, it is particularly critical that those who are oppressed are able to reflect on the nature of their abuse and, if necessary, reject the commitments to family, kin, friendship, or intimacy that bind them to their oppressors.[37] Just so, Harry Potter is able to distance himself from and reject the cruelty, hypocrisy, and resentments of his aunt's family in the context of his allegiance to his dead parents and to a magical community. James recognizes and escapes the oppressive greed and self-aggrandizement of his aunts first through reveries about the world beyond their house on the hill and then by joining an interdependent community of personified insects living in the giant peach. The lesson of the malevolent aunt is that we cannot afford to excuse any relationships—including mothering, familial, and intimate relationships—from critical reflection by all parties involved.[38]

Another ethically promising transgression of the malevolent aunt is her perversion of the "safe haven" conception of home life. For Harry Potter and James, home with auntie is neither physically nor emotionally safe. The centrality of motherlove to home life, the mother *as* home, is denied; what is most familiar and concrete, the places, relations, and experiences that shape childhood, are rendered both suspect and dangerous in depictions of the aunt as a hateful caretaker. This transgression points to the dangers of the homogenizing norms of home life, those taken-for-granted aspects that (supposedly) render home a place of comfort and safety.

The assurances of "home" often obscure historical, material conditions of oppression, suppression, and privilege by ignoring concrete differences and denying relations of domination and exclusion.[39] Taken-for-granted geographic, racial, and class distinctions and exclusions underlie nostalgic fantasies of the suburban utopia, for example. In contrast, these contrary depictions of maternal aunting make a visible display of "the exclusions and repressions which support the seeming homogeneity, stability, and self-evidence" of our most treasured identities, particularly those secured within the mother-centered home.[40] Moreover, the malevolent aunt demonstrates that even middle-class financial resources and comfortable homes can serve as cover for intimate abuse. This critical vision of identity, home, and family life holds family as embedded in concrete, historical, material circumstances as well as personal histories, desires, and possibilities. This is a vision of family life as an uncertain, open, and unfinished process that encourages us to see our most intimate relations as politically and historically situated.

LIKE A MOTHER? IT'S COMPLICATED

The aunt as a hateful caretaker unsettles the ready analogy of the aunt as mother and, in doing so, offers us a critical perspective on our assumptions about the loving mother as an essential figure of family life and childhood and the bad mother as an immoral and unnatural aberration. The outlandishly perverse mothering of this aunt figure can inspire useful reflections on the moral complexities, ethical responsibilities, and relational skills of intimacy and care, reminding us to remain ethically vigilant against the potential for oppression and subjugation in both intimate relations and traditional models of home and family.

The bad-to-good narratives of neotraditional aunts and the implications for relational autonomy that we have culled from narratives of malevolent maternal aunts demonstrate the ambivalences and provocations of aunting as mothering. The maternal aunts we have considered in this chapter literally embody maternal complexity and eschew ready judgments about "bad" mothering. Further, these figures remind us of the impossibility of experiencing or reflecting on families—whether families by biology or choice—apart from the politics of gender.

WISDOM AND WITCHCRAFT

MAGICAL AUNTS AND NIECES

Among the most intriguing of the popular aunt figures are those whose explicit identities are as powerful benevolent witches who share feminine knowledge—both magical and mundane—with their niece(s). Witch aunts are featured in a wide variety of popular texts, such as the TV classic *Bewitched*,[1] *Sabrina, the Teenage Witch*, a popular 1990s teen TV sitcom,[2] the popular novel *Practical Magic*[3] and the movie of the same title,[4] and in the recent popular novel *A Discovery of Witches*,[5] among others. Two popular television sitcom examples spring to mind immediately: Sabrina, a teenaged witch-in-training who lives with and is mentored by her two witch aunts, and *Bewitched*'s Samantha, who has frequent visits from her outrageous yet lovable Aunt Clara. In addition, the magical aunt is a common character in children's fiction. For instance, the popular children's novel *Island of the Aunts* features magical aunts who kidnap children (with great affection) to help them care for all the magical creatures who seek refuge on the aunts' island—and of course, in this case, the women are honorary aunts to the children.[6] The story *Auntie Claus* is about little Sophie's efforts to discern the magical secrets of her glamorous Great-Aunt Claus and her annual "business trip" during the holidays.[7] In this chapter, we explore the witch aunt and her witchcraft as a powerful cultural trope with an enduring legacy of feminine power, mystery, and danger. Popular narratives of the witch aunt demonstrate postfeminist themes while accommodating alternate readings of otherness, sensuality, feminine wisdom, and witchcraft. Any reading of the witch is tinged by the popular legacy of this figure. We discuss the narrative politics of this legacy before exploring contemporary witch aunts in popular media.

THE TALE OF THE WITCHES

The witch has long been marked specifically as a feminine figure in Western cultures.[8] "Within a gendered society, the idea of an ungendered witch [is] unimaginable."[9] While some men were accused of witchcraft, the vast majority of the people tried for witchcraft were women. This gendered rendering of the witch is a mainstay in the received history of the persecution of witches in Europe and the American colonies.[10] Thus, witches in the contemporary popular imagination tend to be women, rather than men. Further, it is not unusual for witches to be aunts rather than mothers in domestic narratives featuring witchcraft. Her marked outsider status makes the witch more suitable in cultural imagination to being an aunt, who is peripheral to the nuclear family, than to being a mother, who is supposed to occupy the heart of the family home. Thus, witchcraft legends and lore often feature women who are biological (mother's sister), legal (uncle's wife), or honorary (community member) aunts.

While tales of the history of witches and witchcraft vary in details, several common threads persist in traditional stories. They feature a traditional healer, always an unmarried wise woman and often a midwife, who is under suspicion by her village for living on the margins of society, vilified by the church and socially rejected even by those who go to her for healing. She is persecuted especially by men and by masculine institutions—governments, the church, and (later in history) the medical establishment. She is deeply associated with the earth (e.g., she keeps undisciplined gardens, has extensive knowledge of herbs, and often lives in a forest). She threatens the institution of motherhood through sexual knowledge, including birth control and abortion, yet her knowledge comes from generations of women before her, clearly bonding her to her female ancestors and framing her magic as a birthright steeped in a family legacy. When she is accused of witchcraft, she is tortured to elicit a confession[11] and then burned at the stake by cruel men who mistakenly accuse her of devil worship, black magic, and threatening the very social fabric of their village, when in fact she alone has the feminine wisdom and magic to help her people.[12]

Popular conceptions of the history of witchcraft in Europe and the U.S. include various stories drawing on the elements above.[13] And popular belief often includes claims that hundreds of thousands of women, half a million women, even as high as the "mythic nine million," were killed for witchcraft, a version of the story that was embraced by feminists in the 1970s.[14] Critical to this feminist version is that the witch is always burned.[15] According to feminist historians of that time, this persecution was inspired by a shift in social and economic orders from feudal to industrial life and impassioned by a struggle over social control among the church, the state, and traditional agrarian and feudal sites of power and relations of authority. Women in particular were marked as heretical or seditious.

Yet the classic versions of the witch story represent an ahistorical simplification and selective interpretation of "what happened." Many feminist historians now discredit any simplistic summary of witch hunts for deviating from historical evidence in a number of significant ways. Certainly, debates persist about the meaning of the *Malleus Maleficarum* (the official medieval guide to witch hunting), the social and political meanings of witch hunts, and the processes through which they were carried out.[16] However, prevailing understandings of history, including those promulgated by most feminist historians, discredit the notion that alleged witches were almost always burned (most were hung) and estimate that tens of thousands (but *not* hundreds of thousands or millions) of women were executed in Europe over alleged witchcraft. Current feminist histories of witch hunts emphasize the need to understand local cultures and gendered customs that influenced the forms that witch hunts took, the variations among witch hunts in different societies, and the complex social and political contexts of witch hunts.[17] This approach contrasts rather sharply with the earlier tendency in scholarship toward trusting oversimplified evidence and relying on exaggerated numbers of victims for dramatic effect.[18]

The simplified stories of unmarried village women who healed with herbs, acted as midwives, and suffered under trumped-up charges of witchcraft by the church enjoys a curious tenacity as a favored tale and is often the preferred back story for contemporary fictional witch characters. As feminists ourselves, we acknowledge that this story is appealing to those whose feminist perspectives seek clear antagonisms. The story of millions of burning but innocent women betrays a longing for a simple truth, a "story with clear oppositions. Everyone can tell who is innocent and who is guilty, who is good and who is bad. . . . This is, above all, a narrative of the Fall, of paradise lost."[19] As scholars of popular culture, we ask of the canonical story of the witch hunts *not* whether it is true, or which parts of it may be true, but rather what cultural longings are reflected in such a tale, and how those longings underlie the meanings of and transgressive possibilities for witch aunt characters in popular narratives. As we will show, in contemporary popular fiction featuring witches, the power of this figure mobilizes both feminist themes of emancipation, women's ways of knowing, and separatism *and* postfeminist themes of empowerment (especially through consumption), cultural savvy, and heteronormativity.

A Bewitching Tale: Beloved Sitcom Witches

The classic TV witch is *Bewitched*'s Samantha Stephens, who lives with her husband Darrin, and later their daughter Tabitha, in an idealized suburban utopia. The comedic plots revolve around the ever-present threat that Samantha's true identity as a witch would become known to the nosy neighbor Gladys Kravitz, to Darrin's boss, Larry Tate (who stops by for cocktails on a regular basis, sometimes with important clients Samantha needs to impress), or to other recurring and one-time characters. The threat of discovery is heightened by a number of Samantha's relatives and magical acquaintances who pop in and out of the household on a regular basis. One of the recurring characters is the elderly Aunt Clara, whose spells become increasingly erratic as she ages. She inevitably screws up or fails to fix the problems Tabitha naively causes with her developing witchcraft skills while under Aunt Clara's indulgent, not-so-watchful eye as she baby-sits her great-niece.

The show, filmed in black and white for the first two seasons and then in color, was immensely popular during its original run from 1964 to 1972. It continues to be viewed in reruns on networks such as TV Land and Nick at Night, streaming on the Internet, and for purchase as DVDs.[20] Though a supporting role, Aunt Clara was a prominent character on the show. One can even purchase a collection made up entirely of episodes featuring Aunt Clara, who appeared in 28 of the original 254 episodes and stopped appearing in the storylines only because the accomplished stage and TV actress who portrayed her, Marion Lorne, died at the age of eighty-four, just ten days before she was posthumously awarded an Emmy for best supporting actress in the series.

The comedic portrayal of Aunt Clara, while skillfully rendered, adheres to many feminine stereotypes. One observer aptly described Aunt Clara as a "mumbling, bumbling" woman, a "befuddled, muttering, doorknob-collecting witch-aunt . . . [who was portrayed] bouncing

Figure 4.1: The witch aunt: Aunt Clara and Samantha Stephens (from Bewitched, *1964–1972). Shown are Marion Lorne as Aunt Clara and Elizabeth Montgomery as Samantha.*

into walls or conjuring up some unintended piece of witchcraft."[21] The aging spinster is a stock aunt character in popular narratives, and here it is deployed in the comedic portrayal of Aunt Clara as a useless, silly, but lovable old woman with no real power to truly endanger the family's way of life (or anything else), nor with sufficient power to save the day when things have gone wrong.

Samantha's goal of being a wife and mother seems less problematic in a postfeminist age than in the 1970s when a resurgent feminism was questioning women's traditional roles. While there have been historical moments in which her choice to remain in the domestic sphere may have been considered troubling by viewers—for example, during the late 1970s and 1980s as women entered the professions in unprecedented numbers—her housewifery can be readily recouped within the present postfeminist culture as "opting out," a sign of her class status.[22] Her professional husband clearly earns sufficient income for them to live in a beautiful home in which Samantha is largely contained, both visually (she is shown outside of the home only for brief periods) and figuratively, as Darrin frequently urges her to rely on her own labor to care for their home and not to use her magic, which presumably would give her time to engage in other, nonhousewifely activities.[23]

Samantha's choice to remain in the home is tangibly supported by Aunt Clara, who babysits Tabitha when Samantha needs to accompany Darrin out of the home in her role as corporate wife. Aunt Clara's unqualified support contrasts with Samantha's mother Endora's disapproval both of her daughter's suburbanite identity and her marriage to the mortal Darrin (whom she refers to by a long list of purposely erroneous names such as Darwood and Dum Dum).[24] Samantha is always caught between mother and husband. In contrast, Aunt Clara, Samantha, and Tabitha (as a young witch) form a feminine triad that leaves out the nonmagical father/husband and also sidesteps the antagonism with Endora's rejection of domesticity. Like every character on the show, Aunt Clara is white and presumably comfortably well off, at least as evidenced by her good grooming, nice clothes, and absence of any discussion of financial strain. This makes Aunt Clara a "model elderly person" who serves as a source of material and emotional support for the nuclear family in the mythic suburban household.

We find several transgressive qualities in the Aunt Clara witch. First, although she seems to be inept but innocuous, Aunt Clara is potentially unruly within the suburban utopia where witchcraft lurks undetected but suspected by the neighbors. While Samantha tries to pass as a housewife, Aunt Clara continually disrupts the masquerade by creating charming mayhem, thereby calling attention to the secret world of witches living in the midst of suburbia. After all, the alternative world that Samantha and her witch kin embody literally threatens the repressive order of the whitewashed suburban community, evoking the ongoing anxiety in white society about integration, immigration, and what type of family might move in next door. At the time that *Bewitched* was originally broadcast, the civil rights movement and racial unrest nationwide, while absent on the sitcom, was a very real part of contemporary life. The breakdown of legal segregation in education and legislation forbidding racial discrimination in housing and mortgage lending (Title VIII of the Civil Rights Act of 1968, the Fair Housing Act) also led to slow but noticeable changes in the composition of neighborhoods that made many white people uncomfortable.[25] Hence, the analogy between racial others and witches as aliens or others whose presence in the neighborhood threatens the safety of the neighborhood is a fitting one. While all of Samantha's relatives threaten Samantha's masquerade and the orderliness of (white) suburban life, it is the elderly aunt who keeps nearly outing Samantha's true identity as a witch, transgressing the smooth performance of appearances that is often taken to mask lurking perversions and danger. Further, she demonstrates the fragility of this suburban order because she is not trying to be disruptive. She enacts her disruptions not by devious strategies but by mistake, by doddering blunders and foolish acts. In this sense, Aunt Clara truly is dangerous.

Little wonder that Clara is cast as an elderly female relative. The stereotype of the dotty old aunt draws on the economic, social, and cultural powerlessness of elderly unmarried women in patriarchal societies. In this guise, Clara's errant magic is less threatening and more palatable. As the lovable, eccentric, powerless, batty spinster, she is readily recouped into acceptable domestic norms. The stereotype of the dotty, asexual, lovable elderly woman remains a stock feature of commercial television.[26] Calling out ageism as a comic device as well as popular representations that denigrate elderly women can contribute to feminist critiques, particularly analyses of how such devices and images inform contemporary issues such as retirement economics, elder abuse, and elderly women's health issues, including sexuality.[27]

Notably, Aunt Clara is depicted as the oldest witch on the series. If we set this fictional character within the popular tales of medieval persecutions and the struggle against witches' power, she becomes a survivor of those struggles.[28] More to the point, while most of the characters appear middle-aged, Clara's age casts her as an "old witch," a character with considerable mythic status. Her own masquerade as a lovable old aunt makes more visible the contrasts between known and unknown, harmless and dangerous, and especially human and nonhuman (or mortals and witches/warlocks) that are central to *Bewitched*. The threat of the alien other in the suburban heart of America is compounded by a fear of feminine mystery and power.

Perhaps the most important transgression is the struggle over identity and allegiance precipitated by Aunt Clara's insistence on the validity and relevance of Samantha's witch identity. Aunt Clara covers the danger of discovery and persecution—in this case, social ostracism and loss of Darrin's income—with comedy, but she still does her part to reinforce Samantha's heritage as a hereditary witch. Unlike Samantha's mother, Endora, who meddles in her daughter's marriage and decries Samantha's efforts to pass as mortal, Aunt Clara's efforts are more ambivalent. She both enables Samantha's ruse and yet requires Samantha to use her powers in order to rectify Clara's unwitting mishaps. Aunt Clara's ongoing befuddlement is not evidence of unease with her identity as a witch but of her comic ineptitude. More effectively than Endora's explicit rejection, Clara makes clear the primacy of Samantha's witch identity and allegiances. Whereas the tension between mother and daughter compels Samantha to reaffirm her commitment to the mortal world, Aunt Clara's support and befuddlement make it impossible for Samantha to deny her identity and powers as a witch. For us, this raises questions about the viability of identity politics and the tenacity of essentialist identities. The two older witches,

Clara and Endora, call Samantha back to her primary allegiances by rejecting or confounding her performance of mortal identity and neo-traditional femininity and calling her to account for denying her witch identity or requiring her to enact it. For Samantha, there are conflicting longings: her essential longing to be a wife and mother versus her essential longing to affirm her heritage and difference. The struggle over identity turns out to be ambivalent, overdetermined, and always unfinished.

Some of the issues raised in *Bewitched*—the fragility of domestic and social order, the threat of the "other," identity struggles—are revisited in another popular series featuring witches. This time it is not an old witch but a young one who engages these concerns.

TRAINING THE TEENAGE WITCH

One of the most popular teen sitcoms during the 1990s was *Sabrina, the Teenage Witch*, and the show continues to be widely viewed in syndication. *Sabrina* features a teen "apprentice" witch who lives with two custodial aunts, Hilda and Zelda, sisters who are practicing witches. They live in an affluent suburb where (for the first four seasons) Sabrina attends high school with her best friend Jenny (who disappears later in the series and is replaced by another girl, Valerie), a boyfriend, Harvey, and her nemesis, the "popular girl," Libby. In seasons 5–7, Sabrina attends college and has various roommates and a different boyfriend (Josh). Her aunts remain part of the storylines even though Sabrina no longer resides with them. Marketed primarily to teen girls, *Sabrina* exemplifies postfeminist lessons reflecting (hetero)sexist roles for women, a focus on class privilege, consumption as a primary means of self-expression, the body as a locus of femininity and sexual empowerment, and assumptions that girls' social, economic, and political opportunities are there for the taking in an era of gender equality (ergo feminism is taken into account).

Aunt Hilda and Aunt Zelda own a large, white, beautifully furnished Victorian house where the three of them reside within the ideal school district. Sabrina attends a public school full of nice suburban kids, including her sensitive and attentive boyfriend Harvey. No violence, deprivation, or material inequities exist in fictional Westbridge,

Massachusetts (where no one has a New England accent). Every student is dressed in clean, new-looking, fashionable clothes, the lockers are pristine and free of scuff marks, the hallway floors always shine. Sabrina walks to school through a lovely residential street of well-kept, single-family homes. Everyone except Sabrina presumably has the requisite two married parents, and the two aunts both date men and obsess about their attractiveness to men, ensuring that they are easily understood as heterosexual. They are sisters, so there is no hint that they may be having an undercover lesbian relationship. Nonwhite characters are few and far between and never figure as primary characters.

Obsession with boys is the order of the day for Sabrina. For young female millennials, "power also comes from judging, dissing, and competing with other girls, especially over guys."[29] Sabrina has a rival, Libby, demonstrating that competing with other girls is normative, even important to the process of adolescent development. In the made-for-TV movie that launched the series, the two girls literally compete with each other for the attention of the captain of the football team.[30] Likewise, in an early episode of the first season, Sabrina gets defensive when grounded by her aunts and is unable to attend a party with Harvey. At school, Libby assures Sabrina that she will be attending the party and will be sure to be available for Harvey, who just shrugs helplessly. Boys are cast as entitled to girls' attention, and competition between girls for the prize of boys' favor is naturalized. Lesbian and gay teens are completely absent from this magical fairy tale, as are girls with better things to do than obsess over boys and how to attract them.

In *Sabrina*, the use of magic blurs fantasy and reality as Sabrina's adolescent troubles are often both the incentive for and site of magical interventions that materialize her impulsive wishes. Witch aunts Hilda and Zelda police the rules of competition—how and why Sabrina uses her fledgling witchcraft skills—but never question the idea of competition for male favor. Indeed, they eagerly seek male attention in their own lives, periodically dating men for whom they elaborately adorn themselves and then feeling angry or sad when rejected in the game of dating. Thus it is not only magic that the witch aunts teach Sabrina but the rules of heterosexual coupling as well: women's competition and being physically attractive specifically to please men are just as important as witchcraft.

Consumption is another preoccupation of the teenaged Sabrina. A plethora of cultural messages assures young women that going to a mall and buying trendy clothes and other items is empowering.[31] The very first thing that Sabrina does after discovering her magical powers is to cast a rapid series of spells to change her clothing repeatedly and to dress her hair differently for each outfit. She thus demonstrates that when given unlimited powers, what a girl really wants is not to save the world or achieve outstanding academic or career success but to maximize her ability to look as attractive as possible in the most current fashions. This theme is carried on in the opening credits of the show, which features Sabrina flashing from one outfit to another, smiling into a full-length mirror in affirmation of her most important asset, her adorned body.

How Zelda and Hilda are able to afford all of the luxuries their niece craves is unclear, for neither of them is ever seen working outside the home. Although Sabrina does work part time during college, her consumption obviously outstrips her earning power. The unstated assumption is that money is readily available and not a cause for concern, except when the longing for a specific expensive luxury item forms a convenient plot device. Poverty is completely erased, along with any societal, economic, or political messiness. The bubble of privilege obscures the reality of a world where the clothes Sabrina prizes so much were sewn by third-world children in sweatshops, most teens cannot afford the latest fashions, and city kids face a likely threat of armed robbery for their athletic shoes.[32] To be fair, this bubble is typical of teenage comedies (e.g., *Saved by the Bell*; *Buffy the Vampire Slayer*). Moreover, the show's focus on consumerism and affluence in Sabrina's life reflects a world in which teens are savvy consumers who make a large number of purchasing decisions: today's teens have more money to spend at their own discretion than previous generations (about $150 per month on average), and they also exert significant influence over family purchases, such as apparel and technology.[33]

On the surface, Sabrina and her aunts do little to trouble postfeminist perspectives of society, and there is little narrative depth below that glossy surface that might hint at other readings. The sitcom exists within a postfeminist dreamworld. Yet it is the taken-for-grantedness of the show as innocent fun for girls that makes it potentially powerful when we rethink the possibilities of witch aunts.

WITCH-HEADED HOUSEHOLDS

Several potentially transgressive elements of *Sabrina, the Teenage Witch* merit discussion. First, Sabrina and her aunts can be read as subverting mainstream ideals in the way in which the show imagines the family unit. The aunts establish a nonnuclear, female-headed household as a meaningful kinship arrangement. When Sabrina's television story opens, her (married, heterosexual) parents have already left her in her aunts' care, allegedly only for a year. Although presumably never parents themselves, the aunts readily accept their niece. Likewise, Sabrina is not angry or hurt to have been abandoned by her biological parents to her aunts' care; she embraces their maternal authority and their love as natural, even before she learns that living away from her parents is part of the witches' code that stipulates nonparental mentors for all adolescent witches. The aunts mentor more than they mother their niece, thus conflating family, kinship, and friendship with apprenticeship and education. While men are sought-after romantic objects, they are never portrayed as necessary to survival. The only male in the household is Salem, a talking cat who is actually a warlock whose punishment for breaking witch laws is a century in cat form (a stereotypically feminine manifestation), so masculine domestic power is firmly rejected. Indeed, the three women are portrayed as in many ways an ideal family unit who truly want to live with each other and encounter no serious social or economic problems doing so, transgressing the continued dominance of nuclear family idealization.

Second, women's power also undeniably—and problematically—functions as a central trope of the show. The sitcom frame of the narrative in which all problems are resolved within thirty minutes (minus commercials) reinforces the perception of the aunts' power to magically fix Sabrina's mistakes or to help her to do so efficiently. These female characters are accepted as innately powerful, with tremendous capacity to affect the course of their own lives; indeed, it appears that women need only snap their fingers or wiggle their noses to effect meaningful change in the real world. While there is tremendous appeal in such representations of women's empowerment (not to mention the joys of immediate wish fulfillment), this vision contrasts sharply with real-world power structures and the overwhelming evidence of continued male control of government, corporate, and social life, including the broadcast entertainment industry.[34] The witch aunts and niece thus embody a caricature of the postfeminist assumption that feminine ways of wielding power and feminine bodies as power wielders can change the world both in and outside the home simply through their own (magical) willpower. This postfeminist promise that girls who work hard enough—on their education, on their careers, on their bodies, on themselves—will realize personal success and happiness while also transforming the world is ultimately oversimplified. Neglected is a more robust, complex vision of the world that depends less on the "magic" of girls with fashion sense and attitude and more on insight into the ways women's educated labor and consuming power have become critical to global capitalism, especially as this system perpetuates traditional power structures in ways that systematically disadvantage girls of color, LGBTQ girls, and girls living in poverty while rendering them all but invisible. All of these forces set the young, savvy, empowered, educated, employable contemporary girl as, paradoxically, the locus of social change and the subject of traditional gender subordination.[35]

It is this last observation that evokes a final transgressive implication: despite their postfeminist guise, the witch aunts take up the ongoing feminist struggle to assert the value of women, girls, and feminine identities. For them and for us, feminism and the need for feminist struggle are far from over. These witch aunts mentor their niece in strategies (social as well as magical) meant to prepare her to counter the subordination of feminine difference. This practical approach to women's struggle and the value of a feminine standpoint sharply contrasts with traditional (and continued) social privileging of masculine values, masculine ways of being, and men. A significant goal of U.S. liberal feminist activism in the 1960s and 1970s was to pass

legislation that secured equal rights for girls in the education system
and to help women engage in consciousness raising to understand the
ways in which women were unfairly and systematically devalued.
Despite these efforts, there is continued evidence of gender-based discrimination and oppression. For example, while female infanticide and
sex selection through abortion are not prevalent cultural practices in
the U.S., parents (particularly fathers) still report a preference for having a son over a daughter.[36] And of course, overwhelming evidence
supports the reality that our society does not live up to its promises
to girls, as mothers continue to face far greater restrictions on career
advancement and work/life balance than do fathers, men continue
to earn higher wages than women (yes, even in the severe economic
recession), women do the vast majority of unpaid and poorly paid elder
care and care for people with chronic illness and disabilities, and one
in four women in the U.S. is sexually assaulted during her lifetime—
need we go on?[37]

By many measures, successful women are still women who manage to act like men while looking and sounding like women. Despite
all the changes in current ideals of masculinity to incorporate hands-
on approaches to fathering and more collaborative forms of management, men face no significant social pressure to act like women while
sounding like men. It is in the context of these realities that we argue
for a liberal feminist impulse in the representation of witches who love
and mentor their niece not despite of her femininity but because of
it. While we have pointed out what we see as serious limitations to
Sabrina and her aunts' very girly, sexualized, heterosexual femininity, we nonetheless believe that the aunts' commitments to mentoring from and valuing a liberal feminist perspective enlist them in the
unfinished goal to eliminate once and for all the cultural bias toward
valuing boys, men, and masculinity over girls, women, and femininity.

Sabrina may offer a thoroughly postfeminist vision of women's
empowerment.[38] Yet the show envisions postpatriarchal kinship, draws
our attention to what is missing from postfeminist promises that girls
are magical and powerful, and reaffirms ongoing feminist struggles
against gender discrimination.

PRACTICING STRONG MAGIC: AUNTS AND FAMILY CURSES

Practical Magic is the title of both a popular novel written by Alice Hoffman and a film adaptation in 1998. The two versions of the story both focus on a multigenerational family of witches, but they diverge quite radically from each other, so we focus exclusively on the film version, a supernatural romance.[39] In the film, two aunts, Jet and Fran, raise their orphaned nieces, Sally and Gillian, after the girls lose their parents to a family curse. The curse afflicts all Owens women—any man they truly love will die a tragic death. So their father died, and their mother, who truly loved him, died of a broken heart. The unmarried aunts provide a loving, if eccentric and permissive, home to the girls, who then grow up as witches themselves. As a romance narrative, the goal is to achieve true love, of course. The aunts magically nudge Sally into a relationship with a handsome young man for whom Sally has been discreetly longing. Since she loves him, he dies tragically several years later while their two daughters are very young, and Sally and her girls move home to live with Aunt Jet and Aunt Fran. Meanwhile Gillian has run away in the middle of the night from the small-town life of her aunts and comes back later pursued by a psychotic ex-boyfriend with a handsome sheriff on his trail. The aunts and nieces must come together, along with several women of the community who both feared and revered the witch family, to break the dangerous curse and let everyone live happily ever after.

The Owens live in a lovely, privileged community, like Samantha and Sabrina, but in their community large houses with big yards full of climbable trees, catchable frogs, and pastoral beauty contrast with the sanitized suburbs. Love is literally at the center of the family curse, and hence at the center of the narrative, and that love is unquestionably and exclusively heterosexual. The witch aunts and nieces use herbs and other natural ingredients to brew their spells, reinforcing a link to nature and further framing heterosexual love as part of the natural order. Money is clearly not an issue, as the aunts do not work outside of the home (other than as witches for hire when local women seek love potions and the like). Although she has moved back to her aunts' home, Sally appears to have made the move more out of a desire for kinship and support rather than as a financial necessity. Indeed, Sally has the resources to open her own shop, where she sells essential oils and homemade soaps infused with flowers and herbs.

Once again, a surface reading of these witch aunts does not trouble the postfeminist worldview. The young women are thin and beautiful; both sport trendy clothes and perfect hair styles. The spinster aunt witches are rendered as nonthreateningly absurd middle-aged women who give their nieces cake for breakfast and brew spells in the blender. They are clearly not to be taken seriously. A popular scene in the movie shows them whipping up a batch of magical "midnight margaritas" in the blender and dancing sensually around the kitchen table while singing "Lime in the Coconut."[40] Eventually the aunts gather the women of the town to perform a group incantation and successfully save the day with an awesomely powerful spell. In the final scene, the witches, in black robes and pointy witch hats, glide effortlessly down from the rooftop to amuse the neighborhood children in a Halloween tableau. And of course the happy ending for Sally and the sheriff comes about as well, as they fall in love.

MAGICAL SOLIDARITY AND NARRATIVE AMBIVALENCE

As with Sabrina, aunting in the Owens family narrative is intertwined with the practice of magic, the nonnuclear, feminine household is affirmed as a meaningful kinship arrangement, and the matrilineal heritage of witchcraft is acknowledged. Loving bonds among women not only make them happy—where men often have failed to do so— but literally save the day at the climax of the story. The aunts shine as examples of strong women in the face of adversity who mobilize their local community—an image of women's solidarity—to fight back against the extreme masculine forces that assault their nieces and their town. As an injunction to feminist solidarity and struggle, *Practical Magic* casts the witch aunts as the dangerous witches of legend, gesturing not so subtly to a radical second-wave feminist vision of an alternative way of being and acting, in which feminine sensuality overcomes the domination of masculine violence. Additionally, as a feminist, transgressive tale, *Practical Magic* complicates the "burn the witch" tale by having the witches do the burning, at least metaphorically, showing strength and solidarity when they come together for collective resistance. While it conforms to the plot of women's romance quite conventionally, *Practical Magic* also includes a vision of cultural life organized around nonrational (magical) forces and women's sensuality. In this vision, sensuality, passion, and impulse are meaningful forces that move beyond rational thought and blur the taken-for-granted order of everyday life.

Narrative ambivalence is apparent: the Hollywood ending notwithstanding, the witch aunts offer hope not of a perfect ending but of endings that are good enough—new love replaces lost love, women reaffirm their bonds with each other, and evil is vanquished, at least for now. The story complicates the "love conquers all" moral and instead offers a more nuanced story of danger that accompanies living, loving, and loss. Far from the sitcom silliness of Samantha and Sabrina, this story's conflicts include death, violence, and both physical and emotional danger, and the witches brew an equally violent revenge to ultimately kill Gillian's ex-boyfriend. The simple fairy tale equation of husbands and boyfriends as sources of everlasting love and happy endings falls apart. Love under patriarchy is revealed in this story to be dangerous, even deadly: Sally and Gillian lose both their parents to the curse, Sally's heart is broken after she loses her husband, and then Gillain's demonic boyfriend sexually assaults her and attempts to rape her. The witch aunts affirm magic as a practical force for fulfilling desire—conveying the warning to be careful what you wish for.

STRANGE ALLIANCES: WITCH AUNTS AND NONHUMAN OTHERS

The recent popular novel *A Discovery of Witches* offers a current version of witchcraft, aunts, and nieces.[41] In some ways, this story echoes themes we observed in other witch aunts; yet it also forwards some bolder reflections that transgress the limits of feminine stereotypes in postfeminist culture.

Diana Bishop is a witch who actively works to deny her magical heritage and suppress and rechannel her magic energies. Her aunts Sarah and Em raised her after the traumatic loss of her parents, who were murdered when she was ten years old. Aunt Em is her mother's sister, Aunt Sarah is Em's life partner. The aunts and their niece are hereditary witches, direct descendants of the first woman executed during the Salem witch trials. They all live in a small town in upstate New York in a magical house that has a character all its own—the house adds rooms at will, offers items previously hidden, and is haunted by family ghosts. The plot begins with Diana, now a tenured professor of history at Yale University, conducting research in a library at Oxford University. There she unknowingly unlocks an enchantment on a long-lost manuscript thought to contain powerful secrets about supernatural creatures.[42] In the world of the book, in addition to humans and witches, vampires and "daemons" populate the earth (and perhaps other species yet to be revealed). The story spirals rapidly not toward conclusion but toward a Tolkien *Fellowship of the Rings*–type ending where a motley, interspecies fellowship has gathered against all odds and then disperses strategically to help the anointed one (Diana) to accomplish her Herculean task to save all of humanity and the supernatural creatures from an epic war.[43]

This updated witch story continues many of the same traditions and old threads—Diana's beauty is praised far more than her intelligence and her heterosexuality is unproblematically assumed and then validated by Matthew, the attractive, provocative male vampire who loves her instantly and passionately pursues her.[44] Her maternal-minded aunts worry about her constantly and keep in close contact with her, admonishing her to take good care of herself and entreating her to guard her safety. While Diana roams the globe, her aunts remain sequestered in the domestic sphere of the Bishop ancestral home in the woods (until the very end of this lengthy novel).

Supernatural Identity Politics

A Discovery of Witches offers a witch aunts story with some transgressive possibilities that are more overt than in the narratives we have explored thus far. What differs is the degree to which the novel offers an explicitly progressive sexual politics, while also affirming tried and true narrative elements of (heterosexual) romantic fiction. The story is in keeping with a recent trend toward including gay subplots to complement primary love stories with straight couples in film, TV, and novels. The book also fits squarely in the current decade's fascination with supernatural species, most notably vampires but also werewolves, fairies, and superheroes.

The novel takes sides on gay marriage and families by explicitly identifying the aunts as a lesbian couple with a long-lasting, loving bond. While the aunts take their niece's lack of romance as problematic and pester her to get a boyfriend, their own sexuality is neither muted nor rendered as spectacle. Instead, a progressive spin on the story normalizes homosexuality—the openly lesbian aunts joke about hiding to have furtive sex when Diana was young, replacing any subtle narrative subtext of spinster aunts as lesbian. In addition, Diana's consistent framing of her biological aunt's partner as also truly her aunt despite the lack of biological or legal connection (the two are repeatedly affirmed as "my aunts are calling") argues for the normalcy of a lesbian family.

Moreover, the story does not merely posit multiple species living alongside one another, but ventures into cross-species romance and invokes racial politics.[45] The book embraces a multiculturalist perspective, implicitly arguing for acceptance of differences that matter equally. The theme of racial prejudice is broached early in the narrative: the aunts initially display an unattractive bigotry toward vampires that is founded in a centuries-old covenant forbidding interspecies romantic ties or breeding. In a *Guess Who's Coming to Dinner*–type meeting,[46] Diana brings her vampire boyfriend home to the aunts, who are soon won over by his personality and obvious devotion to their niece.[47] The story thus addresses intercultural/interracial marriage in the face of institutionalized discrimination (the witch/vampire/daemon governing council prohibits interspecies marriage and reproduction). Also in the assemblage of characters at Aunt Sarah and Aunt Em's house is a young witch-daemon couple, currently pregnant with a witch fetus (in the daemon mother), facing persecution if their interspecies reproduction is found out. In addition, Matthew's son, made not born, is the ultimate example of single-parent reproduction and a single-father family. These challenges to conventional sexual and family dynamics reiterate key themes in earlier stories of witch aunts—once again centering intimacy and caring in female relationships and extolling a flexible, voluntary, communal model of kinship.

Further, the witch aunts invoke a politics of alliance across differences on both personal (romantic love, childbearing) and political (fighting evil forces, cooperation to protect all species) fronts, not by erasing or ignoring differences but by respecting and engaging them.[48] The narrative thus supports contemporary feminist activism promoting antiracist politics, reproductive choices, shifting family forms, gay marriage, cross-cultural relationships, intercultural pluralism, and even intersections across species. The narrative openly recognizes multiple sexualities and allegiances, while addressing ageism, beauty, and power. While still firmly adhering to romantic and supernatural story line conventions, this image of a powerful niece and her witch aunts makes a transgressive nod to a feminist agenda.

MAGICAL IMPLICATIONS OF AUNTING

The witch remains a figure of fascination in popular culture whose visage shifts radically depending on the particular context.[49] Framed by second-wave feminist campaigns against patriarchal domination, the witch becomes a projection of sexual energy and anger emphasizing the violence of persecutions. Admittedly, the popular witch aunts we discuss are thinly drawn caricatures that obscure historical contexts through flip reinventions. At the same time, these figures articulate a persistent fear of and fascination with feminine alliances and power that gain particular force in the context of the ongoing "crisis of masculinity" and the social, political, and cultural "backlash" against feminism.[50] In evoking cultural fears, fascination, and anxieties, even trite popular performances of witch aunts point to the vulnerability of dominant gender and cultural orders and evoke varied images of feminine power and social transformation. In short, images of popular witch aunts implicate transgressive gendered struggles over social traditions and trajectories for change.[51]

Witch aunts—including Clara, Zelda, Hilda, Jet, Fran, Sarah, and Em—talk back to the idea that we are done with the need for collectivist feminism and affirm the possibility of social change through allies and coalition building. Given the persistent association between femininity, female wisdom, and witchcraft as a threat to the established order, it makes sense that some feminists would embrace traditional

associations with witchcraft as a site of potential protest and transformation.[52] Feminist theorist and witch Starhawk defines magic as the
power "to change consciousness at will."[53] She reclaims magic as a
way of thinking about feminine, nurturing power to heal ourselves and
the world, a form of empowerment she calls "power with," contrasted
to a hierarchical and exploitative "power over" that seeks to dominate
others, especially those whom we perceive as different from ourselves.
Other feminists also embrace the contemporary practice of witchcraft
as a secular and/or religious practice of feminist activism that can foster strong bonds among women and transform popular beliefs about
gender and power.[54] Recreating what is accepted as contemporary
postfeminist "reality" is an ambitious project that will require strong
alliances among feminist activists.

ECCENTRIC AUNTS
SANITY, SEXUALITY, AND SPECTACLE

Unruly, disorderly, hysterical, eccentric images of women reveal long-standing Western cultural fears and fascinations with transgressions of the feminine and the female.[1] Feminist theory has celebrated the transformative potential of the feminine eccentric, a figure that moves out of bounds, skirting the limits of theoretical, social, and political conventions and traditions.[2] In this sense, the popular image of the eccentric aunt who engages in outlandish displays or "makes a spectacle of herself" offers a model of feminine transgression that disrupts sexual and social proprieties, rational order, and conventional femininity. The eccentric aunt is a mainstay of popular culture portrayals of extended family relations—for example, popular narratives like *Housekeeping, Arsenic and Old Lace, Auntie Mame,* or *A Series of Unfortunate Events,* which portray the aunt as mad, flamboyant, or hysterical.[3] The humorous frame in which eccentric aunts often are presented renders them seemingly harmless and therefore palatable for broad audiences.[4] However, we contend that such aunts can be reclaimed as fissures that expose the persistently gendered cultural relations circumscribing who we are and who we can be. Laughter is powerful; if we can recognize a gendered norm, make fun of it, and laugh at it, we may become empowered to change it.[5] At the same time, we note the political limitations of irony and caricature: while media scholars once attributed a critical attitude to such forms, there is now a sense that irony in popular culture too often fails critique. We consider why eccentric aunt figures are construed as both deviant and humorous in order to point to transgressive elements that offer opportunities for feminist critique and re-vision.

FEMININE EXCESS: SEXUALITY AND COMING OF AGE

The first examples we focus on are sexually liberated feminine eccentrics: Auntie Mame and Aunt Augusta. Auntie Mame is the title character in the best-selling novel by Patrick Dennis, first published in 1955 and still in print, produced as a Broadway play and twice as a movie, the original starring Rosalind Russell and the remake starring Lucille Ball.[6] Aunt Augusta is a central character in the Graham Greene novel *Travels with My Aunt* and the movie adaptation of the same title starring Maggie Smith. Both are coming-of-age tales in which an older, world-wise, and libertine aunt guides a sexually repressed and unsophisticated nephew through a series of madcap adventures. In both, the mystery and power of feminine desire and excess counters the normative forces of masculine rationality and social propriety.

Mame is depicted as a flamboyant, charming, witty, exuberant, madcap, sophisticated, and passionate 1920s socialite. She becomes the custodial aunt of her orphaned nephew while she is living in a Manhattan apartment in inherited luxury. The coming-of-age story focuses on Mame's ongoing project to loose her nephew from the constrictions of conformity, convention, and stodginess. Published during the conservative retrenchment of the 1950s, it is not surprising that the story of Auntie Mame continually recuperates her eccentricities through her desire for family. Such a desire is always at odds with and threatened by her flamboyant lifestyle and her continually demonstrated inability to conform to expectations of normal family life and feminine conventions.

Auntie Mame differs from the maternal aunts in that she is not tied to the domestic sphere and defies rather than succumbs to the strictures of domesticity and the conventions of "proper" child rearing in favor of the pleasures and challenges of life lived as a public spectacle. The narrative upholds twentieth-century American optimism and faith in liberal capitalism as Mame loses her fortune in the 1929 crash and regains it by marrying an oil tycoon whose death leaves her independently wealthy again. This is a tale of lifestyle triumphing over adversity. In the final scenes, as Mame is writing her memoir, she announces the theme as one of unbridled personal consumption and individualism: "Live! Life's a banquet and most poor suckers are starving to death!"

Figure 5.1: The eccentric aunt exemplar: Auntie Mame (played by Rosalind Russell in the 1958 film directed by Morton DaCosta).

Travels with My Aunt was first published in 1969, adapted for the stage in 1989, and produced as a film in 1972. The story sets eccentric aunting in the context of 1960s cultural tensions between libertine (Aunt Augusta) and conservative (nephew Henry) attitudes and lifestyles. Written by renowned novelist Graham Greene, the story is told by Henry Pulling, a staid retired bank manager, who opens by sharing, "I met my Aunt Augusta for the first time in more than half a century at my mother's funeral" (p. 3). Henry is unmarried, grows dahlias, and leads an unassuming life. After their meeting at the funeral, seventy-five-year-old Aunt Augusta insists that Henry accompany her on a series of trips, first to Brighton, then Paris, then on the Orient Express to Istanbul, and finally Paraguay. In the course of these trips, she continually affronts Henry's conventional attitudes and habits, drawing him into a world of illicit affairs—sexual, political, and business. Though never married, she has had a succession of lovers, and, in drawing out her memories, Henry finds that his father may have been one of those lovers and that his mother may have been his aunt and Aunt Augusta his mother. Yet Aunt Augusta is clearly not a maternal aunt; her efforts to open Henry to the pleasures and thrills of a life lived for the moment are more self-serving instrumental ploys than maternal care. Though a comic character, Aunt Augusta's flamboyance is underwritten by a dark ambivalence toward death, morality, and propriety. For example, at one point, Henry asks her whether she is really a Roman Catholic. "She replied promptly and seriously, 'Yes, my dear, only I just don't believe in all the things they believe in'" (143). Against Henry's pompous and unreflective moral judgments, she espouses a personal commitment to individualism and moral relativism: "Regret your own actions, if you like that kind of wallowing in self-pity, but never, never despise. Never presume yours is a better morality" (103).

Both of these narratives were written and popular prior to the postfeminist moment, yet both speak to postfeminist concerns, notably the celebration of eccentric femininity as a form of individual empowerment, self-fulfillment through consumption, unreflective class privilege, unmarked whiteness, and women's fear of aging. Perhaps most obvious is the celebration of eccentricity as individual empowerment in both *Mame* and *Travels*. The evidence of feminine empowerment in both narratives is not only the free-spirited willfulness and command exercised by both characters but the censure and discipline to which both are subject. Mame's independent choices regarding her nephew's schooling, her unabashedly libertine lifestyle, and her unapologetic support for socially denigrated others, including her unconventional friends and her pregnant unmarried secretary, provoke dire responses from civil authorities. For example, when she insists on a bohemian education for her nephew, the child welfare authorities force her to send him to a boarding school, removing him from her home and daily influence. Her pain at this loss dramatizes the risks of living as a strong, independent woman. Similarly, Augusta's independence informs her ribald past, her reckless lifestyle, and her strong loyalties.

Both Mame and Augusta enjoy class positions that enable their eccentricities, and neither questions her right to luxury or class privilege. Both are deeply enmeshed in racist social formations. Aunt Augusta's affair with her black live-in assistant Wordsworth is particularly troubling. Wordsworth is cast as the "exotic Other," immersed in fortune-telling, prostitution, and drug trafficking and serving Augusta as a "body servant" who is at her beck and call domestically and sexually. Eventually he is discarded, not only as a lover and a manservant but also as a human being, given that he is killed as a vagrant and an intruder outside a party thrown by Augusta and her long-lost paramour, the illicit businessman Mr. Visconti. Perhaps most obvious in both narratives is an underlying despair and desperation over aging that affirms the cultural intolerance for old women. While Auntie Mame defies her age against a biographical narrative that spans several decades, Augusta is introduced as a woman in her seventies. But like Mame, her flamboyance, sexual energies, and recklessness defy the cultural and physical strictures of age. Even so, both characters are disciplined by the normative force of youth and beauty for women.

Both Mame and Augusta are drawn with such exaggeration that the passion for life they embody can be dismissed as too wildly eccentric, a dismissal predicated on a shared belief that such a role is preposterous for a normal, healthy, sane woman.[7] In this sense, the eccentricities of these aunts are recuperated; indeed, they become examples of the extravagances permitted the rich and/or the daft. At the same time, both figures offer an ironic perspective, casting into question the norms defining what is to be taken as sane, normal, natural, and inevitable. This is a perspective readily assimilated to postfeminist perspectives on feminine autonomy, sexuality, and consumption. Mame and Augusta might be cast as protopostfeminists, embodying a sexually liberated and empowered womanhood buoyed by class privilege and male patronage. And yet, we argue that these performances offer a transgressive distance from and a parodic critique of gender conventions.

TRANSGRESSIVE CAMP PERFORMANCES

We suggest that, in inviting us to laugh, the eccentric aunt instigates a transgressive protest against the strictures of conventionality. Mame and Augusta are exaggerations, public spectacles who caricature both the limits of masculine rationality and conventional images of femininity as passive, self-sacrificing, and indecisive.[8] Their exaggerations both caricature and enact eccentric femininity as a strategy of gender struggle and survival rather than a pregiven, essentialized identity.[9]

The analysis of feminine eccentricity as a site of transgressive gender performance is based on the insight that gender is realized in everyday performances, and femininity entails a performative politics.[10] Drawing on psychoanalytic theory, feminists have argued that the "double masquerade" of femininity involves a performance of womanliness in order to appease male desire and anxiety over the feminine.[11] The political potential of such a masquerade is exhibited in carnivalesque exaggerations of female sexuality in which putting on "femininity with a vengeance" explicitly inverts everyday gendered relations of subordination and domination.[12] While much has been made of the transgressive potential of gay drag to reveal the performative nature of gender and create a space of critique and resistance, we find that the eccentric aunts contribute to a feminist "camp" critique of gender and power.[13]

Camp refers to "a parodic, ironic, over-the-top and often nostalgic sensibility that is arguably pervasive in contemporary popular media."[14] The camp aesthetic revels in artifice and excess, taking pleasure in the authentically inauthentic.[15] The incorporation of camp into contemporary popular culture sensibilities is evident in the ubiquity of parody, irony, nostalgia, theatricality and excess, a rampant recycling of images, and a self-proclaimed resistance to convention.[16] The excessive theatricality, convention-flouting, and stereotypic parody of camp performance is evident in both *Mame* and *Travels*, and certainly the movie adaptations of these narratives emphasize a camp aesthetic. What makes these camp performances *feminist* is their integral critique of normative and marginalizing forces regulating gender and sexual identities and relations.

This integral feminist critique is evident in three features characterizing transgressive camp performance: making familiar tropes strange, elaborating on spectacle as a cultural form, and playing off other characters as anchors or foils.[17] The characterizations of Mame and Augusta exhibit feminist critique through each of these three features. First, these characters recall familiar stereotypical feminine tropes including the "rich bitch," the "man-eating vamp," and, for our purposes the most important trope, the "crazy aunt."[18] These tropes entail the persistent pull of heteronormativity and social class: the aunts act out against the forces of social convention and propriety while reproducing heterosexual femininity and class privilege. Yet the ostensible focus of their stories is on the coming of age of a male in their care; hence, Mame and Augusta are continually and ironically repositioned as "like a mother."

It is this ambivalent analogy that gives these performances a transgressive edge. Both Patrick and Henry anchor their aunts' excesses in conservative norms and perspectives and serve as foils for the aunts' parodic performances of self-gratification and feminine empowerment.[19] As a constant reminder of maternal responsibility and domestic conventions, Patrick threatens to subdue the eccentricity of Auntie Mame—he "redeems" the excesses of this figure. Henry, on the other hand, anchors Aunt Augusta in a maternal relationship that is not explicitly declared yet seems affirmed in her efforts to free him from his small-minded, stifled life.[20] In other words, maternal love anchors these eccentric aunts and tempers their unruly femininity. At the same time, as foils, both Patrick and Henry cast the outrageousness of their aunts' excessive behavior in relief. They serve as sidekicks or "straight men," the latter quite literally, as they embody the presence of hetero-sexual masculinity against the aunts' flamboyant femininity. Further, Patrick's developing manhood and Henry's suppressed sexual desires are contrasted with the flagrant feminine sexuality of their aunts/mothers. In this tension there is a constant undermining and reshoring of the familiar feminine dichotomy of the mother/whore that is both a source of humor and disquiet.

It is in these analogies and tensions among tropes, foils, and anchors that the camp performances of eccentric aunts offer a trans-gressive double take. Specifically, the aunts and their nephews parody the repressed sexuality of the mother/son relationship. The analogies inherent to these relationships—mother is to aunt as son is to nephew—ambiguate the well-policed restrictions on the Oedipalized desires of the maternal/filial bond. Neither narrative resolves the incestuous ten-sions at play in this parodic spectacle, transgressing the conventional silence over the sexual desires at the heart of the mother/son bond and opening a space for feminist re-visions of maternal sexuality and patriarchal kinship taboos.[21] In addition, the contrast between male conservatism and female liberalism offers a not-so-subtle commentary on the sexual politics of conventional social life, a point that leads us to consider the potential alliance of camp aunts with gay culture.

Characters like Mame and Augusta have inspired gay camp perfor-mances of feminine excess. While we cannot say that these eccentric aunts bring feminist critique and gay transgression into alliance, the political significance of such alliances bears comment. One strategy for such an alliance is "heterosocial bonding" between heterosexual women and gay men. Heterosocial bonding pairs women as "fag hags" with gay men in a "sistership" that recognizes mutual though different oppressions—for example, the misogyny and homophobia that defend heterosexual maleness—within hetero-patriarchal regimes.[22] Another strategy is an alliance around a "queer" camp aesthetic that enacts a dissonance or distance from the dominant symbolic order, enabling overlapping points of view among heterosexual women, lesbians, and gay men, while providing space for feminist aesthetics and inter-pretations that are "simultaneously non-gay and not stereotypically straight."[23] By denaturalizing the bonds that women, lesbians, and gays hold to straight men, strategies like a political sistership or an aesthetic alliance might energize shared dissent against hegemonic heterosexuality and homophobia. The camp appeal of aunties Mame and Augusta opens space for such alliances as well as for ironic reflection on the fragility of such alliances across differences.[24]

We have argued that eccentric aunts destabilize normative constructions of feminine subjectivity and agency and portend both feminist re-visions of maternal and kinship relations and transgressive alliances in sexual politics. Yet eccentric aunts are readily recuperated into dominant postfeminist discourses of women's lives and desires. This ambivalence troubles another popular figure of feminist transgression: the madwoman.

ECCENTRIC AUNTS: THE MADWOMAN

Feminist scholars frame the association of women with madness in two ways. Female madness may constitute a misogynist mode of control, or, on the contrary, it may be understood as a mode of women's resistance to material and mental oppressions, whether as a mode of rebellion through creative self-destruction or as a mode of survival.[25] The point is made variously but insistently in classic feminist texts that critique the "angel in the house" as shadowed by the "madwoman in the attic," wherein the repression and containment of the one is manifested as deviance, madness, and rebellion in the other.[26] As one social historian put it, "Hysterics and madwomen generally have ended up in the attic or in the asylum, their gestures of pain and defiance having served only to put them out of circulation."[27] And a classic text in women's psychology explained, "What we consider 'madness,' whether it appears in women or in men, is either the acting out of the devalued female role or the total or partial rejection of one's sex-role stereotype."[28] Eccentric aunts in popular culture are readily assimilated to this stereotype of female madness as rebellion against or escape from women's oppressions under patriarchy. At the same time, we argue that these figures offer important transgressions that trouble classic and postfeminist constructions of the madwoman as a rebellious "other." We examine three variations on the eccentric aunt and madness: the two elderly maiden aunts Abby and Martha Brewster in the film *Arsenic and Old Lace* (1944); Aunt Josephine in *The Wide Window*, book 3 of A Series of Unfortunate Events by Lemony Snicket (2000); and Aunt Sylvie in Marilynne Robinson's novel *Housekeeping* (1980) and its film adaptation (1987).

Arsenic and Old Lace, a comedy of homicide and domestic horror, centers on the fear of madness within our most personal and intimate spaces. Written during World War II, the narrative articulates prevailing fears and anxieties over the madness of war. The story centers on a young drama critic who has just married despite his published treatises against marriage. On his way to Niagara Falls for his honeymoon, he stops at his childhood home to inform the maiden aunts who raised him about his marriage. They profess their (maternal) delight, but when he finds a man's corpse in their window seat, the aunts reluctantly admit that they are the murderers. They have killed twelve men, all of them elderly bachelors professing a religious affiliation and without family. Their murders are "charities," they contend, bringing a swift end to these unhappy lives. Complications are provoked by several secondary characters: a second nephew who thinks he is Teddy Roosevelt and who has been burying the murdered men in the cellar under the impression that he is digging locks for the Panama Canal; a third nephew, a murderer wanted by the police, traveling with a plastic surgeon who crafts new faces for him; an Irish policeman with a play manuscript he wants the drama critic to review; and the bride, who lives across the street from the aunts and is hard pressed to understand what is happening as the drama critic nephew becomes more and more frantic about his family's insanity and violence.

The play hardly seems a comedy. And yet, as the situation grows more ludicrous, the dialogue offers more puns and punch lines, the double takes and reactions of the characters become more exaggerated, and the action is at times almost slapstick. The narrative is structured by oppositions: sanity/insanity, benevolence/malevolence, safety/danger, life/death, self/other, feminine/masculine, and of course, the feminine as beatific or monstrous. The drama critic nephew centers the plot around the besieged authority of masculinity and rationality, as a man who has just taken on the role of husband and potential father, whose place in the social order is assured. It is he who drives the resolution of the comic situation, frantic to restore the status quo.

Yet the aunts articulate a mad, "monstrous" feminine otherness that inverts the orderliness of domestic life and love. In one scene, their nephew sits them down and scolds them like children; the camera shows the aunts sitting with their backs to the audience, small and clearly cowed by his disapproval while he stands in front of them beseeching them to be rational and promising them his protection. In this scene, they are shadow figures, beyond the reach of masculine reasoning and entreaties. Just so, the aunts embody a feminine alterity that remains, despite their nephew's efforts, unassimilable to the dominant rational, masculinist order. They are not harmless old spinsters; they are the monsters that we fear behind the rational, controlled façade of normal domestic life. And they are dangerous because they enact the irrationality at the heart of rational order in the name of maternal benevolence—the horror of murder as charity carried out within the domestic serenity of home. The aunts are "like a mother" except they are not: they are the monstrous feminine other.

Another mad aunt, Aunt Josephine, appears in book 3, *The Wide Window* (2000), in author/narrator Lemony Snicket's A Series of Unfortunate Events, a chronicle of the misfortunes and resourcefulness of the three Baudelaire orphans (Klaus, Violet, and Sunny) against the greedy malevolence of their nemesis, Count Olaf. A movie adaptation of the first three books in the series was produced in 2004. In *The Wide Window*, the orphans move in with their Aunt Josephine Anwhistle, whose irrational fears over the possibilities of danger in her own home belie her wildly adventurous youth. She entreats the children to avoid all manner of domestic deathtraps: tripping over the welcome mat could lead to decapitation, the radiator could explode, glass doorknobs might heat up and shatter, the stove might burst into flames, the refrigerator could fall and crush a body. In the course of the story, these fears come to fruition—raising the question of whether they are irrational after all. The narrative blurs the lines between appearance and illusion, safety and danger, rationality and irrationality, care and neglect. Aunt Josephine, charitable enough to take the children in ("like a mother"), hands them over to Count Olaf to save herself. Her passion for grammar saves her when she codes a message about her disappearance by riddling it with grammatical errors as clues. However, when she corrects Captain Sham's grammar (Count Olaf in disguise), he leaves her in a sinking rowboat to be devoured by "ill-behaved" leeches.

Aunt Josephine's house perches on a cliff over Lake Lachrymose (the name means "tending to tears or weeping"), where her husband Ike Anwhistle (i.e., "I can whistle") was devoured by the lake's leeches.[29] She spends her days anxiously watching the foreboding lake with a telescope out of a very wide window in her library. The psychoanalytic overtones of this narrative suggest that Aunt Josephine's phobias manifest a repressed sexual trauma. Yet we contend that Aunt Josephine's anxieties can be understood as postfeminist, given the proliferation and normalization of a plethora of feminine anxieties and ills, including weight, age, body image, and the demands of careers and perfect motherhood as well as epidemics of low self-esteem, meanness, binge drinking, anorexia, depression, and suicide.[30] It is as if "seeking to achieve a feminine identity makes women and girls ill" (97).[31] The seemingly endless choices and possibilities that postfeminism locates "at the end of feminism" confront young women particularly with inexorable demands for perfection and happiness accomplished through individual effort and motivation. In her internalization of impossible imperatives, is it any wonder that Aunt Josephine is overwhelmed by anxiety?

Housekeeping is a girl's coming-of-age narrative, a multigenerational story of women and the divergent paths of sisters succumbing to or resisting hegemonic femininity, social order, and the psychic and physical discipline of women's conventional domesticity.[32] The story is set in Fingerbone, Idaho, a remote town dominated by Fingerbone Lake, where the girls' grandfather and later their mother drowned. After their mother's suicide, Ruth and Lucille are raised for five years by their maternal grandmother, then briefly by two elderly maiden aunts, and finally by their eccentric Aunt Sylvie. Sylvie cooks and attends to the girls, but she is not a mother, not a homemaker, not capable of the discipline of housekeeping. She leaves the doors open so that leaves and animals enter the house, piles tin cans and old newspapers everywhere, spends her days wandering the woods and the lake, prefers moonlight to lamplight, and deals ineptly with the authorities of conventional life—the school, the townswomen, the sheriff. As they become teenagers, Lucille is gradually repelled by Sylvie's world and drawn into the normative desires and conventional practices of mainstream social life (she eventually moves in with her home economics teacher). Meanwhile, Ruth is drawn into Sylvie's existential transience. Eventually, Sylvie's housekeeping incompetence draws the concern of the local community, but, before Ruth can be taken from her, Sylvie and Ruth burn their house down and disappear into a life of vagrancy: "Now truly we were cast out to wander and there was an end to housekeeping."[33]

While Ruth is the narrator of the story, some critics argue that Aunt Sylvie is the protagonist. Sylvie suffers the ambivalence of the feminine eccentric, unable to conform yet terrorized by the sanctions of nonconformance. Feminist critics have argued that this imagistic narrative blurs the imaginary and mythic to convey an image of feminine experience as radically sensual.[34] For example, images of water, its flows and depths in lakes, floods, and damp spaces, show us feminine energies and desire, especially when overflowing the house, the place of patriarchal order and feminine containment. Sylvie's everyday existence is not contained by her housekeeping duties; instead, she is defined by a *jouissance* beyond the patriarchal order, realized in a sensual relation with the natural world and the small elements of subsistence living.[35] She enacts housekeeping as a fluid process without fixed boundaries: inside/outside, clean/dirty, order/disorder, stability/instability, permanence/impermanence are not fixed but permeable categories—the outside (leaves, dead birds, water) comes inside, too. She "mistakes accumulation for housekeeping," accumulating and keeping (worthless) property (e.g., piles of old newspapers and tin cans).[36] Her failure at housekeeping, that is, at maintaining proper domestic order, subjects her to scrutiny by the townswomen who ineffectually counter her eccentricity with casseroles and other signs of their own domesticity,[37] but particularly by the sheriff, charged with carrying out the dictates of patriarchal law and order. Madness, patriarchal repression, and feminine otherness clearly inhabit the figure of Aunt Sylvie.

Mad Aunts Return Us to Feminism

These crazy aunts make the classic feminist case for madness and hysteria as forms of feminine otherness and rebellion. All three of the mad aunts enact an antagonism between feminine otherness and patriarchal order. However, we resist casting the mad aunt as a figure of resistance. Instead, we offer three re-visions of these mad aunt performances. First, we argue for a distinction between madness as a critique of women's oppression and mental illness as a feminist political issue. Second, we critique the normalization of feminine anxieties and recover an impulse to feminist solidarity. Third, we argue that the gender performances of these mad aunts can ultimately contribute to energizing the collective political force of feminism.

First, we urge rethinking the mad aunt through the perspective of a feminist disability studies theory that addresses embodiment and mental illness. The madwoman as an icon of feminist resistance has been soundly critiqued elsewhere on a variety of grounds, including essentialism, heterosexism, colonialism, and racism.[38] Yet this image persists; indeed, the persuasiveness of our own interpretations draws in part on the antagonisms inherent to this model. However, we are aware of the danger of romanticizing madness and the failure to distinguish this trope from mental illness. The power of such a romance is that it is not distinct from but can become integral to lived realities, and even as a feminist trope for women's oppression and struggle, it runs the danger of reinforcing the stigma of chronic mental illness.[39]

Further, such a vision of women's struggle against illness as oppression is readily articulated to the postfeminist celebration of the autonomous, heroic individual. Such a neoliberal vision plays into a larger "discourse of democratic citizenship in which will and self are imagined as inviolable," thereby holding the madwoman accountable for her failure to conform to social norms.[40] Feminist scholars have productively critiqued the medical, scientific, legal, and political tropes associating women with madness, hysteria, anxieties, and psychological deviations from the (male) norm, convincingly showing how such tropes have justified perceptions, practices, and policies of constraint, discrimination, and harmful intervention enacted upon women with disabilities. Yet the power of this trope is culturally tenacious.

In this sense the aunts in these narratives call our attention to the need for reconsidering the relationship between the material and cultural subject of disability as a critical aspect of a robust feminist agenda for social justice.[41] How we represent women with mental illnesses and instabilities matters to such an agenda. To this end, we re-vision the figures in the narratives we have highlighted as provocations for imaginative reflection. How might the madness and eccentricities of aunt figures like the Brewster sisters, Aunt Josephine, and Sophie expand on and complicate the ways family life and kinship are imagined and lived?[42] We think these figures offer invitations to rethink relations of care and death; the sexual energies of anxiety, resilience, and hope; and struggles over and against the gendered discipline of housekeeping.

Although we have just critiqued the classic feminist case for women's madness as a trope of subjugation and resistance, we want to offer our own re-vision of this conception of madness and feminism. The relevance of the mad aunts is not only the way they might energize a feminist agenda that holds disabilities to be a cornerstone of feminism but also the ways in which they inspire new stories in our collective cultural imagination. After all, before we can enact change, we must be able to imagine its possibilities. So we revisit two aspects of the mad aunt narratives. First, we look at the implications of the monstrous madwoman in the context of home and household. These mad aunts are not confined to the attic; they enact the threat of the monstrous maternal in the midst of the safety and comfort of home. We consider how the aunts threaten the ideal of home and the normative order of the patriarchal household.[43] Second, we focus on the aunt narratives as re-visions of feminist solidarity in the context of the move beyond feminism characteristic of postfeminist culture. The intensity of desire and madness shared by the Brewster spinster aunts and Sylvie and Ruth in *Housekeeping* models the emotional and political intensities of women's relationships. Analogously, we find the mad aunts to be hopeful indices of the viability of feminism as a social force.

We begin with reflections on eccentric aunts and home. In each mad aunt narrative, female insanity is cast as out of place in the context of patriarchal domestic order.[44] This reading coincides with the classic feminist version of women and madness—the mad aunt disrupts and resists her place of subjugation. So the house as a space of home, comfort, and safety becomes a site of danger, even murder, and this can be read in accord with a feminist indictment of the home as a place of women's social, physical, and psychological confinement.[45] For example, the complacent, familiar feminine domestic orderliness of the Brewster house belies the horror of the murders the aunts commit there. Aunt Josephine's house, at first a place of safety for the Baudelaire orphans, becomes the site of chaos and disorder—it literally flies apart, giving tangible form to their aunt's anxieties. Finally, even though she recognizes the promises of domestic order and is called to housekeeping, Aunt Sylvie ultimately resists the dictates of conventional domesticity and a woman's "proper place" by setting fire to her house and becoming a vagrant again, a person who has no place as home.

Yet even in these narratives, the links between conceptions of home and women's madness are ambivalent. For the Brewster house is not only a place of madness and murder but a place for acts of charity—after all, the aunts advance utilitarian, almost Swiftian arguments justifying their murders.[46] Aunt Josephine's house is not only the site of her neuroses and repressed passions but a gathering place for her memories and the keepsakes of her life, a place of "preservation" that affirms her past and present.[47] The house in *Housekeeping* resists in itself the efforts to "keep" it intact, an indictment of the ideal of wholeness, stability, and the maternal. While it burns, Ruth imagines the soul of the house escaping in the fire just as she and Sylvie escape the disciplinary force of housekeeping. House and home are not only confining and disciplining but necessary to soul and survival; these are "deeply ambivalent values."[48] Our cultural and existential ambivalences of house and home encourage an ongoing re-visioning of domestic spaces, identities, and values beyond conventional chains of equivalence linking home, femininity, and fulfillment or feminist critiques linking entrapment, madness, and resistance.

In addition to problematizing domestic space, house, and home, we find in these narratives of madness an appeal for a feminist solidarity. Women's desire for women is implicit in the sisterly love and madness of the Brewster spinsters and in the merging of Ruth and Sylvie in *Housekeeping*.[49] This express desire among women for women is both entertained and denied in postfeminist culture. Women's relationships with women—friends, sisters, mothers—are mediated by consumption and romance and undermined by competition and anxiety. Further, while women can now be "anything they desire," being powerful remains problematic: being a powerful woman threatens the masquerade of neotraditional femininity necessary for maintaining desirability in the heteronormative market.[50] Hence, the political, social, and cultural desire of women acting with and for other women is distracted, expressed in the ambivalence of the phrase "I'm not a feminist but. . . ." Yet we see in these tales of crazy aunts a longing for women's company, embodied female sensuality, and a resolute alterity that cannot be reincorporated into prevailing modes of heterosexuality. These yearnings can be deemed political in the sense in which feminist scholars have argued for a "lesbian continuum" through which women's yearning for women, regardless of sexual orientation, articulates resistances and alternatives to heteronormativity.[51] As one feminist scholar put it, such yearnings are the basis for the "political love for 'womanhood' which feminism advocated and encouraged." Hence, while we do not condone the madwoman as a symbol of feminist resistance, the portraits of women's bonds with women in *Arsenic and Old Lace* and *Housekeeping* recall these conceptions of feminist solidarity.

In this chapter, we have considered the popular image of the eccentric aunt as a basis for questioning contemporary discourses about women's lives and desires. In particular, we have argued that in the context of contemporary postfeminist discourses, these aunt figures offer critical distance from the contention that feminism is finished, has failed, or is to blame for social ills. Further, the aunts counter popular postfeminist discourses about women's desire for heterosexual romance, children, and family. By exploiting the instability of the analogy linking aunts to mothers (my aunt is like a mother) we drew attention to assumptions about women and maternality. The eccentric excesses of such figures as Auntie Mame and Aunt Josephine move beyond and often against normative conceptions of and social sanctions over femininity, maternality, and kinship. In revisioning the link between women and madness, we have questioned the feminist trope of madness as resistance and the postfeminist normalization of the link between womanhood and mental illness (anxiety, anorexia, etc.). For us, the mad aunt inspires creative and collective reflections that can contribute to a feminist agenda for social justice and that introduce ambivalences into the classic feminist case against the chains of equivalence binding women to home and domesticity. These popular aunt figures offer critical opportunities to deconstruct the tendentious links among femininity, family, sexuality, and sanity that continue to shape women's lives.

COMMODIFYING THE AUNT

A surprising number of businesses identify their products and services—from pretzels to pet-walking—with the aunt, most explicitly by using that kinship title in the company name. A quick Web search for "aunt" will turn up hundreds of thousands of pages (33,100,000 in January 2010) for commercial sites using the aunt in the company name. For example, we found:

> Aunt Bertha's Kitchen, Aunt Kizzy's Back Porch Restaurant, Aunt Jeni's Home Made Pet Food, Aunt Verna's Orange Cake, Aunt Pearlie's Food Products, Inc., Aunt Ilene's Devils Food Cake, Aunt Susie's Child Care, Aunt Minnie's Food Service, Aunt Granny's All-You-Care-to-Eat Buffet, Aunt Annie's Crafts, Aunt Dimity's Christmas, Aunt Izzy's Gnocchi, Aunt Irene's Care Packages, Aunt Wilma's Companion Home Care, Inc., Aunt Patty's Natural Foods, Aunt Sally's Market, Aunt Mary's Country Store & Bakery, Aunt Susie's 10 Minute Low Fat Recipe Books, Aunt Midi's Fresh Quality Produce, Aunt Ann's Elder Home Care, Aunt Martha's Youth Service Center, Aunt Sue's Country Corner, Aunt Margaret's Gift Basket, Aunt Bessie's Golden Syrup Sponge Puddings, Aunt Polly's Fried Chicken Restaurant, Aunt Vi's Garden Bath Care Products, Aunt Tesa's Toy Box, Aunt Sally's Praline Shop Inc., Aunt Bee's

All Natural Skin Products, Aunt Edna's Kitchen, Aunt Sarah's Restaurant, Aunt Aggie De's Pralines, Aunt Betty's Steamed Puddings, Aunt Leah's House, Aunt Sarah's Casual Clothing, Aunt Chilada's Mexican Food, Aunt Nellie's Farm Kitchen, Aunt Ann's Home Care

. . . to name just a few!

On the surface, the aunt image that sells everything from real estate to cleaning services is beneficent, female-gendered, and happily domestic. Importantly, the aunt image is relational because the aunt is an aunt only by virtue of a recognized kinship relationship—biological, legal, or voluntary. This relationship appeals to cultural images of aunting as mothering ("my aunt is like a mother"), as friendship (as the title of one popular book puts it, *Aunts: Our Older, Cooler, Wiser Friends*),[1] as mentoring, and as generational caretaking (a recent study emphasizes generativity—caretaking across generations—as the hallmark of the aunt relationship).[2] This point is critical because, as a marketing image, the iconic aunt associates whatever product or service is on offer with the emotional connections and loyalty evoked by the cultural ideal of the aunt. The aunt as a brand image is a form of emotional branding; as such, emotional connections conjured by the image overwhelm our relationship to the product.[3] The aunt image is, in this sense, akin to the "lovemark," an idealistic and sentiment-infused relational connection that invokes intense loyalty and desire.[4] The repercussions are daunting, for brands and their loyalties are not peripheral to but constitutive of lived culture; brands shape our understandings of and conflicts over personal, cultural, and national identities.[5]

Accordingly, the first part of this chapter documents the qualities associated with the aunt image and the cultural associations and relational bonds evoked in such associations. We question the appeal of the aunt as a marketing image by "interrogating the image."[6] A cultural image is a "sign" that circulates within the semiotic economy of cultural life in any given historical moment. From a feminist interpretive perspective, we question the intersections of representation, power, and cultural imagination and memory within which the image comes to be meaningful. Importantly, meaning-making entails the play of differences—what is included or excluded, familiar or strange, legitimate or deviant, and so forth.

In considering the dominant marketing image of the aunt from a feminist perspective, we argue that this image is not just benignly appealing but also baldly stereotyped, ahistorical, and morally bereft. In the second part of this chapter, we deconstruct the appeals that recall our emotional attachment to an ideal aunting relationship as a means of promoting a market transaction. We address the question: What are the links between the gendered image of the aunt and the rampant contemporary commodification of family life?[7] The argument is this: family labor—caregiving, homemaking, affective relations, and so on—cannot be valued in strictly market exchange and monetary terms. Rather, the value of family labor is incommensurate with economic exchange because the ineffable qualities of such labor—love, care, mutual respect, familial loyalty, and the like—cannot be reduced to market exchange values without objectifying and degrading these qualities and, to follow Marx's original analysis of the commodification of human labor, eroding the conditions of human flourishing.[8] We adopt this argument to critique the trivialization of familial relations and the moral degradation inherent in the manipulation of the popular image of the aunt to sell loving care in the new "service economy."[9] Our purpose in burdening a seemingly trivial marketing image with these charges is to urge more reflective practices of consumption that recognize and respond to the dangers of commodifying affective bonds, ignoring domestic exploitation, and devaluing caring labor even as the demand for loving care becomes more critical. In this, we transgress the appeal of the aunt image.

FINDING E-AUNTS

We began our analysis by accessing examples of the aunt as a marketing logo in the commercial online marketplace. Using a popular search engine, we searched for the term "aunt," yielding over 33 million links. The sheer number of such sites in itself testifies to the appeal of the aunt as a cultural image. While many sites had to do with personal aunts and aunting relationships, thousands of links were for commercial ventures using the aunt as a figurehead and/or in the title of the enterprise. We printed out the search pages displaying the first six hundred links and visited the websites for the first hundred commercial sites that use the aunt as a commercial logo. We logged the website and URL along with descriptions of the page and the products and services associated with the aunt (see Appendix I for this log). In our discussion, we identify these websites by their number on this log to enhance readability and flow.[10]

The websites we sampled were concentrated on products and services in domestic and leisure industries: retail venues selling crafts, antiques, specialty food products, and jewelry; services including home management, elder care, child care, pet care, pet kennels, housekeeping, and vacation planning; restaurants, bed and breakfast facilities, and cabin rentals. We focused on the language used on the homepage and the "About Us" page (if available) that explained the meaning of the aunt image, that is, the reasons, qualities, or associations warranting the use of this image. While some sites paid tribute to an actual aunt figure or referred to the qualities of a fictional or culturally ideal aunt, others made no comment but relied on implied associations. These reasons, qualities, and associations offer an explicit construction of the aunt's appeal and a focus for our initial analysis.

THE APPEAL OF E-AUNTS

Promising Care

Some sites paid tribute to an actual aunt figure. In their explanations, these sites typically emphasized the sterling qualities of the woman herself, often in terms that recall traditional feminine characteristics and roles, especially beneficence, domesticity, and care. For example, Gail Stewart, executive director of Aunt Leah's [47], a facility teaching life skills to youth and single moms, credits her grandmother, Leah, as her inspiration for a facility that seeks to provide an alternative source of support. On a page featuring a photograph of her paternal grandmother, Stewart explains, "From an early age I developed a keen sense of love, loyalty and passion for this special person . . . [her spirit imparts] a warm, vital and creative energy. . . . We attempt to become that strong alternate caregiver that Leah was for me."

The website for "Auntie Annie's" [5], a national chain serving soft pretzels and other treats, features stories and images of the founder, Anne Beiler, the original Auntie Annie, that link her pretzels to both a brand promise to be "better than the best you ever tasted" and an altruistic narrative about the company's origins in a farmer's market and a delivery order mistake. Aunt Martha's [57], a full-spectrum social service agency serving nine counties in northeastern Illinois, uses the name to convey a "warm family atmosphere" for children, teens, and families using their services. According to the "About Us" page on their website, "The name 'Aunt Martha's' was chosen because a founding member recalled that when she was a teenager and was having trouble at home she could go to her aunt to air grievances and seek help. It was hoped that the name would suggest concern and caring and that young people would find at the agency an atmosphere like one finds at the home of a close relative." The rationale for Aunt Polly's Children's Clothes website [76] claims to enact Aunt Polly's altruism: "If I could sum up my Great Aunt's life in one word, it would be *service*. She sacrificed many things in life simply to help and serve others. . . . Of course, her character of service and sacrifice was rooted in love. She was a selfless woman, full of love and concern for others." "Cool Aunt Designs" [24] was named as such because "I wanted a more creative name." A narrative relates how a college-age niece's spontaneous expression of pleasure over one of the jewelry designs inspired the name "Cool Aunt Designs." The appeal of a "cool" aunt is the appeal of aunting as friendship, the aunt as "older, cooler, wiser." The website "Oh My Giddy Aunt" [35], selling original jewelry designs and keepsakes, also trades on the aunt as an "older, cooler, wiser" friend and kinkeeper. The site offers the following definition of a "giddy aunt" as "a person who plays by her own rules, isn't afraid"; "Giddy aunts are keepers of family stories and the tellers of wonderful tales." Tracy Tee, owner of Aunt Beep [13], maintains a blogsite where she explains that Aunt Beep "knew how to shop," gave "a sea of presents" to her nieces and nephews "in awe-inspiring quantities," "had a thing for tacky" but "knew the value of a long lasting gift," "loved glamour," "had a flair for the unusual," and "single-handedly started the Customer Service movement" by always demanding personalized service.

These sites extol not the actual women they are named for but the cultural values associated with aunts. Often using hyperbole and caricature, these sites naturalize the characteristics of the aunt with claims that both celebrate and idealize nurture, familial service, feminine domestic roles, and kinkeeping functions. They use language about feminine warmth and energy, unqualified concern and care for loved ones, selfless service, and sacrifice rooted in love, personal strength, loving generosity, and demanding carefulness. What goes without saying in these depictions is the promise of caring service modeled on feminine or maternal beneficence and sacrifice (the analogy of the aunt as mother). The aunt image thus offers psychosocial assurance of loving care while at the same time perpetuating a cultural caricature of feminine beneficence.

Other websites exploit this conflation of loving care and contractual care services. For example, the slogan for an in-home care agency implies that their services are motivated by care, not payment: "Aunt Ann's Elder Home Care is people caring for people" [8]. Similarly, the slogan for Aunt Ann's Agency [9], a nationwide leader in household management services, suggests a lifelong kinship relation: Aunt Ann's has been "helping you through all the stages of life." The mission statement for a foster care agency for children, Aunt Hattie's Place, Inc. [37], promises a loving home experience for which the nurturing associations of the aunt image stand as a warrant: "Dedicated to providing a safe, stable, nurturing, and long-term home" where foster children "feel love and stability." Similarly, Aunt Martha's [57] youth service center in Illinois promises, "The world will give up on you . . . but Aunt Martha's won't." Across these examples, the aunt image reframes contractual relations as affective kinship relations, standing in for the promise of home and family as a marker of quality personal care.

Leaving a beloved pet in the care of a trusted aunt entails a similar conflation of love and money. Aunt Cynthia's Bed and Biscuit [25], a pet boarding and pet-sitting service, states: "Our purpose is to pet, pamper, and provide your dog with the highest quality loving care available!" Aunt Ruthie's Animal Care and Wellness Center [83] claims to be a "special place run by caring professionals" that offer pets "a truly caring environment" recognized by several awards for "premier" certified care and grooming. At Aunt Susie's Pet Sitting [95], "We look forward to working for you and loving and caring for your furry friends (or scaly or feathery)!" Aunt Jeni's Home Made [43] is an all-natural pet food company; the "Who Is Aunt Jeni?" page features a thirty-something woman described as an "Animal lover!" with a degree in animal nutrition who not only researches and sells pet food but lectures on animal welfare. The image of the aunt throughout these websites is one of a loving family member whose caring services are offered not so much in exchange for a contractual fee but out of love and a desire to care for others.

Selling Nostalgia

Many websites alluded to particular qualities of products and services associated with a nurturing aunt stereotype linked to "down-home" tastes and smells, neighborly hospitality, idealized family images, and nostalgia for childhood and innocence. For example, Aunt Cookie's Red Rhubarb Jams and Jellies [23] links the aunt to wholesomeness, natural goodness, and hand-picked care. Along with a picture of a man and woman standing in front of a farm field, the site proclaims: "Aunt Cookie's Red Rhubarb Spreadable Fruit is all natural and Minnesota Grown. . . . Because we do not use artificial additives, you can be sure of the goodness in each jar. . . . We hand pick only choice fresh red rhubarb and use only Minnesota grown fruit. . . . Aunt Cookie's uses NO preservatives or food coloring. Our red color is obtained from using only 100% red rhubarb." The assurance of wholesome goodness is underwritten by the image of the aunt—it is the relationship of care promised by Aunt Cookie that guarantees the products' quality.

Childhood innocence and nostalgia were frequent themes. For example, Aunt Belle's Confectionery [14] explicitly invokes nostalgia for a time of childhood innocence, community friendliness, and sensory pleasures: "step back in time and be a kid in a candy store again!" Family owned and operated, the shop is "'known as the 'friendliest store in town!'. . . Home of Sweet Smells and Sunny Smiles!" Similarly, Aunt Sadie's Gourmet Cookie Company links the aunt to nostalgia for childhood security and homemade quality: "Do you remember when you were little and your grandmother made you cookies from scratch? They tasted so wonderfully. They made you tingle inside and feel warm and safe. Aunt Sadie does too! . . . Now you can have the delicious cookies you remember as a child." The conflation of lost

innocence—as childhood or community—with the promise of gratifi-
cation seems a blatant appeal to the indulgence of desire through consumption and the ideal of the mother as the source of satisfaction. The
aunt as an asexual yet maternal figure can promise indulgence without
incurring the guilt that plagues the cultural image of the mother. An
aunt is like a mother but she is not a mother; we do not owe her the debt
of gratitude or feel the same emotional dependencies that can make
gifts from the mother a source of ambivalence. The aunt, in short, is
an ideal advertising image because she promises to fulfill our desires
with no strings attached.

In an interesting variation, several sites admitted that the aunt in
their company name was a fictional character but that her qualities
were not. For example, the website for Aunt Maude's supper club [60]
extols the ideal attributes of the aunt: "Although Aunt Maude the person is mythical, we cherish the ideals of her with our casual personal
style, superb service, and excellent cuisine." Aunt Millie's Bakeries
[62] explicitly acknowledges the power of the aunt image to evoke nostalgia and desire—their slogan is "at Aunt Millie's, we bake more than
bread; we bake memories." Their history page reveals that the Aunt
Millie icon was developed in 1991 to represent a line of "authentic,
'home-style' breads": "Customers readily identified her as caring, loving, and always baking something wonderful. Aunt Millie became so
popular that in 2005, the company was renamed 'Aunt Millie's Bakeries.'" Aunt Mae's Home Care [61] website features a cartoon aunt
meant to embody the agency's values: "Aunt Mae is our icon in more
ways than one. She is the embodiment of all the values that our agency
is founded on: genuine concern, friendly companionship, gentle care
and love." These attributes characterize the cultural ideal of the loving
aunt. Further, as attested in the Aunt Millie website, customers readily
recognize this ideal.

Across these sites, the aunt image evokes sentimental nostalgia for
home, childhood innocence, sensory pleasures, and homemade goodness, implicitly reassuring consumers that they can buy nurturance and
comfort. In the rushed pace of contemporary life, a nostalgic longing
for "the good old days" when auntie baked you cookies and casseroles
clearly remains part of an idealized construction of childhood, home,

and family. The affective power of the aunt relationship underwrites and obscures the economic function of these commercial sites.

Trading on Auntness

Some sites admitted to using the aunt as a commercial figurehead simply to cut through the marketing clutter and "noise" of competitive appeals. The "About Us" page for Aunt Clara's Kitchen [22], a restaurant specializing in Dominican cooking, includes a confession: "Amateur cook and part-time Internet junkie, Aunt Clara is not really anyone's aunt, but she needed a catchy name for a website about cooking." Here the "aunt" is admittedly a ploy, appealing to a constellation of associations invoked by the promises of female kin in the kitchen.

An unusual use of the aunt as figurehead is AuntMinnie.com [64], a news and forum site for the radiology and medical imaging community and its associated YouTube channel, AuntMinnie TV. The site's logo is a cartoon of an elderly woman's face. The name AuntMinnie was coined by a University of Cincinnati radiologist, Dr. Ben Felson, to suggest a compelling case diagnosis: "'a case with radiologic findings so specific and compelling that no realistic differential diagnosis exists.' In other words: If it looks like your Aunt Minnie, then it's your Aunt Minnie." Recognizing someone as an aunt makes her an aunt, a practice endorsed by the AuntMinnie site's emphasis on a concrete mode of diagnosis.

Many websites featured highly stylized cartoon representations of an aunt as a company logo. While we have not focused on the visual aspects of any of these websites, the cartoon images are worthy of note. Of the one hundred websites we reviewed, eighteen included a visual image. Of those, fifteen employed an image that pictured the aunt as old-fashioned and domestic, highlighting features such as bun hairstyles, spectacles, aprons, and housedresses. These visualizations of the marketing aunt's idealized qualities are remarkably consistent. For example, Aunt Bessie's Foods [15], a division of Tryton Foods, Ltd., features a cartoon image of an elderly woman in an apron with her hair in a bun and a mixing bowl in her arms; a business school case study by DataMonitor, a private business information group, attributed Aunt Bessie's "strong growth" in the frozen food business to the company's emphasis on "tradition, convenience, value and the family," attributes of the idealized aunt image.[11] Aunt Agatha's Books [3] features a cartoon silhouette of a middle-aged woman with a flower hat, handbag, and a bloody knife—perhaps an allusion to Agatha Christie's famous detective figure, Miss Marple, also a dowdy, middle-aged woman, whose keen attention to detail and intuitive reasoning often triumph over masculine reasoning.

Notably absent from these depictions is racial diversity. Almost all of the depictions are clearly Anglo-American; indeed, the textual descriptions of the aunt usually implied a white, middle-class identity. Only in the case of an ethnically or regionally marked service or product, usually restaurants or travel locations, is the aunt depicted as other than Caucasian. For example, the homepage for Aunt I's Jamaican Restaurant [38] claims, "Aunt I's was built on the foundation of preparing good wholesome Jamaican cuisine in an environment that makes you feel at home." The "About Us" page explains, "Started at home in 1986, the word got out that 'dis lady can really cook' and in a short time the house was filled with people from all over." Aunt I's is one of the few websites in our sample that depicted an aunt of color, calling attention to the assumption that the aunt is Caucasian except when the product or service is obviously ethnic or racially inflected, as in Jamaican cooking.

Finally, some websites offered no explicit verbal or visual rationale for using "aunt" in the company name. These sites depended on the cultural associations of the aunt for the marketing value of this image. Some of the sites seemed to capitalize on the "old-fashioned" associations of the aunt. For example, Aunt Ellen's Attic [31] is a down-home mom-and-pop antique and collectibles store, while Aunt Fanny's Olde Egg Shoppe [32] sells antiques along with rustic and country style furnishings. Several websites advertised bed and breakfast facilities with an historic or rustic appeal: Aunt Bug's Log Cabin Rentals [19] offers premium log cabins in the Smoky Mountains; Aunt Louise's Lake House [51] is a bed and breakfast featuring Victorian-style accommodations. These sites implicitly market their services and facilities by evoking the cultural associations of "aunt" with old-fashioned quality and care. Another uncommented usage was by publishers: the Aunt

Publishing Corporation [1] and the Aunt Lute Publishing Company [53]. The former site stated the company's encouragement of both established and new writers, suggesting a social supportiveness associated with the aunt. The Aunt Lute site advertises a feminist publisher.[12]

A final use of the aunt without comment was restaurants: Aunt Josie's Italian restaurant [45], Aunt Mary's Café [59], Aunt Sue's Tea Room [95]. As evident in the picture of Aunt Carrie's Seafood Restaurant [21] on their homepage, these sites feature associations with homemade, old-fashioned quality and hospitality as well as family traditions, although a rationale for using "aunt" in the name of the restaurant was not mentioned explicitly.

One other uncommented usage of the aunt image is worth noting because the product is neither domestic nor feminine: the use of the title "aunt" by popular music artists. Rock artist Frank Zappa titled an album released in the 1990s *Electric Aunt Jemima* without further comment (Aunt Jemima as a marketing image is discussed in chapter 3). Aunt Flossie [34] is the name of a "high velocity" rock quartet managed by Crown Records out of Austin, Texas (they won the famous South by Southwest music festival in 2005). Aunt Rubie's Sweet Jazz Babies [80] is a jazz and swing band specializing in 1930s- and 1940s-era songs and promising "family-oriented entertainment." Aunt Sandra [88] is the performance name of Sandra Pajovic, a popular singer and model in Belgrade. Aunt Netta [71] is the stage name of Nimmi Harasgama, a Sri Lankan comedian who performs shows about her immigration to Great Britain. In these cases, we assume that the title "aunt" is used as a parody of the dominant cultural image. Its effectiveness in garnering attention in the popular music scene is both an acknowledgment and an ironic juxtaposition of a band's associations with commercial entertainment against the aunt's market associations with nonsexualized femininity, domesticity, and family.

In summary, we found that most sites touted their wares or services in terms of traditional qualities of care, especially beneficence, unqualified affection, and various forms of devoted caretaking, particularly loving care, comfort, and carefulness, often manifested as an old-fashioned attention to quality and detail. Despite this link with feminine and feminized care, the aunt image was never overtly sexualized. Notwithstanding the prevalence of sexual images of women in advertising, these marketing images of the aunt appeared predominantly bound to nonsexualized feminine stereotypes of domesticity and family. In addition, the majority were depicted as mature in age or old-fashioned in attitude or as living in another era. The most caricatured depictions featured elderly women, and verbal depictions often referred to "old-fashioned" or "home-style" attributes. Finally, race was not mentioned unless the product or service carried an ethnic identification; indeed, almost all visual depictions represented the aunt as white.

The consistency across these images suggests that the aunt as a marketing image naturalizes certain cultural constructions: feminzed service as asexual, domestic, careful and caring, embodying traditional middle-class values; a woman whose bounteous goodwill and homemaking talents overflow the confines of her home and family, whose neighborliness overrides the instrumentality of commercial market relations. The image of the aunt, in other words, encapsulates a stubborn cultural caricature of feminine bounty, domesticity, and nurture. Feminist critiques have long decried the relationally oppressive and economically exploitive effects of such stereotypes, yet, as we have suggested, they carry powerful implicit promises of care, comfort, and fulfillment through consumption.

WHY WORRY? TROUBLING IMPLICATIONS OF THE COMMODIFIED AUNT

What are the links between the marketing image of the aunt and the rampant contemporary commodification of family life? The commodified image of the aunt draws on a juncture of historical, cultural, social, and economic forces that are both visible and obscured in the dominant cultural ideal of the aunt as a feminine kinship figure associated with beneficent giving and affectionate care. We interrogate the aunt image for the implicit associations that confound kinship and market transactions. Specifically, we explore the expectation that the aunt image guarantees that we get more than we pay for; that this image exploits intimacy relations while excusing us from the responsibilities of intimacy ("intimacy at a distance");[13] that the aunt image participates in the commodification of the family; and that racial tensions infuse the seemingly benign marketing image of the aunt.

Getting More than We Pay For

When we purchase Aunt Jane's Jams and Jellies or engage Aunt Sally's Maid Service, we expect to get the quality reserved for family. In other words, the aunt guarantees that *we will get more than we pay for.* For example, a customer tribute on Aunt LuLu's Embroidery website [52] exclaims over the bargain price for careful craftsmanship: "Each embroidery detail was so intricately stitched with the richest of colors, I was embarrassed to pay the small fee I was charged."

The aunt image offers cultural assurances that we deserve to get what we desire regardless of effort or merit—you don't have to be the best, work hard, or be needy to receive the bounty of the aunt's gifts and affection. This image thus feeds a sense of entitlement, both for material goods and emotional benefits. But getting more than you pay for may increase rather than appease the desire for personal indulgence: while the aunt image promises to fulfill emotional as well as material needs through purchase, the image may also evoke psychosocial anxieties—fears of abandonment, unfulfilled desires, and disappointment—particularly given the image's appeal to a nostalgic portrayal of the family and the cultural ideal of childhood happiness and innocence. The ambivalence of the aunt image is thus a powerful marketing ploy because the image positions the consumer as beloved and promises emotional fulfillment through self-indulgent consumption while evoking the anxieties of childhood dependencies and intimacy.

(Not) Just Like Family

The aunt as a marketing image both affirms and corrupts the family values and relationships of home and kin that it exploits. When intimate life is commercialized, that is, when the intangible goods of family life become commodities or services that can be marketed for profit, the affective qualities and commitments of intimacy are eroded.[14] In addition, the basis for intimate relations shifts if everyone who makes a purchase is treated "like family": a short-term, contractual basis for commercial exchanges comes to substitute for the long-term and moral nature of familial relations. More insidiously, exchanging money for love and comfort relieves us of any moral responsibility for reciprocity; we buy our way out of emotional commitment, emotional work, and reciprocal intimacy, out of the cooperation and mutual contributions of domestic labor undertaken with and in the interests of those we love. In short, we purchase "intimacy at a distance."[15] The aunt is a particularly suitable figurehead for promoting both the value of affective relations for purchase and the promise of "intimacy at a distance." An aunt may be a close relative, physically, emotionally, and personally, but she might just as well be quite distant. Receiving gifts from an aunt you do not know very well is not unusual. Exploiting this familiar experience in the guise of the commodified aunt encourages unreflective participation in purchases that enact intimacy at a distance.

Selling (Out) the Family

The economy of family relations trades in affective exchange, that is, nonmarket values like personal responsibility and obligation, compassion, care, and love.[16] In contrast, the competitive pursuit of self-interest and profit motivates market forces and works on the basis of a self-regulating tension between supply and demand. But care and compassion are not amenable to competitive markets; loving and caring, being loved and receiving care produce intangible, affective, and long-term benefits that cannot be reduced to monetary values.

Commodifying familial values threatens to undermine the personal basis of care, love, respect, and familial affection because the basis for exchange is changed: reciprocal affection and moral obligation are supplanted by monetary advantage and self-interest. When Aunt Martha's child welfare services promises, "The world will give up on you . . . but Aunt Martha's won't," the promise is for more than conscientious welfare services—this is a promise of unwavering support and care. Such intangible goods are not amenable to either rational measure or cost-benefit calculations. Further, when services and products are focused on aspects of our lives that have considerable personal and emotional investment—child or elder caretaking, home management, pet care, or even home cleaning services—the emotional investments make rational cost-benefit decisions difficult or beside the point.[17]

In sum, confounding the logics of familial and market relations promotes a moral shortsightedness—by corrupting these values, we alter them: love becomes a commodity to be had at a bargain.[18] But the quality of social life depends on the affective lessons of family and kin so, by commodifying those intangible values, we ultimately degrade social relations. The aunt image assures us that we will get more than we pay for—but at what price?

An Economy of Aunts

We live today in what has been called a "servant economy" in which domestic service and personal convenience are both commodities and values.[19] After all, mainstream life in the U.S. has come to depend on products that cut the time and effort necessary for accomplishing everyday tasks and for services that once were affordable only to the wealthy. Consider, for example, the expansion of all kinds of domestic services and products, from fast foods to closet organizing. However, it appears that U.S. families are experiencing a "care deficit"; that is, in the face of depleted private and public resources for care, they engage in a variety of domestic arrangements and spend a considerable amount of money to take care of familial responsibilities.[20]

The aunt image frames labor-saving products and services in terms of the "old-fashioned quality" associated with the cultural myths of home as a "haven," domestic labor as a sign of care, and family time as "quality time" unsullied by domestic chores and responsibilities. For example, Aunt B's Cleaning Service website [11] asks, "Do you have a busy life? Are you always on the go? Well, then you've come to the right place. I love to clean"; Aunt Bessie's [15] convenience foods assures us that because "cooking dinner for the family from scratch takes time" their foods provide an "expert help-ing hand" to create a "meal to be proud of"; and Aunt Jessica Cares [44], a domestic service agency, waxes eloquent about their services: "As our lives become increasingly chaotic, entangled in the web that life weaves about us, time is scarce. Our staff can provide a haven in the storm, ensuring that your free time is quality time." Taking care of the family now becomes a matter of purchasing the aunt's old-fashioned goods and services.

Given a care deficit and the commodification of home-style care, families are drawn into the servant economy that both responds to their needs and perpetuates the failure of social policy makers to create adequate domestic infrastructures. This servant economy is increasingly two-tiered: while the upper tier is college educated and engaged in some form of knowledge work, the lower tier is less educated, underpaid, employed part time and in largely service-oriented industries concentrated in fast food, retail, tourist, care, or in light manufacturing.[21] Women, youth, minorities, immigrants, and other groups of disadvantaged workers comprise the majority of people in the lower tier. Romanticizing the conditions of caring labor by identifying the service provider as an "aunt" affects a pretense of emotional connections, kinship obligations, and service expectations that deflects attention from the harsh realities of distinctly unromantic work and makes it possible to ignore the persistent social, legal, and global economic policies that perpetuate the suffering of marginalized workers for the benefit of an economic elite.[22]

Indeed, the aunt image, as the online consumer's first contact with the contracting service company, mediates the contractual relationship between the consumer tier of this caring labor market, the company contracting the care service or home-style product, and the actual labor provider. Taking those who care for us for granted, expecting caring quality for a bargain, purchasing intimacy at a distance, refusing to see or pay for the labor of care as labor, these are issues that are redirecting the moral forces of social and familial life. Those who purchase services and products under the auspices of brand promises anchored by the image of the aunt as a sign of care, home, and family risk developing the "callousness and solipsism of the served."[23] That is, unreflective consumerism facilitates instrumental relations with others that render the consumer hardened to the humanity of the other and concerned with nothing beyond the self. While we do not claim that using an aunt icon as a marketing brand is the basis for such moral reductionism, we are concerned that the aunt's associations can be readily aligned with such a calloused social morality.

(RE)LEARNING THE LESSONS OF E-AUNTING

We have pointed out material, historical, cultural, and psychosocial bases for the popularity of the aunt image as a marketing sign. It is little wonder that the aunt proves to be a popular marketing image. This image attests to the importance of and desire for nonnuclear family relationships, kincare, and kinwork as critical social resources. Our concern is that the aunt as a marketing tool reproduces stereotypes of women, families, care, and comfort that obscure the conditions of domestic labor, limit women's agency, and celebrate relations of servitude. The aunt image conflates familial and market logics, promoting the commodification of intangible goods and bargain hunting for care. In this sense, the aunt as a marketing image encourages us to consume with and for the family by promoting a sentimentalized vision of extended familial relations and home. This privatized demand for care deflects attention from the role of civil and state resources in meeting family needs. The aunt image, in short, invites us to engage in the economic and affective exploitations that characterize a "servant economy." The upshot may be a moral callousness that undermines compassion, connection, and intimacy by prioritizing market exchange as the basis for social relations. The aunt image assures us that we will get more than we pay for, but this appeal brings with it hidden social-ethical costs.

THE IMPACT OF AUNTS

Our feminist re-visioning of aunts in popular culture situates the aunt as a rallying point for progressive feminist issues and as a site of struggle over our collective sense of what women, femininity, family, kinship, and social life can—or should—become. The small transgressions of aunts in popular culture are easily overlooked. By drawing them out, we have attempted to demonstrate that feminist concerns and perspectives remain critical to the ways we understand everyday life and to our hopes for social change. In doing this, we have cast the figure of the aunt as a "double agent" whose narrative moves can be seen as both neotraditional and postfeminist but also as transgressive and feminist. There is Aunt Bee, the happy homemaker living in a transgressively nonnuclear family of choice, Aunt Jemima perpetuating oppressively racist images yet inspiring a new generation of antiracist activists, or Auntie Mame, an icon of empowered womanhood whose camp alliances with gay culture deny heteronormative boundaries. Our hope is that in highlighting the transgressions of popular aunts, we call attention to the need for, urgency of, and desire for feminist agendas.

We want to concretize this hope by applying the insights and extending the implications of our re-visions of popular aunts in five arenas: feminism and postfeminism, everyday gender politics, kinship and family, commerce, and the productive tensions inherent in

133

recognizing and celebrating aunts. We begin by reflecting on our perspective on feminism and postfeminism and the ways that popular aunts have illuminated their antagonisms. Then we elaborate the implications of popular aunt representations for the ways we think about and engage in social and cultural change.

AUNTING FEMINISM

A bit of reflection is in order regarding our take on feminism and the way we have examined postfeminist discourses. The subversive, often feisty, aunts of TV, film, and fiction inspire us to question the cultural assumptions about women's lives that are portrayed in the domestic fictions in popular media. The issues we have raised in our encounters with various representations of the aunt outline an ambitious agenda for social change that is unabashedly feminist. Throughout, we have identified the shortcomings of the current postfeminist discourses that permeate mainstream popular culture to counter what we see as dangerous reversals and limitations affecting women's identities and ambitions. Our effort has been to urge ongoing work toward conditions of social justice that recognize the differences among us as critically and productively divergent and that support well-being for all in as wide an array of possibilities as that might entail.

The antagonism between postfeminism and feminism has structured our explorations into popular aunt representations, and we want to reflect on our own understandings of this antagonism and its implications. Postfeminism is multifaceted but includes a multicultural celebration of women's power and possibilities that moves beyond feminist political struggle, that is, it "takes feminism into account" as finished and no longer necessary or as to blame for various socio-material ills—loneliness, singlehood, childlessness, workaholism, to name a few. At the same time, a postfeminist culture encourages its own array of discontent, anxieties, and inequities that dovetail with contemporary neotraditional emphases on the family, the market, and personal, community, and national security. All of the problems we face in these arenas are supposedly resolvable if only women properly exercise their power as leaders, consumers, mothers, and lovers. We think this is all too neat! While feminism has been accused of being perpetually dissatisfied, there are good reasons to reject the assumptions, arguments, and trajectories in postfeminist discourses. At the same time, we are conscious that we have ventured into "either/or" territory—either feminism is correct and postfeminism is wrong or vice versa. By exploring the ambivalences and complexities that popular aunt representations show us, we have tried to steer clear of such polarizations. In addition, we have been careful not to be drawn into the confusion over what constitutes feminism today. There is much talk of "waves" and "post-postfeminism." While we have at times identified strands of feminist thinking—radical feminism or liberal feminism, for example—we are concerned to offer a sense of feminism as a viable assemblage of different though conjoined people, issues, and perspectives. Feminism itself can be thought of as political and historical energies resisting and mobilizing social change. In this sense, there have been both many feminisms and various ebbs and flows of feminist energies. At the same time, feminism remains an ongoing, vital, and transformative force that is just as important now as it has ever been if we are to continue pursuing progressive trajectories of social development.

A note on methodology: we have tried to respond to the call for new feminist "reading strategies to counteract the popularized feminism, figurations of female agency, and canny neutralization of traditional feminist critiques" in popular culture texts.[1] By reading transgressive trajectories into the domestic narratives that feature aunt figures—we have revived the classic feminist concept of "re-visioning" to describe this strategy—we have attempted to take a feminist turn that recovers progressive directions within postfeminism. Aunts prove to be "double agents" in popular narratives about family, femininity, and culture because, while they conform, they also subtly call into question social and cultural conventions and ideologies. We hang much of our analysis of this double agent status on the troubled analogy "the aunt is like a mother." Our point is that the aunt is "like a mother" but "not a mother," thus also a postfeminist but not a postfeminist.

So Aunt Bee, the white, asexual, maternal ideal of the "good aunt" popularized in the 1960s sitcom *The Andy Griffith Show*, is surprisingly transgressive of those very norms she seems to embody.

Similarly, the maternal aunts in black sitcoms transgress the postracial and postfeminist reassurances they embody. The black aunt remains entangled in webs of intersecting discourses—sexist, masculinist, racist, and ageist discourses—that perpetuate denigrations of black womanhood and the racialization of the domestic sphere. This is most evident in the ongoing popularity of the black mammy, especially in the figure of Aunt Jemima. This mammy has outed herself as a double agent: not only did we find her in souvenir shops and on pancake boxes as a subservient domestic accoutrement to white hegemony but as a provocateur for creative expressions of resistance and protest.

In contrast to Aunt Jemima, the neotraditional maternal aunt is well-ensconced in the maternalism of postfeminist visions of womanhood. Even those maternal aunts who never make the move from "bad" mothering to "good" mothers serve as reminders of what can happen to women who deny or distort their mothering instincts and desires. Yet while all of these figures affirm familialism and an essential maternalism as the "happy ending" to social and domestic woes, these aunts can be read as double agents who subtly question the normative force of the ideal maternal aunt and the seemingly inexorable links among women, marriage, domesticity, and heteronormativity.

Then there are aunt figures that have been claimed by feminism as powerful and thus dangerous and denigrated feminine "others"—the witch and the madwoman. These figures have been reframed in postfeminist texts as exemplars of feminine empowerment and individualism. So, as "dangerous" feminine subjects, popular witch aunts are titillating teases who pretend to challenge masculine dominance but are bound to heteronormative positions as exemplary consumers of material luxuries and heterosexual pleasures. Nonetheless, witch aunts are double agents who ultimately fail to conform to the prohibitions structuring kinship, reproduction, rationality, and social order. These magical aunts give us a transgressive vision of women's culture as well as a critique of feminism's own fable of the witch.

We take feminism's metaphor of the madwoman as feminist rebel to task as well for failing to engage with the actualities of such conditions. However, Auntie Mame's popularity as a feminine eccentric casts her as a double agent moving between straight and gay cultures and suggesting the possibility for political alliances among those of differing sexualities. The madwoman and feminine hysteric also gives us hope for revitalizing feminist collective action by taking disability not only as a feminist issue but also as the basis for re-visioning embodied relations to the world and each other. Finally, our analysis of the "e-aunt" or the aunt figure as a brand icon found the marketing popularity of this figure to be drawn on the analogy of the mother and aunt. As a brand image, the aunt can be read indexically: she points to our nostalgic longing for those feminine and maternal virtues of maternality that have been embraced in postfeminist culture. At the same time, this aunt is also a double agent whose contradictory evocations of loving care and market exchange carry troubling moral and social implications.

Aunts in popular culture are a varied lot, blatantly caricatured yet richly nuanced. They are double agents operating as both postfeminist and feminist subjects. By reading for transgressive impulses and implications, we find that popular aunts afford us feminist re-visions of both the issues and the possibilities of living as gendered subjects under conditions of justice, peace, and well-being. We remain intrigued by the dense associations and trajectories they inspire and their amusing, provocative, and ultimately hopeful transgressions.

AUNTING AND THE EVERYDAY POLITICS OF GENDER

While we have identified many issues for a feminist agenda, we do not mean such an agenda as a prescriptive or definitive list. Rather, our intent has been to provoke recognition of the yet-to-be finished struggles in which feminism is engaged or should be engaged and to encourage progressive practices that are not focused solely on redressing wrongs but on creating more equitable patterns of gendered living. In that light, we propose a few feminist re-visions informed by our analyses of aunts that address the gendered politics shaping everyday social life.

First, the various renditions of aunts as the "woman of the house" point to a continued reliance on women to do the unpaid reproductive labor necessary for society. While we value nurturing and domesticity, we also recognize that cultural expectations of selfless nurturing place a disproportionate burden on women, particularly those who are economically disadvantaged. From mammies (e.g., Aunt Jemima) to hip and trendy urbanite aunties (e.g., *Raising Helen*), the availability and willingness of aunts to take on the unpaid work of child care and domestic labor, taking maternal fulfillment as the basis for their physical and mental well-being, is a taken-for-granted premise of these aunting stories. The neotraditional message of these stories is that a woman's "natural" place is as a homemaker and nurturer of children. We think not. Instead, we have argued for feminist critiques of dominant cultural assumptions about women's maternal nature, the romance of home, and the conflation of race, class, and gender in the delegation of caring labor. In addition, there is a critical need for more adequate social policies and institutional support for all kinds of family care needs. If the "care deficit" that U.S. families face is met by privatized caring labor, there are steep social and moral costs, as we pointed out in chapter 6. Popular culture aunts gesture to the ways in which we have come to take for granted feminine nurturing and urge us to re-vision nurturing not as an innate female impulse or a devalued form of labor but as a social practice vital to us all.

Second, a primary site of feminist struggle over everyday life involves the intense focus on young women and girls in popular narratives of femininity and domestic life. Feminist media scholars analyzing popular postfeminist representations of girls and young women offer a reason for this focus: "Postfeminism frequently imagines femininity as a state of vitality in opposition to the symbolically deathly social and economic fields of contemporary Western cultures, and the highest-profile forms of postfeminist femininity are empowered to recharge a culture defined by exhaustion, uncertainty, and moral ambiguity."[2] In other words, girls and young women are our hope for resolving cultural ills, and the dominant cultural message is that girls are only limited by their innate timidity and anxieties. Not surprisingly, "growing up too fast" is both encouraged and condemned.

One problem is that transitional moments in moving from girlhood to womanhood seem overwhelmed by messages about how girls must empower themselves by being obsessed with self-transformation through savvy consumption, heterosexual desirability, and social achievements. While popular aunt narratives are complicit in promoting such messages, they also offer alternative visions of mentoring and ritual that redirect girls' anxieties about self-development and acceptance. In particular, representations of witches and magical aunts and their nieces bring to the fore the importance of extended periods in which the girl is mentored to womanhood and the significance of rituals marking her transitions. Recall Sabrina and her Aunts Hilda and Zelda or Aunts Jet and Fran and their nieces Sally and Gillian Owens from *Practical Magic*: these narratives of magical aunting cast ritual as a critical feature of the mentoring aunt and her nieces. Cultural rituals are prescribed acts that pay homage to the symbolic or sacred value that a group invests in a person, place, thing, or event.[3] Rituals associated with popular culture witch aunts and magical aunts are often depicted as extremely powerful. Their everyday lives are filled with ritual preparations, lyrical (often rhyming) incantations, exotic ingredients, and prescribed ceremonies. Admittedly, the witches are postfeminist subjects for whom beauty and diet rituals seem just as important as magical rituals. Nonetheless, these rituals connect aunts and nieces to feminine legacies, commitments, and communities beyond themselves.

This vision of feminine ritual need not cast girls as the agents of social transformation; instead, these images might just as readily redefine girlhood in the context of women's history and community. Common girls' rituals of passage at the juncture of race, ethnicity, religion, and region include the Jewish bat mitzvah at age thirteen, the Mexican American quinseñera at age fifteen, the "sweet sixteen" birthday party, and the debutante's coming out ball. All have been hypercommercialized and reduced to spectacles of consumption in such reality TV productions as MTV's *My Super Sweet 16*. Yet reclaiming such rituals of passage and the investments in community and culture that they entail might affirm a girl's sense of belonging within and responsibility to her community and frame the transition to womanhood as a positive coming of age without linking this transition to heteronormative expectations.

A related re-vision based on our analysis of popular aunts affirms the value of women's culture and women's friendships. Despite the sentimentalism and neotraditionalism of "chick" genres in literature and film, these modes of women's culture invoke powerful emotional connections among women based on shared recognition of the frustrations and limitations of heterosexual romance, familiar pleasures in the conventions of the genre, and a sense of hope that life will work out.[4] We have argued as well for the significance of women's friendships and networks as a basis for personal well-being, day-to-day support, and potential political alliances.[5] We need to take women's experiences seriously and have spaces that are dedicated to the issues and opportunities shaping women's lives.[6]

Third, we are struck by the intersecting oppressions and privileges that structure all aspects of experience and culture.[7] Our discussion of white and black maternal aunts in chapter 2 points to the impossibility of understanding these representations of motherhood, families, and social life without considering multiple forces of power and subjugation, especially the overlapping of race, class, and gender. For example, the black sitcom aunts—such as Aunt Vivian Banks from *The Fresh Prince of Bel-Air* and Ella Payne from *Tyler Perry's House of Payne*—draw on and defer a legacy of black female stereotypes related to class and race while negotiating contemporary postracial and postfeminist sensibilities. Likewise, Aunt Bee in whitewashed Mayberry occupies a place of both domestic oppression *and* enormous yet completely ignored—even denied—white privilege. Here popular culture aunts remind us of the dangers of essentializing any particular cultural identities, that is, reducing them to one dimension, and the necessity of striving for more complex understandings of individuals, groups, and institutions.[8]

Finally, feminist analyses of media representations are timely and critical to ongoing interventions in neotraditional and conservative cultural ideologies and social projects. Gender roles, expectations, and realities continue to fluctuate over time; no gender stasis exists. While much is made of the progress toward gender equity in this postfeminist moment, we contend—and our analyses here demonstrate—that equity is still an unmet goal and that both women and men continue to suffer from prescriptive gender norms. Across the variety of aunt characters—witches, eccentrics, substitute mothers, brand icons, mammies—entrenched assumptions and stereotypes persist. We have interrogated the work of these representations not only to critique their limitations but to offer feminist re-visions of small transgressions that unsettle those entrenched meanings. Admittedly, the circulation of popular images is bound to larger systems of capital and commerce. And yet, re-visioning feminist alternatives matters if, as one feminist scholar put it, "relations of power are indeed made and unmade within texts of enjoyment."[9]

AUNTING KINSHIP

We have made much of the alternative configurations of aunt-niece and aunt-nephew relationships, extended families, and nonpatriarchal kinship in popular representations of aunts. We suggest that these representations can be read in terms of multiplicity, choice, and creative approaches to relationships. Feminists have long argued against traditional, patriarchal family and kinship forms and in favor of practices and policies endorsing the great variety of configurations that enable people to manage material conditions and live well together.[10] Family remains a site of political struggle. Recent studies suggest that public conceptions of family remain wedded to a genetic, legal, and racially monolithic nuclear family ideal.[11] In contrast, demographic portraits of the U.S. family depict a multiplicity of configurations:

- multiple forms of family—childless, nonheterosexual, single parent, step-parent, multigenerational, and nonrelated custodial parenting;
- functionally focused relationships that count as voluntary family or chosen kin;
- varieties of cohabitation including heterosexual/homosexual partners and friends, commuting marriages, cross-racial adoption and caregiving, and life-stage support communities;
- changing patterns of marriage, divorce and family size—marriage rates and family size have decreased while rates of divorce have remained at 50 percent or higher over the past thirty years.

The contradictions between the perceived ideals and the lived conditions of family life create challenges, anxieties, and struggle. Yet the pervasiveness of such myths and the passionate defense of conservative family values mark a hegemonic struggle over the location and nature of the intimate connections and emotionally powerful social bonds constituting personal and social life.[12] For example, if features of family life such as intactness, children, and biolegal ties are enforced as cultural standards, then alternative features like an aunt-headed household or the aunt as mother are likely to be assessed as either unacceptable or deviant in relation to such criteria.[13]

One television historian persuasively argues that the nuclear model of the family is a nostalgic and patently ahistoric myth perpetuated in popular culture and epitomized by TV sitcoms.[14] She warns that deeply entrenched popular myths of family deny the diversity, creativity, and lived conditions of family life past and present and the possibilities for the future of families: "As long as our view of family change is refracted through the lens of nostalgia for the past, we will not be able to see a way forward."[15] We have argued that the narratives of popular aunts not only reinforce but often unwittingly complicate normative conceptions of family life, frequently normalizing alternative arrangements despite the inherent conservatism of the sitcom genre itself. Such representations do not mirror lived configurations so much as chip away at the unreflective acceptance of normative conceptions. By drawing attention to their transgressive family arrangements, we have cast the popular aunts as feminist allies in the struggle to expand on what counts as family in popular imagination.

Our reading of popular aunts also encourages more expansive conceptions of kinship. Cultural conceptions of kinship have been the site of some of the more vociferous "culture wars" during the last quarter of the twentieth century and continuing into the twenty-first. Who is related to whom has become a source of considerable confusion, destabilizing family lineages and personal identities, contesting seemingly indisputable claims based on genetic conceptions of kinship. Anthropologists and social historians alike have decried the restrictive and patently ideological nature of structuralist models of kinship. Progeny and property can no longer be straightforwardly attested to by bloodlines or marriages.

It is not hard to find evidence that traditional models of kinship are being replaced by more dynamic conceptions. In anthropology, kinship is recognized as an enacted practice, increasingly indistinct from friendship, community, and a plethora of other relational phenomena.[16] Popular undertakings like the *National Geographic*'s human genealogy project forgo the specifics of particular family lines to aggregate migration patterns and genetic codes, suggesting that if there are meaningful distinctions to be made among humans, our common social classifications are inadequate to the task. Likewise, the Human Genome Project continues to issue unsettling announcements, finding smaller and smaller genetic differences supporting sociobiological classifications distinguishing race, gender, and family.[17] The questions that arise in cases of surrogate births, organ donations, property rights over cell lines, or cross-species transmutations underline the need for more responsive conceptions of kinship.[18] In short, commonsense conceptions of kinship as biological lineage or legally ordained linkages have been strongly disputed. Yet despite scientific, legal, and even personal experiences of their inadequacies, traditional definitions of biolegal kinship remain the bedrock of common-sense understandings of kinship.[19] People continue to hold that "real" kinship means direct genetic lineage, and those who openly counter this ideal are often subject to personal challenges and social stigma.[20] Hence, these ongoing struggles over what we know as kinship and how kin relations refigure not just extended family forms but our sense of humanness and connectedness are of critical importance in feminist arguments for social transformations.

By re-visioning the aunt from a feminist perspective, we have enlisted this figure in the struggle over progressive reforms in the high-stakes struggles over what family and kinship can and should be. In each chapter, we highlighted aunt characters who occupy spaces that are simultaneously outside of the nuclear family but also overlap with it in critical ways. Beloved classic characters such as Aunt Bee and Auntie Mame subtly but inexorably point to the impossibility or undesirability of living out the nuclear family ideal for many families, and yet they still offer a portrait of a family so vivid and real that it is widely taken as upholding traditional "family values." Likewise,

Sabrina, the teenage witch, resides with her aunts Hilda and Zelda in a tightly knit family unit that is affluent, attractive, and competent; we can almost—but not quite—forget that no men live in that woman-defined domestic space.

Rather than arguing for or against particular configurations of family as valid or invalid, morally superior or suspect, functional or dysfunctional, we advocate for the acceptance of multiple forms of families. In honoring the aunt-headed household and alternative kinship conceptions, we hope to defer nostalgia for "the way we never were" and instead embrace and develop the many ways in which we live today.

AUNTING COMMERCE

Consumerism as well as the underlying capitalist ideology that pervades contemporary culture has been a recurrent theme in this book, as all stories—including aunt stories—exist in a world in which money matters, whether that serves as a central tenet of the plot lines and dialogue or remains unspoken, as a taken-for-granted premise of a sitcom. Popular culture aunts both participate in and resist consumerism in postfeminist culture. Sabrina's aunts pay as much attention to the acquisition of just the right clothes as their niece does. Eccentric Auntie Mame's affluence and loss of it is central to her relationship with her nephew Patrick. Aunt Petunia's stinginess with Harry Potter and her contrasting material indulgence of her son Dudley are crucial to the tale. Aunt Bee could not support herself without Andy to provide her with a place to live. The Fresh Prince's move from lower-class apartment to his wealthy aunt and uncle's home in Bel-Air, along with his ghetto persona in contrast to that of his cousins, who were raised in the world of wealth, is the very premise of the show. Money matters, yet naturalizing class, race, and gender as aspects of consumption and lifestyle is morally troubling. But it is the moral corruption inherent in the use of aunts as brand icons that provoked our most critical analysis of aunts and consumption.

We offer the following points that emerge from our analysis of commodifying nostalgia and nurture through the brand image aunt.

First, we (re)learn the potency of family values in the marketplace. The aunt recalls the importance of family values while at the same time constituting those values as negotiable and available for sale. Two points are relevant. First, this is a sterile and impersonal image of family values. The aunt does not require the relationship work of a parental figure: you do not have to work at getting along, you do not get stuck with onerous responsibilities thanks to your kinship obligations. The aunt has an advantage in this sense over the mother as a marketing image. While the mother might evoke more intense emotional responses, the potential for negative emotions—guilt, anger, resentment, and so on—is strong. With an aunt, such negative emotions are tempered by the aunt's more flexible cultural role. Further, while the aunts who promote products and services might also be working mothers, the image of the aunt does not evoke the intense concerns over neglect and care or balancing priorities that the mother does. Once again, we get family values without the complications.

In addition, the use of the aunt as a symbol to sell domestic and leisure services and products reveals troubling trends in consumer demands and production processes. As we note, the aunt image positions the consumer as deserving and desiring, longing for the security and comforts of an idealized childhood and family. The commodified aunt contributes to the social and commercial relations of consumer society in which individual comfort and convenience have become paramount social values. In domestic and leisure arenas, this association encourages self-indulgence, but in other arenas the associations might not play as well. For example, what might we expect of a bank that advertises "Aunt Mae's interest rates" or a dealership by the name of "Aunt Jane's Used Cars." The image of the aunt constitutes a nonthreatening, nonrational, even noncompetitive basis for transaction.

The nostalgic aunt as an advertising icon is part of the taken-for-granted fabric of our "free market" economic system. Yet her presence troubles us and offers a critical lesson in the danger of dismissing seemingly trivial imagery. Invoking the aunt as shorthand for commodified caring points to the ways in which caring is morally devalued in contemporary U.S. culture.

An unmarked shadow haunts many of the images of aunts in women's popular fiction today: the spinster aunt. While we have not called her out, she has been a presence across the chapters, and we want to give this figure her due. The spinster aunt is a critical figure in both post-feminist and feminist accounts of social life and women's possibilities. Indeed, the spinster serves as a locus for the tensions that connect and divide feminist and postfeminist perspectives on the aunt.

Take Aunt Bee, the prototypical spinster aunt dedicated to nurturing her kin: a web of historical and cultural associations attend Aunt Bee's spinster arrangement with her nephew Andy. The exchange of her domestic service for his patronage not only casts her as a "prisoner of love" as we argued in chapter 1 but entails a legacy of kinservice among unmarried women. This legacy informs both postfeminist and feminist revisions of the maternal spinster aunt, though with differing implications. Thus the legacy is worth a brief digression: the traditional stereotype of the spinster condenses and caricatures the economic disadvantage and social stigma of the unmarried woman under patrilineal kinship and patriarchal social systems. "Spinster" was originally an occupational designation (unmarried women earned their keep as spinners of wool); the term became a legal description of a woman's unmarried status in eighteenth century Britain. Legal, economic, and social disadvantage accompanied such status; it was not uncommon for unmarried women in the working classes to take on grueling physical labor while those in the "servant-keeping" classes had little waged employment options and often resorted to living with kin in exchange for service as nannies and domestics.[21] Aunt Bee's spinster contract and her characterization as a fussy homebody set her in the patrilineal traditions of the unmarried kinswoman bound to familial servitude.

From a neotraditional postfeminist perspective, the spinster contract is made all the more palatable by the assumption that this arrangement fulfills Aunt Bee's frustrated maternalism—she needs to mother and to be of (domestic) service. Further, as we pointed out in chapter 3 regarding neotraditional aunts, not only does spinster maternalism fulfill a woman's innate need to nurture, but such service also can enhance her value in the marriage market. Contemporary popular narratives often depict the spinster with children attracting a desirable man. Hence, feminism is taken into account: these women can "have it all," under conditions of personal choice. However, from a feminist perspective, the historical legacy of spinsterhood cannot be denied or dismissed. Rather, the figure of the maternal spinster aunt conjoins a suspect nostalgia for the comforts of home and kin linked to a pernicious justification for exploiting women's domestic labor and loving care. Further, the popular chick flick resolution of the spinster's self-alienation (her failure to realize her own desires for children and marriage) reconciles the feminine subject to prevailing ideologies of family, sexuality, and maternality. The differences in the postfeminist and feminist images of the spinster aunt are politically significant: much is at stake in refiguring the neotraditional spinster aunt as personally and socially fulfilled or as ideologically, socially, and economically conscripted into kinservice.

Similarly, the spinster aunt as a culturally marginalized figure has been reclaimed in both postfeminist and feminist perspectives by linking this figure to women's desire for freedom and autonomy and to psychosocial anxieties and fears. In postfeminist narratives, this palpable cultural ambivalence over women independent of men and marriage informs two contrasting images of the spinster aunt. One is the savvy auntie, a figure we explored in chapter 3 as the "neotraditional" aunt but that also encompasses the beautiful witches in chapter 4 and the world-wise eccentric aunts in chapter 5. While this aunt is often posed as the "cool" aunt and an icon of women's independence,[22] she is also subject to the "pathologization of the single woman" prevalent in postfeminist culture.[23] For example, the spinster witch or eccentric is hailed as an icon of women's autonomy and freedom not only from outdated social mores against women's explicit display of sexual desire but also from outdated feminist mandates calling for women's dissolution of the heterosexual contract and social institutions like marriage. In popular narratives like *A Discovery of Witches* or *Auntie Mame*, witches and eccentrics are cast as defying conventional mores. Nonetheless, these same figures are unreflectively governed by heteronormative desire. In contrast, the other prevalent postfeminist spinster aunt figure is the fussy homebody, whether subsumed by maternalism or depicted as an unmarried, unfulfilled, hence failed, woman. For example, the apron-wearing figure we identified as one of the aunt brand images in online commercial websites is depicted as "like a mother," who loves to serve her family. In this image, nostalgia for mother care and home are on offer. In contrast, the spinster aunt as a failed woman is depicted in the dispirited old maid or in her more extreme form, the embittered, mad old hag. For example, the horror film *Aunt Rose* offers a cautionary image of the spinster's deformation of feminine nature, a spinster aunt in the attic whose kin care turns to killing intruders in her home.[24] Hence, the postfeminist spinster aunt celebrates autonomy yet is subject to harshly disciplining normative forces.

Feminists have reclaimed the spinster as an image of defiance and rebellion against status quo social structures and power relations.[25] Feminism's challenge to dominant social and psychic structures is embodied in the figures of the spinster aunt as witch or eccentric, women without children, or men whose satisfaction with alternative ways of living and loving threaten the status quo. As one feminist put it, "If women are allowed to flee on their broomsticks, couldn't they possibly destroy all that has been so carefully put together by men?"[26] We have argued that feminism's own popular narratives of the witch and the madwoman are suspect; nonetheless, these figures of women sans men remain potent images of feminist challenge and alterity. The spinster aunt thus embodies contrary sanctions in contemporary popular culture—a figure of autonomy and empowerment in both feminist and postfeminist narratives, yet one whose marginality inspires personal and cultural anxieties, whether of an unfulfilled life or a persecuted one. The ambivalences that trouble the figure of the spinster are likely to come to the fore in both popular culture and social issues, given that women now outnumber men in the U.S. and only half of all adults are married (the lowest percentage in the past 100 years).[27] These demographics provoke "the marriage question" anew, raising in its contemporary manifestation issues such as the sanctity of marriage, recession unemployment rates among men and women, incarceration and immigration policies, and the privatization of social services for children and families. Hence, we anticipate that the spinster aunt may become increasingly visible across genres of women's popular culture.

We caution against embracing this figure as a feminist icon. Instead, we urge feminists to engage the ambivalences and issues that attend this figure, including postfeminist celebrations and denigrations, making the spinster aunt a key to mapping critical alliances and affiliations across myriad struggles to advance or retain progressive social changes.

CELEBRATING AUNTS

As we have mentioned previously, several popular books have appeared in the past few years celebrating the aunt, and several websites and blogs celebrate aunts and aunting. Infant clothing manufacturers now market "my aunt loves me" outfits to complement those referencing mothers, fathers, and grandparents. Cards appear on the racks each Mother's Day that pay tribute to aunts because they are "like a mother" to us, and birthday cards for nieces and nephews abound. While we appreciate these capitalist odes to the significance of aunts, we acknowledge a tension between our deep appreciation for the increased cultural recognition of aunts and our concern over the dangers of mainstream celebration.

On the one hand, increased cultural recognition of the centrality of aunts in our lives is important because, in a very real sense, we name what exists. That is, the designation of the second Sunday of July as Aunt's Day—following Mother's Day in May and Father's Day in June—is an acknowledgment of the existing (and historical) contribution of aunts as nonnuclear family members to their nieces and nephews' lives. In particular, celebrating aunts is a way for women without children to affirm a nurturing identity distinct from mothering. Rates of voluntary and involuntary childlessness among women have increased markedly in the last thirty years,[28] and many women delay childbearing until their thirties or even forties. Hence, aunting can be a source of deep meaning for many women without children and a way to participate in children's lives without taking on the responsibilities of full-time parenting.[29] Such nurturing can be a tremendous help to besieged parents balancing careers, marriage or partnership, and childrearing and for single parents who need support in caring for their children. A designated day for aunts and the opportunity to buy T-shirts that signify aunt-niece and aunt-nephew relationships may seem like trivial matters, but as cultural symbols they tap into a trend toward understanding women as nurturers in multiple ways, rather than only in traditional maternal roles. We celebrate that message and see the continued popularity of aunt characters in media to be a contributing factor to the recent surge in aunts' cultural status.

Yet, on the other hand, we admit concern about the dangers of mainstreaming aunts and the pitfalls of commercialization and devaluation. Can our representations of aunts continue to pose transgressive challenges to dominant gender roles once they join the ranks of mothers, fathers, and grandparents as the focus of marketing campaigns? Mother's Day, for example, is the single biggest day for sales of flower arrangements, making it the focus of an epic onslaught of advertising each year, guaranteed to generate feelings of guilt, competition, and inadequacy if one fails to acknowledge a mother through good, or at least adequate, consumption of goods and services in her honor.[30] To render celebration as equivalent to an act of consumption cheapens aunt-niece and aunt-nephew bonds and may, in the end, do more to undermine them than celebrate them. Likewise, savvyauntie.com, a site we think offers useful content, also offers up the aunt-niece and aunt-nephew bond as a commercial market niche. One of the auntie-types on the site includes the "PANK"—the professional aunt, no kids: "PANKs are the new Pink—the new segment of women that marketers should be focusing on,"[31] presumably because these aunts have disposable income to spend on nieces and nephews. While we embrace celebration of aunts and aunting, we caution against the ready equation of aunts, care, and the purchase of goods and services or the practice of honoring aunts with equivalent purchases.

FINAL THOUGHTS

Exploring popular culture aunts has been a fun yet challenging experience for us as feminist scholars. We continue to enjoy watching *Bewitched* reruns and the black-and-white *Arsenic and Old Lace* when it comes on. And we continue to find more aunt characters than we could possibly address in one book. We find the aunt in popular culture to be an impetus to question continually how the domestic sphere

and its persistent, attendant gender roles form the seemingly innocuous background of the TV shows we watch, the films we see, and the
books we read for pleasure and for our research. We choose not to be
disheartened by the regressive and oppressive representations of gender that permeate women's popular culture. Instead, we pay attention
to the multitude of small but significant ways in which aunt characters
point us toward a more hopeful vision of gender equity and justice,
one that includes humor and playfulness as well as serious challenges
to status quo arrangements and understandings. Where are the aunts?
They are everywhere in our cultural narratives, mainstream caricatures but also rallying points for feminist progressive change.

APPENDIX I

AUNT WEBSITES[‡]

	Name	URL	Description
1	Aunt Publishing Corp	Aunt.com	Independent vanity publishing house encouraging rookie writers.
2	Aunt Abigail's Software	Auntabigail.com*	"Don't be afraid to ask"
3	Aunt Agatha's books	Auntagathas.com	New & used mysteries, detection [sic] & true crime books, Ann Arbor
4	My Great Aunt Agnes	Heelstone.com/agnes	Collectible & affordable American art pottery
5	Auntie Annie's	Auntieannes.com	Pretzel franchise org since 1988: "A shining LIGHT in the business community"
6	Aunt Annie's Crafts	Auntannie.com	Craft Web books and software
7	Aunt Annie's Quilt Nook	Auntanniesquiltnook.com*	Online store selling fabrics, patterns, books, kits, notions
8	Aunt Ann's Elder Home Care	Auntannshomecare.com	In-home elder care in SF since 1958

[‡] *Accessed January–February 2010*

* These websites are data sources rather than citations. Although some are now defunct as websites, they remain pertinent as data relevant to our analyses. We note with an asterisk those sites that were no longer viable as of May 2012.

	Name	*URL*	*Description*
9	Aunt Ann's Agency	Auntanns.com	In-house staffing @ Aunt Ann's SF; household staff & home care
10	Aunt Art Clothing	auntart.blogspot.com/	Children's clothing w/art designs
11	Aunt B's Cleaning Service	Ilove2clean.zoomshare. com	Residential and commercial cleaning; clean and safe
12	Aunt Barbie's Dolls	Mylinuxisp.com/ ~appelomega/ABB	Hard to find Barbie dolls and collectibles
13	Aunt Beep	thisnext.com/by/ auntbeep/	Artists consignment gallery
14	Aunt Belle's Confectionary	Auntbelles.com	Gourmet & handmade chocolates & candies
15	Aunt Bessie's	http://www.auntbessies. co.uk/	Mixes & convenience foods esp. Yorkshire pudding
16	Aunt Betsy's Photography	Auntbetsy.com* (*see* tollerproductions.com)	Portrait studio esp. maternity, breastfeeding, kids, family
17	Aunt Betty's	Auntbettys.co.nz* (*see* hansells.com/ourfoods/ browseourrange/ auntbettys.aspx)	Old Fashioned Foods, Ltd.; Steamed puddings & desserts
18	Aunt Book	Auntbook.com	Ask Aunt Book Children's Book Identification Site
19	Aunt Bug's Log Cabin Rental	Auntbug.com	Gatlinburg cabins, Pigeon Forge cabins & Smoky Mtn cabins
20	Aunt Candice Foods	Auntcandicefoods.com* (*see* candicefoods.com)	Gluten- & casein-free foods
21	Aunt Carrie's Restaurant	auntcarriesri.com	Birthplace of the clam cake
22	Aunt Clara's Kitchen	Dominicancooking.com	Dominican recipes & cooking
23	Aunt Cookie's Red Rhubarb	Redrhubarb.com* (*see* armplate.com/local-food/ preserve-maker/aunt -cookies-red-rhubarb -warren-mn)	Red rhubarb spreadable fruit
24	Cool Aunt Designs	Coolauntdesigns.com	Handcrafted jewelry
25	Aunt Cynthia's Bed & Biscuit	Auntcynthiasbnb.com	Doggie day & night care at our home—cage free! Friendly dogs welcome!

	Name	URL	Description
26	Aunt Daisy's Bed & Breakfast	auntdaisy.net	B&B in 1890 Midwestern home
27	Aunt Deb's Attic	Auntdebsattic.com	Antiques & books
28	Aunt Debbie's Knit and Stitch	Knit-and-stitch.co	Yarns & needlepoint materials in British Columbia
29	Aunt Edie's Miniatures	Ediespage.com/ miniatures*	Dollhouse miniatures, related books and videos
30	Aunt Edna's Kitchen	Auntedna.com	Nonprofit, personal webpage about cooking
31	Aunt Ellen's Attic	Mei.net/~golftang	Antiques, collectibles, hard-to-find rarities
32	Aunt Fanny's Olde Egg Shoppe	Auntfannys.com*	Antiques, rustic & country-style furnishings
33	Aunt Fannies Bloomers	Auntfannies.net* (now on Facebook)	Family-owned & operated florist shop
34	Aunt Flossie	crownrecords.com/ music_gap/af_music/ auntflossie.html	High-velocity rock quartet in Austin, Tex.
35	Oh my giddy aunt	Ohmygiddyaunt.com.au	Personalized jewelry & keepsakes
36	Aunt Glenda's Cakes	Auntglendascakes.com	Family-owned custom cake shop
37	Aunt Hattie's Place Inc.	Aunthattiesplace.net	Nonprofit residential child care facility for young boys w/ special needs
38	Aunt I's Jamaican Restaurant	Auntis.net	Two locations in South Florida
39	Aunt Irene's Recipes	1001medrecipes.com*	Personal website w/ Mediterranean recipes, diet, maps
40	Aunt Irene's	auntieirenes.com	Aunt Irene's Espresso, Pastries, Ice Cream
41	Aunt Jan's Candles	Auntjanscandles.com*	Family business: scented candles in fanceful shapes
42	Aunt Jane's Victorian Manor	Auntjanes.com	Vacation lodging
43	Aunt Jeni's Home Made	Auntjeni.com	All-natural pet food
44	Aunt Jessica Cares	Auntjessicacares.co.uk	Agency for domestic recruitment services

	Name	*URL*	*Description*
45	Aunt Josie's Restaurant	Auntjosies.com	Family owned & operated since 1961 in Syracuse
46	Aunt LaLi's Treats	Auntlali.com	Ice cream trucks
47	Aunt Leah's	Auntleahs.org	Housing, job training, life skills for youth and single moms
48	Aunt Leah's Fudge	Auntleahs.com	Family-run shop: "The best fudge in the world"
49	Aunt Lizzie's	Auntlizzie.com	Food product: cheese straws in Memphis
50	Aunt Lois's Homemade Soap	Auntloissoap.com* (now on Facebook)	Soaps and bath salts in Texas
51	Aunt Louise's Lake House	Auntlouiseslakehouse.com	B & B in N.Y. wine country
52	Aunt LuLu's Embroidery	Stitchesbyauntlulu.com/	Custom embroidery
53	Aunt Lute Feminist Publishing	Auntlute.com	Independent feminist book publisher
54	Aunt Lynnie's kitchen	Auntlynnie.freeservers.com/	Holiday and Egyptian recipes
55	Aunt Mahalia's Candies	Auntmahalias.com	Gatlinburg, Tenn., since 1939
56	Aunt Manny's	Auntmanny.com	Vintage & primitive folk art
57	Aunt Martha's Youth Service Center	http://www.auntmarthas.org/	Child, teen, family social services in Danville, Ill.
58	Aunt Martha's Bed and Breakfast	Auntmarthasbedandbreakfast.com	Fort Walton Beach, Fla.
59	Aunt Mary's Café	Auntmaryscafe.com	Southern comfort food in Oakland, Calif.
60	Aunt Maude's Restaurant	Auntmaudesames.com	Supper club in Ames, Iowa
61	Aunt Mae's Home Care	Auntmae.com	In-home care provider, Dallas, Tex.
62	Aunt Millie's Bakeries	Auntmillies.com	Breads and other bakery in Ind.
63	Aunt Millie's Pizzas and Subs	Auntmilliespizza.com	Milton, N.C.
64	Aunt Minnie Radiology MISYS	Auntminnie.com	Radiologist news

	Name	URL	Description
65	Aunt Minnie's Southern-Style	Auntminniesfood.com	Southern comfort frozen foods
66	Aunt Molly's Bead Street	Home.flash.net/~ mjtafoya* (*see* beadwork. about.com/library/weekly/ blmarytafoya.htm)	Bead art
67	Aunt Myra Quilt Designs	Auntmyras.com	Quilt designs and tips
68	Aunt Myrna's Cabin	Aunt-myrnas-cabin.com	Nebraska; also on Facebook
69	Aunt Nea's Inn	1neasalley.com	St. Georges, Bermuda
70	Aunt Nellie's Vegetables	Senecafoods.com/store/ contents/en-us/d1.html	Glass-packed beets, onions, beans
71	Auntie Netta	auntienetta.tamasha. org.uk/	Sri Lankan comedian in Britain
72	Aunt Nette Children's Jokes, Songs, Car Games	beachnet. com/~jeanettem/	Resources for entertaining nieces and nephews
73	Aunt Philly's Toothbrush Rugs	Auntphillys.com	Denver, Colo.
74	Aunt Patty's Natural Foods	http://auntpattys. glorybee.com/	Natural foods
75	Aunt Patty's Attic	Auntpattysattic.com	Lincoln, Neb.
76	Aunt Polly's Children's Clothes	Southernchild.com* (now on Facebook)	Used clothing
77	Aunt Polly's B&B	Auntpollysbb.com*	Inn and stables in Adirondacks
78	Aunt Polly's B&B	pollysbnb.com	Middletown, R.I.
79	Aunt Polly's Dreams	Auntpolly.com	Porn
80	Aunt Ruby's Sweet Jazz Babies	Arsjb.com	Band—hot jazz & swing from 1910–1940 era
81	Aunt Ruby's Peanuts	Auntrubyspeanuts.com	North Carolina's finest peanuts
82	Aunt Ruthie's Sugar Pie Farmhouse	Sugarpiefarmhouse.com	Branson, Mo.; product endorsements
83	Aunt Ruth's Animal Care	Auntieruth.com	Minnetonka, Minn.
84	Aunt Ruth's Kitchen	Auntruthskitchen.com	Recipes and home and cooking items
85	Aunt Sadie's Candles	Auntsadiesinc.com	Scented candles, Boston, Mass.

	Name	URL	Description
86	Aunt Sadie's Bed & Breakfast	Auntsadies.com	Branson, Mo.
87	Aunt Sally's Original Creole Pralines	Auntsallys.com	New Orleans, La.
88	Aunt Sandra	Myspace.com/auntsandra	Belgrade, Serbia
89	Aunt Sandra's Candy Factory	Auntsandras.com	1950s style shop in Belfast, Ireland
90	Aunt Sarah's General Store	Auntsarah.com	Arthur, Ill., heart of Illinois Amish country
91	Aunt Sarah's Meeting Planner	Auntsarah.org	Caribbean tours and sassy seniors in Fla.
92	Aunt Sue's Country Corner	Auntsues.com	Pickens, S.C.
93	Aunt Sue Sustainable Urban	Aunt-sue.info	London
94	Aunt Sue's Tea Room	Auntsuestearoom.com	Marion, Ind.
95	Aunt Susie's Pet Sitting	Auntsusiespetsit.com*	Neenah, Wis., in-home pet sitting
96	Aunt Susie's Country Vacation Homes	Auntsusies.com	Raystown Lakes
97	Aunt Susie's House	Auntsusieshouse.com	Ogden, Utah, Punch needle crafts
98	Aunt Thelma Studio	Thelmas.com	Portland, Ore., recording studio
99	Aunt Vi's	Auntvis.com	Color and aroma therapy
100	Aunt Violet Productions	Auntviolet.com	Bay area graphics, marketing, and design
101	Aunt Wilma's Companion Homecare	Auntwilmas.com	St. Petersburg, Fla.

APPENDIX II

POPULAR SOURCES

BOOKS

Dahl, Roald. (1961). *James and the Giant Peach*. New York: Penguin.

Dennis, Patrick. (1955). *Auntie Mame: An Irreverent Escapade*. New York: Vanguard Press.

Esquivel, L. (1995). *Like Water for Chocolate: A Novel in Monthly Installments with Recipes, Romances, and Home Remedies*. Garden City, NY: Anchor Books.

Greene, Graham. (1969). *Travels with My Aunt*. London: The Bodley Head.

Harkness, Deborah. (2011). *A Discovery of Witches*. New York: Viking.

Hoffman, Alice. (1995). *Practical Magic*. New York: Berkley Books.

Ibbotson, Eva. (1999). *The Island of the Aunts*. New York: Penguin.

Kleypas, L. (2009). *Smooth Talking Stranger*. New York: St. Martin's.

Mitchell, Margaret. (1936). *Gone with the Wind*. New York: Warner Books.

Primavera, E. (2010). *Auntie Claus* (repr. ed.). San Anselmo, CA: Sandpiper.

Randall, Alice. (2001). *The Wind Done Gone*. New York: Houghton Mifflin.

Robinson, Marilynne. (1980). *Housekeeping*. New York: Picador.

Rowlings, J. K. (2003). *Harry Potter and the Order of the Phoenix*. New York: Arthur A. Levine Books.

Snicket, Lemony. (2007). *The Wide Window: Or, Disappearance!* A Series of Unfortunate Events, bk 3. New York: HarperCollins.

Stowe, Harriet Beecher. (1851). *Uncle Tom's Cabin.* New York: Bantam.

Tolkien, J. R. R. (1999). *The Fellowship of the Ring* [1954]. Mariner Books.

Twain, Mark. (1887). *The Adventures of Tom Sawyer.* New York: Penguin.

Wiggin, Kate Douglas Smith. (1903). *Rebecca of Sunnybrook Farm.* New York: Houghton Mifflin.

MOVIES

A Princess for Christmas (2011). M. Damien (director). Hallmark Channel.

Alice. (1990). Woody Allen (director), Woody Allen (writer). Orion Pictures.

Arsenic and Old Lace. (1944). Frank Capra (director), Julius J. Epstein, Philip G. Epstein, Joseph Kesselring (writers). Warner Brothers Pictures.

Auntie Mame. (1958). Morton DaCosta (director), Betty Comden, Adolph Green, Patrick Dennis (writers). Warner Brothers Pictures.

Aunt Rose. (2005). James Tucker (director), Joshua Nelson (writer). Savage Roses Productions.

Bewitched (2005). Nora Ephron (director), Nora Ephron, Delia Ephron (writers). Columbia Pictures.

Bringing Down the House. (2003). Adam Shankman (director), Jason Filardi (writer). Touchstones Pictures, Hyde Park Films.

Driving Miss Daisy. (1989). Bruce Beresford (director), Alfred Uhry (writer). The Zanuck Company, Majestic Films International.

The F Word: Who Wants to Be a Feminist? (2011). Michael McNamara (director), Michael McNamara, Judy Holm (writers). Markham Street Films.

Ghost. (1990). Jerry Zucker (director), Bruce Joel Rubin (writer). Paramount Pictures.

Gone with the Wind. (1939). Victor Fleming, George Cukor, Sam Wood (directors), Margaret Mitchell, Sidney Howard, Oliver H. P. Garrett, Ben Hecht, Jo Swerling, John Van Druten (writers). Selznick International Pictures, Metro-Goldwyn-Mayer.

Grave of the Fireflies. (1988). Isao Takahata (director), Akiyuki Nosaka, Isaso Takahahta (writers). Shinchosha Company, Studio Ghibli.

Housekeeping. (1987). Bill Forsyth (director), Marilynne Robinson, Bill Forsyth (writers). Columbia Pictures.

Imitation of Life. (1956). Douglas Sirk (director), Eleanore Griffin, Allan Scott, Fannie Hurst (writers). Universal International Pictures.

James and the Giant Peach. (1996). Henry Selick (director), Roald Dahl, Karey Kirkpartrick, Jonathan Riberts, Steve Bloom (writers). Allied Filmmakers.

Lemony Snicket's A Series of Unfortunate Events. (2005). Brad Silberling (director), Daniel Handler, Robert Gordon (writers). Paramount Studios.

Mame. (1974). Gene Saks (director), Patrick Dennis, Jerome Lawrence, Robert E. Lee, Paul Zindel (writers). American Broadcasting Company, Warner Brothers Pictures.

Mostly Martha. (2001). Sandra Nettelbeck (director), Sandra Nettelbeck (writer). Arte, Bavaria Film, Kinowelt Filmproduktion, Palomar, Pandora Filmproduktion, Prisma Film, Rai Cinemafiction, SRG SSR idée suisse, Schweizer Fernsehen, Südwestrundfunk, T&C Film AG, Teleclub AG, Westdeutscher Rundfunck, Österreichischer Rundfunk.

My Big Fat Greek Wedding. (2002). Joel Zwick (director), Nia Vardalos (writer). Gold Circle Films, Home Box Office, MPH Entertainment Productions, Playtone, Ontario Film Development Corporation, Big Wedding.

No Reservations. (2007). Scott Hicks (director), Carol Fuchs, Sandra Nettelbeck (writers). Castle Rock Entertainment, Storefront Pictures, Village Roadshow Pictures, WV Films III, Warner Brothers Pictures.

Of Boys and Men. (2008). Carl Seaton (director), Shebeta Carter (producer). USA: Anointed Harvesters.

Passion Fish. (1992). John Sayles (director), John Sayles (writer). Atchafalaya.

Practical Magic. (1998). Griffin Dunne (director), Alice Hoffman, Robin Swicord, Akiva Goldsman, Adam Brooks (writers). Village Roadshow Pictures Entertainment, Fortis Films, Di Novi Pictures.

Raising Helen. (2004). Garry Marshall (director), Patrick J. Clifton, Bath Rigazio, Jack Amiel, Michael Begler (writers). Touchstone Pictures, Beacon Pictures, Mandeville Films, High Arc Productions.

Rebecca of Sunnybrook Farm. (1938). Allan Dwan (director), Kate Douglas Wiggin, Don Ettlinger, Karl Turnberg (writers). Twentieth Century Fox Film.

Rosewood. (1997). John Singleton (director), Gregory Poirier (writer). Warner Brothers Pictures, Peters Entertainment, New Deal Productions.

Sabrina, the Teenage Witch. (1996). Tibor Takács (director), Barney Cohen, Kathryn Wallack, Nicholas Factor (writers). Hartbreak Films, Viacom Productions, Barney Cohen/Kathryn Wallack Productions, Once & Future Films.

Three Weeks, Three Kids. (2011). Mark Jean (director), Jean Abounader, J. B. White (writers). Johnson Production Groups.

Travels with My Aunt. (1972). George Cukor (director), Graham Greene, Jay Presson Allen, Hugh Wheeler (writers). Metro-Goldwyn-Mayer (MGM) Studios.

Volver. (2006). Pedro Almodóvar (director), Pedro Almodóvar (writer). Canal + España, El Deseo S.A., Ministerio de Cultura, Televisión Española.

The Wizard of Oz. (1939). Victor Fleming, George Cukor, Mervyn LeRoy, King Vidor (directors), Noel Langley, Florence Ryerson, Edgar Allan Woolf, L. Frank Baum, Irvine Brecher, William H. Cannon, Herbert Fields, Arthur Freed, Jack Haley, E. Y. Harburg, Samuel Hoffenstein, Bert Lahr, John Lee Martin, Herman J. Mankiewicz, Jack Mintz, Ogden Nash, Robert Pirosh, George Seaton, Sid Silvers (writers). Metro-Goldwyn-Mayer, Loew's.

TELEVISION

The Andy Griffith Show. (1960–1968). Sheldon Leonard (creator). CBS.

The Bernie Mac Show. (2001–2006). Larry Wilmore (creator). Fox.

Bewitched. (1964–1972). Sol Saks (creator). ABC.

The Bill Cosby Show. (1984–1992). Bill Cosby, Michael Leeson, Ed. Weinberger (creators). NBC.

Charmed. (1998–2006). Constance M. Burge (creator). The WB.

The Fresh Prince of Bel-Air. (1990–1996). Andy Borowitz, Susan Borowitz (creators). NBC.

The Jamie Foxx Show. (1996–2001). Jamie Foxx, Bentley Kyle Evans (creators). The WB.

Mayberry R.F.D. (1968–1971). Bob Ross (producer), Christian Nyby, Hal Cooper (directors). Hollywood: Paramount Studies/CBS.

Pushing Daisies. (2007–2009). Bryan Fuller (creator). ABC.

Sabrina, the Teenage Witch. (1996–2003). N. Scovell (creator). ABC.

Tyler Perry's House of Payne. (2006–2012). Tyler Perry (creator). TBS.

WEBSITES

Ask an Aunt. http://www.askanaunt.org/.

Book Aunt. http://bookaunt.blogspot.com/2009/05/blog-award-from
-charlottes-library.html.

The Canadian Aunt's Blog. http://estherbyer.blogspot.com/.

Savvy Auntie. http://blog.savvyauntie.com/.

OTHER

"I ain't yr mama" (2004). Opal P. Adisa [digital image/poem]. Santa
Clara, Calif.: DeSaisset Museum.

The Liberation of Aunt Jemima. (1972). Betye Saar. Berkeley Art
Museum.

The New Aunt Jemima. (1964). Joe Overstreet. Menil Collection, Houston, Tex.

Sabrina, the Teenage Witch. (1971–1983). George Gladir (writer), Dan
Decarlo (artist). Archie Comics.

Workers + Warriors: The Return of Aunt Jemima. (1998). Betye Saar,
Michael Rosenfeld Gallery.

NOTES

Introduction

1 Re-visioning was articulated by feminist poet and theorist Adrienne Rich (1972) as a rallying mode of feminist critique aimed at both deconstructing the taken-for-granted assumptions that self-entrap marginalized peoples within intersecting oppressions and creating new visions of gendered life. She called revision not just critique but an act of survival: "Re-vision—the act of looking back, of seeing with fresh eyes, of entering an old text from a new critical direction—is for women more than a chapter in cultural history: it is an act of survival" (p. 18).

2 Gerson, 2010.

3 Eng, 2010.

4 Banyard, 2010; Douglas, 2010; McRobbie, 2009.

5 In *The Female Complaint*, Lauren Berlant (2008) offers an elegant exposition of the ways women's fiction genres or women's culture has created an "intimate public" around the pleasures of consuming sentimental narratives expressing complaints about the disappointments, frustrations, and small oppressions of being a woman. Berlant is an apologist for conventional women's genres, arguing that, rather than dismissing these forms, there is need to engage with the affective *communitas* they inspire that makes them such enduring and powerful features of the popular culture landscape. As she puts it, "My claim is that the gender-marked texts of women's popular culture cultivate fantasies of vague belonging as an alleviation of what is hard to manage in the lived real—social antagonisms, exploitation, compromised intimacies, the attrition of life" (p. 5). The conventional narratives of "chick lit" and other forms of women's culture circulate sentimental fantasies of a "better good life" based on the ultimate value of emotional recognition and reciprocity enhanced by good intentions. In addition, they engage

in complaint formulas based on "a view of power that blames flawed men and bad
ideologies for women's intimate suffering" (p. 2); one such bad ideology in the
postfeminist version of these complaint narratives is feminism.

6   Cultural media analysis has been criticized for failing to tap audience perceptions and relying too heavily on textual analyses. One recent example is Schiappa's (2008) charge that critical media analyses are plagued by a normative
schema of "representational correctness" that leads to condemnations of popular
fare without assessing audience interpretations. Schiappa urges media critics to
adopt social-psychological measures to support their analyses. Such demands for
"audience verification" imply that interpretive analysis is divorced from what
"real" audiences perceive and understand. The suggestion misunderstands critical interpretive engagement and oversimplifies empirical-analytic instrumenta-
tion. Yet we acknowledge that when we identify "dominant" interpretations of
aunt figures—the maternality of Aunt Bee, for example—we are making claims
that might seem to require such verification. How do we know that these interpretations are dominant or widely understood and shared? While we have talked
with many people about popular cultural representations of aunts and have in
that way received personal anecdotal evidence that our interpretations are not
off the mark, we have drawn on popular documentation for corroboration—film
reviews, blogs, popular magazines, TV ratings, and the like—rather than conducting formal interviews or surveys. More importantly, we make this case by
drawing out the connections and resonances among these figures and contexts
of cultural, political, and material elements and relations. We argue that it is not
merely verifying an interpretation with a particular audience but drawing out the
contextual relations that create the resonances, associations, and power of any
figure that is critical. In short, "dominance" is not constituted solely on the basis
of how many people assent to a particular interpretation but is a more complexly
contextualized claim.

7   We use "feminism" as a singular noun with the recognition that feminism has
never been a monolithic movement, discourse, or struggle. Our own allegiances
are to poststructuralist feminisms, as we will discuss shortly. Nonetheless, we
concur with those who argue that feminisms are characterized by commitments
to social justice and interventions in sexual and gendered oppressions.

8   See Projansky (2001, p. 67) for an extended explanation of the following postfeminist discursive strands:
   1.   a linear postfeminist perspective: In this chronological view, we have
         moved from prefeminism to feminism and now beyond feminism; femi-
         nism is outdated or has already been taken into account and is supplanted
         by postfeminism;
   2.   backlash postfeminism or "new traditionalism": "these discourses aggres-
         sively lash back at feminism" and include an "'antifeminist feminist post-
         feminism'" that takes feminists to task for representing women as victims
         and advances an antivictim critique (see, e.g., critiques by Ropie [1994] or
         Hoff Sommers [1995]); this discursive strand also includes a "'new tradi-
         tionalist postfeminism' marked by a nostalgia for a prefeminist past as an
         ideal that feminism has supposedly destroyed";

3. equality and choice postfeminism: "narratives about feminism's 'success' in achieving gender 'equity' and having given women 'choice' particularly with regard to labor and family";

4. (hetero)sex-positive postfeminism: disparages feminism as man-hating and as opposed to heterosexual relations and embraces individuality, independence, and personal empowerment through (hetero)sexual expression; and

5. postfeminist men: the principle of equality means men can be feminists too—sometimes better ones than women.

9   Projansky, 2001, p. 68.

10   Johnson, 2004, p. 331.

11   See the analyses of girl power in Harris, 2004; or Pecora & Mazzarella, 2001.

12   Banyard, 2010; Brunsdon, 2005; Coleman, 2009; Douglas, 2010; Genz & Brabon, 2009; McRobbie, 2009; Negra, 2009; Probyn, 1990; 2006.

13   Vavrus, 2002, p. 23.

14   Even the words "aunt" and "uncle" are fairly recent in the linguistic record. According to anthropologist Jack Goody in *The Development of Family and Marriage in Europe*, "aunt" and "uncle" as linguistic categories appeared during the late Roman Empire in vernacular Latin. The Romans distinguished a maternal aunt, *matertera*, from a paternal aunt, *amita*; the English term "aunt" derives from the latter. Eventually, the term "aunt" or "auntie" was applied not just to kinswomen but to any older woman of friendly acquaintance.

15   The growing presence of the aunt during this time can be traced in English usages of the term "aunt," which expanded during the seventeenth and eighteenth centuries. Many of the meanings of the term that emerged then remain in use. According to linguist Susan Harvey, a.k.a. the Virtual Linguist,

> In Shakespeare's day, the term "aunt" referred to both a gossipy old woman and a bawd, procuress or prostitute (cf. Shakespeare's *The Winter's Tale* "Are summer songs for me and my aunts, As we lie tumbling in the hay"). In the 17th century, students from Oxford called Cambridge University their "Aunt" and vice versa. The BBC is affectionately known as Auntie and aunt appears in a few mild exclamations eg [*sic*] my giddy aunt, my sacred aunt, my holy aunt or even just "my aunt." Then there's an Aunt Edna, a lowbrow theatre-goer, an Aunt Emma, an unenterprising croquet player, Aunt Sally, a fairground game or the wicket-keeper in cricket, and "my Aunt Fanny," used in sentences expressing disbelief, eg [*sic*] Tell that to my old Aunt Fanny.

16   Literary historian Ruth Perry's excellent treatise *Novel Relations* (2004) traces the transformation of the English family through the eighteenth and nineteenth centuries in the context of concurrent social, economic, and political changes including the development of a market economy, wage labor, and economic class stratifications, including the rise of the middle class, enclosure and the redistribution of land, urbanization, and the development of print culture.

17   Perry, 2004, 348, 349.

18   Perry, 2004, 363–71.

19   We draw here on literary critic Rupert Christiansen's delightful volume *The Complete Book of Aunts* (2006), in which he scours literary sources from the

nineteenth through the twentieth centuries for evidence of the aunt's presence. Christiansen acknowledges that, between Tacitus's account of the Emperor Nero's aunt in 41 B.C.E. and the initial appearance of the powerful maternal aunt in the late seventeenth century, there is little evidence of aunts in existing historical and literary work.

20 Christiansen, 2006, 22.

21 Rose, 1999.

22 Christiansen, 2006, 25.

23 See Cunningham, 1997; Sturgis, 2004; Traeder & Bennett, 1998.

24 Traeder & Bennett, 1998.

25 Sturgis, 2004.

26 http://www.savvyauntie.com/.

27 Notkin, 2011b.

28 Although we appreciate these claims for the significance of aunting, our analyses will show that such popular accolades too often limit the cultural power of aunting by drawing facile analogies between the aunt and the cultural ideal of the mother ("my aunt is like a mother to me") and linking aunting to the nuclear family and patriarchal kinship. We contend that such associations undermine the progressive potential of aunts and aunting for challenging and changing conventional understandings and practices of women's roles, especially within the family.

29 See Bengtson, 2001; Hanks & Ponzetti, 2004; Langer & Ribarich, 2007; Loury, 2006; Pashos & McBurney, 2008; and Wenger & Burholt, 2001.

30 Family scholar Robert Milardo's *Forgotten Kin* (2010) analyzes the roles of both aunts and uncles from a social science perspective.

31 Davis-Sowers, 2006, 2012.

32 See Ellingson & Sotirin, 2010; Ellingson & Sotirin, 2008; Sotirin & Ellingson, 2007; Ellingson & Sotirin, 2006; Sotirin & Ellingson, 2005.

33 Ellingson & Sotirin, 2010.

34 See Ellingson & Sotirin, 2008.

35 For two alternative perspectives, see Eng, 2010; Franklin & MacKinnon, 2001b.

36 We concur here with Negra, 2009, p. 9.

37 Adaptation is a fraught process; the issues are beyond the scope of the present book. See the arguments in Hutcheon, 2006; Leitch, 2007; Sanders, 2007; or Stam & Raengo, 2005.

38 See the London *Daily Mail* (January 1, 2011): "Sales of bodice-ripping e-books soar as women use digital readers to hide their romantic novels." The article cites research that confirms "new figures from market researchers Nielsen BookScan show digital sales of the genre have overtaken print copies for the first time—which the gadget users can read without anyone else knowing" (¶2). *Library Journal* blogger Roy Tennant (2011) suggested that "reading is going underground at the speed of e-reader adoption" (¶3). That is, he believes that people's choices will be shaped by their inability to impress others with their choice of prestigious reading material and by the privacy that means we are no longer shamed by "the trashy novels many of us secretly wish we could but were too embarrassed to take onto the street" (¶4).

39 See Moody's (2011) recent conference presentation, "'Convergence Culture':

Exploring the Literacy Practices of Online Romance Fiction Communities," in which she argues that online media are reshaping how fans read romance fiction because digital spaces "make romance reading more participatory, personal, and elastic but . . . in doing so they also package producer/consumer relations through a discourse of familiarity" (n.p.).

40 Kompare (2004) documents the emergence and entrenchment of this regime in business practices like off-network strip syndication (this involves packaging a number of shows from a series to be broadcast one after another—as a "strip"— across a time segment), production conventions like genre formulas, local programming strategies aimed at cost-effectiveness and counterprogramming, and conceptions of audiences through aggregating audience demographics focused on consumption patterns (see also Williams, 1994). Even the small fraction of an audience share created in contemporary postnetwork television's "narrowcasting" practices contributes to the regime of repetition by refiguring any particular strategy (reality shows, viewer voting) or issue (abortion, polygamy) to repeat across television series, channels, and markets (Lotz, 2006).

41 U.S. consumers are equipped to access such rebroadcasts through a variety of media. According to Nielsen's Television Audience Report in 2009, the average American home had 2.86 TV sets, 38 percent had digital cable, and 88 percent had a DVD player.

42 This phrase is from Kompare's excellent analysis of the industry's turn to rebroadcast in *Rerun Nation* (2004), cited above, n. 40.

43 Feminist media historian Lynn Spigel realized the stakes involved when she asked her television history students about their perceptions of women's lives in the U.S. during the fifties and sixties. She reports that the historical sensibility promoted by the jumble of historically situated narratives available to and assembled by today's television viewers like her students is the basis for popular memory as a "history for the present," "a form of storytelling in which people make sense of their own lives and culture" (Spigel, 1995, p. 21). Popular memory glosses over the historical contradictions between the way we imagine we were in the fifties and the ways we really were during that time in favor of addressing sociohistorical tensions through nostalgia and selective memory. Spigel observed that, in particular, the dominance of female-focused programming in reruns—sitcoms and soap operas—means that the eclectic mix of shows from different eras in any given day's lineup offers an implicit narrative of women's roles over the past sixty years from a white, middle-class perspective (Spigel, 1995, p. 19).

44 Spigel, 1995, p. 27.

45 From Adrienne Rich's classic essay on feminist re-visioning (1972, p. 18). We are encouraged in this appropriation by Rich's poem "Aunt Jennifer's Tigers" included in her essay. In the figure of this aunt, Rich articulates a sense of her own capitulation to heteronormative pressures and her avenue for escape through creative acts. Aunt Jennifer embodies for Rich the strategies of ambivalence, irony, and critique that we adopt in our analyses.

46 We adopt a poststructuralist interpretive approach that takes the logics of a text to be deeply contextual and intertextual. As McKee puts it in his primer on

poststructuralist interpretive analysis, "by analyzing a text you can find out about the sense-making practices that were in place in a culture where it is circulated as meaningful" (2003, p. 49).

47 According to Weedon (1997), feminist poststructuralist critique entails challenging the constitutive force of dominant ideologies of gender to advance definitions of reality, gendered subject positions, and moral orders that are taken as natural, politically neutral, ahistorical, and commonsensical but that, under scrutiny, are revealed as partial, partisan, historically situated, and materially oppressive.

48 We draw here on Ferguson's (1993) work on feminist irony.

49 Ferguson, 1993, pp. xi, 30.

50 Ferguson (1993) uses the evocative phrase the "manyness of things" to refer to this strategy. See p. 154.

51 Negra, 2009, p. 7.

Chapter 1

1 Laclau and Mouffe (1998) refer to such inherent oppositions as "antagonisms," those principles that negate the basis upon which a chain of associations is premised; for example, our interjection that "the aunt is like a mother but not a mother" negates the basis for the signifying chain: mother—aunt—maternal care—self-sacrifice. Such antagonisms provoke alternative associations, setting off processes of critique and, eventually, re-vision. For a useful overview situating LaClau and Mouffe's perspective within a theory of articulation, see Slack, 1996.

2 Leonard, 1960–1968.

3 The Aunt Bee character appeared on all eight seasons of the popular *Andy Griffith Show* (1960–1968) as the maternal substitute in her widowed nephew's home. The character was carried over as the (maternal) housekeeper in another widowed father's home in the spin-off *Mayberry R.F.D.* (1968–1971).

4 On the historical recency of this model of the family, see Glenn, 1994.

5 Throughout the book we use the terms *black* and *African American* interchangeably to signify U.S. citizens of African descent.

6 The cast included Andy Griffith as widower and sheriff Andy Taylor, Ron Howard as his son Opie, popular comedian Don Knots as Andy's cousin and inept sidekick, Deputy Barney Fife, and Frances Bavier as Andy and Barney's Aunt Beatrice (Aunt Bee). Aunt Bee became Bavier's signature character. For a profile of the show and information about all the characters, see the fansite The Andy Griffith Show Rerun Watchers Club (Clark, n.d.). There are also numerous fan books, chief among them Clark and Beck, *The Andy Griffith Show Book* (2000), and Robinson and Fernandes, *The Definitive Andy Griffith Show Reference* (2004).

7 For evidence of this popularity, see Clark, n.d.; Clark & Beck, 2000; Robinson & Fernandez, 2004.

8 See *Rerun Nation*, Kompare's (2004) insightful discussion of the industry strategies, institutional changes, and cultural trends that contributed to the development of this heritage.

9   Leonard, S. [director], Elinson, J. & Stewart, C. [writers]; originally aired October 3, 1960.
10   See Benedict Anderson's (1983) classic argument for nationalism as "imagined communities."
11   This Mayberry vision of American life was an especially potent formulation at this point in television history when the networks were engaged in an effort to create a "TV Nation" through a confluence of strategies such as content formulas, standardized affiliate marketing, the common denominator audience, and industry consolidation (Spigel & Curtin, 1997, p. 3).
12   For plot summaries of all eight seasons of *The Andy Griffith Show* and three seasons of Mayberry R.F.D., see the online Internet Movie Database, http://www.imdb .com (hereafter IMDb) or *The Andy Griffith Show Episode Guide* (Zille, n.d.).
13   "Andy and Opie, Housekeepers" (Sweeney, B. [director], Tarloff, F. [writer], originally aired March 13, 1961). IMDb.
14   "The Bed Jacket" (Sweeney, B. [director], Bullock, H. & Allen, R. S. [writers], originally aired December 17, 1962). IMDb.
15   For recent feminist analyses of the ongoing oppressions and inequities attending women's household and child care responsibilities, see Baxter, Hewitt, & Western, 2005; Bianchi, Robinson, & Milkie, 2006; McDonald, Phipps, & Lethbridge, 2005.
16   The idea that women as domestic caregivers are "prisoners of love" is feminist economist Nancy Folbre's (2001) conception, and we draw on her work to make this point about the spinster aunt. In addition, see our concluding chapter for a discussion of the spinster aunt's legacy and contemporary political significance.
17   For examples of recent feminist analyses of gender inequities in domestic responsibilities, especially caretaking labor, and calls for more public policies supporting caretaking and household labor, see Alberts, Tracy, & Trethewey, 2011; Duffy, 2007; England, Budig, & Folbre, 2002; Hochschild, 1989; Kirby, Golden, Medved, Jorgenson, & Buzzanell, 2003; Sayer, 2005; Wilkie, Ferree, & Ratcliff, 1998; Wood & Dow, 2010.
18   For analyses of the conditions of caring labor and calls for a labor movement, see the papers presented at the 2005 Caring Labor Conference sponsored by the Harry Bridges Center for Labor Studies, University of Washington (http://depts .washington.edu/pcls/caringlaborconference/caring_labor_conference.htm) and the resulting special issue in *Politics & Society* (Jacoby, 2006). An interesting ongoing forum is maintained at caringlabor.wordpress.com.
19   In their research among family viewers, Hoover, Clark, and Alters (2004) report an interview between researcher Diane Alters and Jim Mills, the father in a blended family, about the influence of television depictions of the family on Mills' own ideas and practices of family. Mills singled out *The Andy Griffith Show* as an example of the classic television shows that "contained many stories of goodness and demonstrated values that Mills felt had been important for his own moral growth" (p. 63). Hoover, et al., add a footnote about the show's Bible study fan groups that, according to Jerry Fann, who developed the "Mayberry Bible Study" concept, were formed around the premise that "'the show is filled with basic morals and Christian principles taught by the Scriptures'" (Terwilliger,

2001, 2D; cited in Hoover, et al., 2004, p. 183 n. 14). Also see BarneyFife
.com (Fann, 1998), a website for developing Bible studies drawn on the morals
and values illustrated in specific episodes of *The Andy Griffith Show*. A promo-
tional paragraph for the related book *The Way Back to Mayberry: Lessons from a
Simpler Time* (Fann & Lindsey, 2001) states that the book "draws out the subtle
parables found in thirty favorite episodes."

20   Frank, 2004; Coontz, 1992.

21   This language is drawn from the conservative "Doctrine for Natural Families"
advanced by the World Congress of Families (1997–2005).

22   "Wedding Bells for Aunt Bee" (Sweeney, B. [director] & Bullock, H. [writer],
originally aired April 2, 1962). IMDb.

23   Coontz, 1999.

24   This argument is drawn on anthropologist Judith Stacey's important work on
family and kinship. See Stacey, 1999, p. 398.

25   Our analyses in this chapter are informed by black feminist and womanist scholars who have called into question the value of the persistent cultural images of
black womanhood, challenging the intersectionality of historical, material, and
cultural forces of oppression that underwrite them. However, as black scholar
Lisa Thompson explains, "Black feminist and womanist theories were born out
of black women's shared experiences of oppression and their shared efforts to
resist it" (2009, p. 153). We recognize that as white feminists, our critical interpretations are affected by our own experiences, privileges, and perspectives, and
we are sensitive to the charge of cultural critic and theorist bell hooks that non-
blacks intent on critical analysis "may simply recreate the imperial gaze—the
look that seeks to dominate, subjugate, and colonize" (hooks, 1992, p. 7). We are
also aware of the need to get out of the way and let black women speak for themselves (Coogan-Gehr, 2011). Yet we could not ignore the significance of black
maternal aunts, and we believe that struggles over embedded cultural representations matter. Accordingly, our approach has been to learn from the scholars
whose work we have read, both about the images, experiences, and issues affecting black women's lives and about the limitations of our own habitual ways of
thinking and being in the world.

26   Indeed, Mayberry is reassuringly white, and none of the episodes over the show's
eight-year run addressed racial tensions. Only one show even included a black
character: episode 215, "Opie's Piano Lesson" (Philips, L. [director], Townsend,
L. & Townsend, P. [writers], originally aired March 13, 1967. IMDb) featured
the character Flip Conroy, a former professional football star and the new high
school football coach, who also played classical piano, resolving Opie's masculinity dilemma over playing the instrument (the episode was originally telecast
March 13, 1967).

27   Despite locating *The Andy Griffith Show* in the rural South—Mayberry was modeled on Andy Griffith's hometown, Mt. Airy, North Carolina (Beck & Clark,
2000, p. xv)—there is little explicit acknowledgment of the racial disparities and
tensions that characterized the American South historically or more specifically,
throughout the sixties when the show was produced. One scholar documenting
the cultural history of hillbilly Americana said of *The Andy Griffith Show*, "the

show offered a romanticized image of a benign southern past free of social tensions, a placidity largely made possible through the whitewashing of blacks from the southern landscape" (Harkins, 2005, p. 197).

28   For a classic and poignant essay on this point, see Minnie Bruce Pratt, "Identity: Skin Blood Heart" (1984), in which she chronicles her awakening to the intersections and implications of racial oppression, white privilege, heteronormativity, and classism, the invisible infrastructures of her Southern upbringing.

29   Just as postfeminist discourses frame sexism as a problem of the past that is now a subtle and largely culturally contained issue for women, postracial or transracial discourses entail a contemporary social perception that we know about racism and have taken care of the most egregious aspects of racial injustice and oppression.

30   The white rural South was the context for several popular sitcoms, all of which were canceled during the "rural purge": *Mayberry R.F.D.* (1968–1970), *Petticoat Junction* (1963–1970), *The Beverly Hillbillies* (1962–1971), and *Green Acres* (1965–1971).

31   Harkins (2005) contends that CBS executive Fred Silverman purged his network of rural-themed shows and shows appealing to rural audiences in response to analyses showing that the shows did not appeal to the twenty-five- to forty-year-old urban demographic. Several of the canceled shows were replaced by a wave of socially conscious "quality" offerings such as *The Mary Tyler Moore Show* and *All in the Family*. Another reason for changing the prime time lineup had to do with the FCC's prime time access rule issued in 1970 which limited the amount of prime time network programming, leading to realignments of the prime time schedule.

32   See media theorist Kirsten Lentz's insightful argument about the emergence of and distractions between quality and relevance programming in her article "Quality versus Relevance: Feminism, Race, and the Politics of the Sign in 1970s Television" (2000). Lentz argues that these shows are characterized by a "politics of the referent" because they based a claim to social relevance on seemingly authentic representations of racial reality, from sets that depicted ghetto conditions to characters whose talk and behavior were based on patterns of black urban life.

33   In the representational struggle over race on television, "keeping it real" is a politically charged, semiotically fraught injunction. Stuart Hall, in a well-known essay exploring the question of "What Is This 'Black' in Black Popular Culture?" (1992), engages the essentialist arguments about "keeping it real" that boil down to questions of whether a show is "black enough" or "really black." He argues that blackness is not adequately understood as an "is/is not" determination but rather must be held as a mark of difference that operates inside yet remains defiant of assimilationist forces. Black is not an empty signifier but a political one strategically representing black community, the black aesthetic, and black counternarratives, thus making good on the promise of "keeping it real." This representational strategy is not based on essentialist polarities (black or not) but on linking and hybridization (black and gendered, classed, sexually oriented, aged, etc.); it does not dehistoricize and naturalize signs of blackness but takes

them as "political, symbolic, and positional"; it is not apart from and subordinate to experience itself but integral to the struggle over representations of race. Hall warns that there is much at stake in the representational struggles over blackness because "it is only through the way in which we represent and imagine ourselves that we come to know how we are constituted and who we are. There is no escape from the politics of representation, and we cannot wield 'how life really is out there' as a kind of test against which the political rightness or wrongness of a particular cultural strategy or text can be measured" (p. 473).

34 In the words of E. Patrick Johnson, "Authenticity, then, is yet another trope manipulated for cultural capital." He quickly acknowledges, however, that authenticity claims can give marginalized groups a basis for self-representation that counter oppressive stereotypes, particularly those that maintain dominant racial hierarchies (2003, pp. 2–6).

35 What is televisually "real" must generate ratings, the "real" determining factor in whether a black sitcom remains on the air. Despite the emergence of BET and other programming aimed at black audience share, black sitcoms are notoriously short-lived. To stay on the air requires these shows to both conform to genre expectations and appeal to white as well as black audiences (Means Coleman, 2000). This is why blog commentator Amyar Christian, arguing recently that black audiences are turning to cable over network TV in search of relevant content, opined, "The 'keep it real' aspect is key. If a series can keep it real—we know, and don't know, what that means—and manage to be as creative and witty as the acclaimed group of broadcast sitcoms (*Community, Parks and Recreation, 30 Rock, Big Bang Theory, The Office*) we might have the next *Cosby Show* coming soon to a TV near you" (2011). Christian's observation affirms the necessity for building audience share by linking depictions of blackness to mainstream (white) expectations of the sitcom genre. Yet, according to media scholar Robin Means Coleman (2003), this strategy for marketing black sitcoms runs into a problem: the "keeping it real" aspect, which may verge on essentialist identity claims that can marginalize white audiences, is in tension with market dynamics that appropriate and commodify black histories, cultures, and politics, assimilate their specificities, and "skew Black identity symbols in response to dominant, mainstream expectations" (p. 60). She warns that while "claims of authenticity are unwieldy—hard to pin down and even discriminatory . . . they do confront market forces that seek to appropriate, or, at worse, exploit Blackness for profit" (p. 63).

36 See Jhally & Lewis, 1992; Gates, 1989. As media scholar Herman Gray argues, while differences in public attitudes about race and changes in national circumstances across the decades from the 1970s through the 2000s affect televisual representations, it is the "persistence of the assimilationist vision, sustained and reinforced through television images and situations, that is ideological" (Gray, 2005, p. 227).

37 This strategy has been facilitated by industry shifts including niche cable channels, lifestyle brand marketing, targeted demographics, and media convergence, allowing a keener focus on specific audience/market groups (Gray, 2005, p. 84).

38 Although Tyler Perry is only an occasional character in the show that bears his name, the show trades on his popularity as a comedy actor, writer, and producer.

39 Gray's (1995b) hope that black production teams and black ownership would alter stereotype-ridden television fare has not been realized. Notably, all four of the black sitcoms we discuss were created and produced by African Americans. Even so, all four adopted the blatantly stereotypic characterizations that have dominated black sitcoms in the 1990s and 2000s.

40 Urban blackness has become "cool" in popular culture, and all four sitcoms cast urban hipness as a cultural and personal style that is not limited to African Americans. The shows diffuse black culture in the context of a multicultural view of American society. This diffusion and multiculturalism occur across the regional settings of the four black sitcoms: all of the shows are set in mixed neighborhoods, although one might think that Bel Air is largely black on *Fresh Prince* while the Philadelphia location of the King's Towers hotel in *The Jamie Foxx Show* implies that theirs is a predominantly black area. *The Bernie Mac Show* is set in an upper-middle-class, progressive neighborhood in Encino, California, while *House of Payne* is set in a working-class, mixed-minorities neighborhood in Atlanta, Georgia.

41 The affirmation of difference obscures systemic racial disparities. For example, despite the struggle for equal educational opportunities and the landmark legislation and social changes over the past fifty years that seemed to realize this goal, the Massachusetts-based Schott Foundation on Public Education (2010) reported that 53 percent of black male students did not graduate from high school in 2007–2008 compared to a 22 percent drop-out rate for white males. Further, in 2009, 9.4 percent of white Americans lived below the poverty line compared with 25.8 percent of African Americans. In August 2011 the U.S. Bureau of Labor Statistics reported that, while the unemployment rate was at 9.1 percent, the rate of unemployment among African Americans was 16.7 percent. Finally, incarceration rates for African Americans have been extraordinarily high compared with other racial groups since the 1970s. For example, one in nine African American males between the ages of twenty and twenty-nine was incarcerated in 2005; out of the total population of African Americans, 2.3 percent were in prison compared with 0.4 percent of whites and 0.7 percent of Hispanics (Mauer & King, 2007, p. 3). Allusions to these stark differences are few and politically anemic on television sitcoms.

42 Means Coleman (2000) argues that contemporary popular culture is populated by stereotypic black characters drawn on the legacy of minstrel shows—the black coon, the shuck and jive man, the young buck. She labeled current television sitcom fare as *neominstrel* for the reliance on such characters. See also Crouch (2011).

43 Nelson (2008) points out that masculinity and blackness are both naturalized and depoliticized on *Bernie Mac* (p. 205), constructing Bernie Mac as "one of us" in a logic of equivalence that makes race not a point of antagonism but simply an idiosyncratic element in his multicultural upper-middle-class lifestyle. See also Norris (2002).

44   These sitcoms create black middle-class worlds that interface with but are sepa-
      rate from the white middle-class world as well as the struggles of other racial/
      ethnic groups. In this way, blackness is repositioned as part of a complexly strati-
      fied multicultural social order. Gray notes that the television industry has long
      promulgated "mirror sitcoms" offering "separate but equal discourses" that "sit-
      uate Black characters in domestically centered Black worlds and circumstances
      that essentially parallel those of whites. Like their white counterparts, these
      shows . . . maintain a commitment to the universal acceptance into the trans-
      parent 'normative' middle class" (1995b, p. 87). He warns that it is "more and
      more difficult to distinguish progressive political possibilities from neoliberal
      and conservative rewrites of the same old racial narratives" (1995b, pp. 162–63).
45   Each of the shows included episodes given over to vignettes of the black expe-
      rience of slavery, the civil rights movement, or historic achievements of Afri-
      can Americans. For example, *Fresh Prince* aired an episode centered on the
      importance of teaching black history in high school ("The Ethnic Tip"; originally
      aired February 4, 1991). *House of Payne* devoted one episode to recounting the
      achievements of baseball's Negro Leagues, while in another, Ella and Curtis
      treat C.J.'s daughter as a house slave to teach her about slavery and the value
      of civil rights. Such vignettes sanitize past oppressions for comedic effect, pro-
      mote a communal pride in blackness as a sign of noble struggle, and attest to the
      promise of social equality and the dream of an integrated society. While they
      may reclaim the triumphs of African American history, they repress the anger,
      militance, and violence of black nationalism and black power (Gray, 1995). In
      effect, they conform cultural memory and visions to the postracial assurance that
      civil rights antagonisms are safely past.
46   All of these shows have been subject to criticism for their hegemonic capitula-
      tion in the struggle over cultural representations of black identities, culture, and
      experience. For example, protests over nominations for the NAACP's Image
      Award explicitly questioned the damaging stereotypes promoted in *The Jamie
      Foxx Show*, while producers of the show defended their representations. More
      recently, criticisms of *Tyler Perry's House of Payne* have culminated in a public
      war of words between Perry and filmmaker Spike Lee in which Lee decried the
      "coonery and buffoonery" of Perry's shows, while Perry defended the authentic-
      ity of his narratives for the African American community (for recent commen-
      tary, see Izrael, 2011; Keyes, 2010; Lapowsky, 2009). See n. 65 below.
47   See Douglas, *Enlightened Sexism* (2010) and Means Coleman (2003) on the
      commodification of blackness in popular media.
48   There are numerous lists of the racist media stereotypes of black women, among
      them "mammies, matriarchs, jezebels, welfare mothers, and tragic mulattoes"
      (Brooks and Hébert, 2006, p. 299); contemporary stereotypes like the sapphire,
      that is, the "angry black woman" (Samuels, 2011, p. 62), the "sassy, hyper-
      sexualized sistah," or the "Oprah" entrepreneur (Moore, 2008; Samuels, 2011);
      the diva, black lady, and angry black woman along with reality TV caricatures
      like "the black bitch," "the loud black woman," and "the sistah with attitude"
      (Springer, 2007, pp. 254, 267); and the welfare queen and urban teen mother
      (Jordan-Zachary, 2009, p. 6).

49   U.S. Department of Labor, 1965. For a critical analysis of the treatment of black
     women in this report, see Giddings. More recent criticisms of the black mother
     focus on the alarming rate of incarceration and imprisonment among young Afri-
     can American men. Black mothers have been charged with "failed mothering"
     for fostering an enabling/dependent relationship with sons, explained in part as
     a reaction to the "endangered black male" construction. Black feminists have
     argued that this charge of "failed mothering" is largely misdirected and that cri-
     tique should focus on the institutionalized racism in educational, law enforce-
     ment, criminal justice, and public policy systems. See, e.g., Jordan-Zachery,
     2009; Radford-Hill, 2002.
50   See E. Patrick Johnson's discussion of the significance of the mother as trope in
     black gay discourse. He observes, "In general, the black mother is 'fierce' in that
     she does not suffer fools lightly, works hard but makes it look easy, and is the
     epitome of grace, style, and flair" (2003, p. 94). This description is recognizable
     in Tyler Perry's description of the black mother caricatures in his successful
     Madea movies and black sitcoms, including *House of Payne* (see n. 64 below).
51   Thompson, 2009, p. 4.
52   We follow Thompson's (2009) argument that in talking about popular culture
     representations of the black middle class, the black lady designation is not merely
     an economic determination but has to do with cultural capital and social status
     as well. She notes that in popular culture depictions in the 1960s through the
     1980s, "the black middle class was overwhelmingly depicted as status-obsessed,
     self-serving cultural imposters more interested in copying whites than fighting
     for social justice," a suspicion of racial betrayal and artifice casting middle-class
     blacks as "oreos." But by the 1990s, a "new black aesthetic," open to middle
     class lifestyles and status, allowed for "a much more fluid view of blackness. If
     middle-class characters no longer have to act as cultural police in order to uphold
     narrow, essentialist ideals of blackness, then there is room for diverse representa-
     tions of middle-class black women" including, we suggest, the black maternal
     aunt (p. 5).
53   On the strong black woman as a stereotype hearkening back to American slav-
     ery, see Giddings, 1996; Harris, 1995; and Harris-Lacewell, 2001. For a criti-
     cal analysis of the repercussions of the "strong black woman" image for black
     women, see Beauboeuf-Lafontant, 2009.
54   In the 1990–1991 season, Clair's distant cousin Pam, a seventeen-year-old high
     school student, joins the family while her mother cares for an ailing relative in
     another state. While this is an example of the extended kinship care we discuss
     later, the emphasis in the series is on Clair as a mother, not as a maternal aunt.
55   After her focus groups conveyed their enthusiasm for such figures as Clair
     Huxtable and Vivian Banks, Means Coleman argued that fan response should
     not be discounted; instead, she urged scholars to recognize that, for fans, these
     characters offer an image of hope and possibility against the lived constraints
     of daily experience. Boylorn (2011) argues that black women viewers negotiate
     positive and negative stereotypes of black women.
56   For example, *Madame Noir*, a Web magazine for women devoted to black popular
     entertainment, ranked Vivian Banks second only to Clair Huxtable as a positive

maternal role model, and comments by fans enthusiastically endorsed this rank-ing (Edwards, 2011); the *Grio*, a black news and entertainment website, named Vivian Banks one of the top ten black sitcom mothers, again in the company of Clair Huxtable (Witherspoon, 2011). That the Aunt Vivian character is indebted to *The Cosby Show*'s Clair Huxtable is explicitly alluded to in the show itself; for example, in a Season 3 episode, Fresh Prince Will admonishes his uncle Phil, "Clair would never talk to Cliff like that."

57   The family sitcom has been the focus of ongoing critique for its commercial-ism, conventionalism, and conservatism. According to Mills, the genre has been "criticized for its simplistic use of stereotypes, outmoded representations, and an apparent failure to engage with social or political developments" beyond reaffirming dominant social norms and ideologies (2004, p. 63). He observes that both the format of the sitcom and its content have remained unchanged for decades.

58   The exception is Helen King on *The Jamie Foxx Show*, who owns and manages the King's Towers hotel, although it can be argued that the hotel is her domestic space given that she lives there as well.

59   "The idea of being both black and a lady is a dichotomy that continues to haunt African American women" (Thompson, 2009, p. 6). Black feminist theorist Patricia Hill Collins (1998) decried the bifurcated images of black women in popular television and movies—black women appear as either intensely raced poor black women (p. 36) or as the "black lady overachiever" who is relatively "'unraced' and assimilated" (p. 38). She identifies this as a representational strategy of containment, although, writing in the late nineties, she also identified a "rhetoric of tolerance" in which race and other social categories were embraced as differences that no longer mattered (p. 35). As Thompson adds, "The per-formance of middle-class black womanhood is tied to impossible standards of respectability. No other group of African Americans find themselves responsible for setting professional, aesthetic, political, moral, ethical, historical, and cul-tural values" (2009, pp. 3–4). For more on the significance of the black lady in African American culture, see Springer, 2007, p. 273.

60   In an interview in the *New York Times*, *Fresh Prince* producer Quincy Jones recalled:

> In the pilot of "Fresh Prince of Bel Air," Mr. Smith's street-smart charac-ter bumps up against the father, who has embraced upper-class manners, a preppy teen-age son and a teen-age daughter who is a classic BAP— "black American princess"—not unlike his own daughter, Mr. Jones says with a laugh. "The black experience is a funny experience," he adds. "It's very rich. It's colorful. It's the juice of American pop culture." Casting Mr. Smith as the lead enables the show to tap into the language, dress and style of rap, as well as the music. (Gunther, 1990)

61   "Love at First Fight" (Melman, J. [director], originally aired on February 18, 1991). IMDb.

62   "The Big Four-Oh" (Falcon, E. [director], originally aired on October 21, 1991). IMDb.

63   In the second episode of Season 3, "Will Gets Committed" (Jensen, S. [director],

originally aired September 21, 1992. IMDb), we learn that Aunt Vivian is pregnant, a surprising plot twist and apparently not one scripted by the writers.
Rather, the actress playing Aunt Vivian, Janet Hubert, was herself pregnant, and
the show followed the course of her pregnancy as part of the narrative. However,
because she violated her contract and had ongoing creative differences with Will
Smith, Hubert was fired after the baby arrived (on screen and off). In the first episode of the following television season, the much lighter-skinned actress Daphne
Maxwell Reid appeared as Aunt Vivian. The actress Janet Hubert wrote about
her dismissal from the show in a 2009 memoir, *Perfection Is not a Sitcom Mom*.

64   Auter & Davis, 1991.

65   The show's producer, director, and occasional actor, Tyler Perry, gained popular
attention for his gospel plays and outrageous portrayals of the fictional black
woman character Madea, a stereotypic large, loud, and angry black matriarch.
The name "Madea" is an acronym for "Mother Dear." In an interview, movie
director Spike Lee said that he believes Tyler Perry's television shows like
"House of Payne" and "Madea" movies amount to "coonery and buffoonery."
Responding in a *60 Minutes* interview, Perry defended his caricature of black
women, stating, "Madea is a cross between my mother and my aunt. She's the
type of grandmother that was on every corner when I was growing up. She
smoked. She walked out of the house with her curlers and her muumuu and she
watched everybody's kids. She didn't take no crap. She's a strong figure where
I come from. In my part of the African-American community. And I say that
because I'm sure that there are some other parts of the African-American community that may be looking at me now going, 'Who does he think he's speaking
of?' But, for me, this woman was very, very visible" (Streeter, 2010).

66   Originally, Ella was depicted as C.J.'s mother, but, in the first season, their col-
lege-attending son Calvin appeared, and C.J. was abruptly restoried as a nephew.

67   *House of Payne* has been generally panned for poor directing, shallow writing,
uneven acting, and poor comedic timing but, like Perry's films, is acknowledged as engaging an otherwise neglected audience niche. Despite perennially
bad reviews, *House of Payne* was named "best television comedy" five times
(2008–2012) by the NAACP Image Awards honoring the accomplishments of
the black entertainment industry (http://www.naacpimageawards.net/; Harris,
2011). The show was rated the number one comedy among African American
viewers ages eighteen to forty-nine in 2007 and 2008 (Saval, 2009). Nonetheless, in a review of the DVD release of *House of Payne*, critic Clark Douglas
called it "one of the most payneful shows I've ever seen"; *Toronto Star* reviewer
characterized Perry's work as "gross-out humour, black-on-black racism, thinly
veiled misogyny, cussing, slapping, caterwauling and more caterwauling and
melodrama, heaps and loads of melodrama"; and Robert Bianco of *USA Today*
(2007) intoned, "Glaringly, shamefully, insultingly inept, this new cable comedy
from filmmaker Tyler Perry isn't just the worst sitcom of the year, it's one of the
worst of the modern era." More recently, Hilton Als, a black critic for *The New
Yorker*, accused Perry of populating his productions with plots and characterizations that betrayed "internal racism" and promoting "lazy cultural stereotypes
about blackness" (2010). The contradiction between critics' denouncements and

its popularity and success with the NAACP and black viewers points to the tensions that riddle contemporary racial representations.

68 "We've Come This Far by Faith" (Perry, T. [director], Giles, J.V. and Griffin, K. [writers], originally aired August 6, 2008). IMDb.

69 "Payneful Visit" (Perry, T. [director & writer], originally aired April 6, 2011). IMDb. A similar depiction occurs in the recent film *Of Boys and Men* (2008), in which a black family is devastated by the death of the mother in a random car accident and the father's sister, Aunt Janay, moves in to care for the children and nurture the family in their grief. Aunt Janay counsels a trust in Jesus, often against the anger and grief of the family members. Unlike the sitcom aunts, she is with the family only temporarily (Stephanie, 2010).

70 Harris-Lacewell points out that black religiosity is a critical element of black culture. She argues that jeremiad and liberation theologies provided a basis for collective resistance, resilience, and hope against conditions of slavery, discrimination, and injustice. More recently, a prosperity gospel has become popular, advancing individualistic narratives of personal accumulation and success that undermine the collective mandates of the older theological perspectives. Harris-Lacewell observes,

> Through the narrative of jeremiad and liberation theology there is a mandate for a collective approach to politics and critiques systems of inequality. Christians are called by Jesus' example both to serve the poor and to destroy the structures that create and reproduce poverty. The prosperity gospel advances a pervasively individualistic conception of Christ. To the extent that the prosperity gospel promotes an individualized, dispositional understanding of the world, it discourages collective political action. Beliefs in more instrumental and individual ideas of Christ, like those prosperity gospel, make black Americans less likely to engage politically. (2000, p. 187)

71 Collins (2004) offers a powerful treatise on the urgency for a black politics of community premised in loving ethics. West (2000) offers an alternative plea for a black political theology marked by hope, loving compassion, and revolution (see esp. the section "Prophetic Christian Thought," pp. 357–442).

72 In a recent essay, Banet-Weiser and Gray (2009) argue that this proliferation of racial and social differences in popular media is a "technology of power" that produces the normativity of whiteness, masculinity, and heterosexuality (p. 17).

73 All of the maternal aunts are portrayed as sexually attractive women, whether their bodies are conventionally shaped, like Vivian Banks or Wanda McCullough, full figured, like Helen King, or quite overweight, like Ella Payne. In "Growing Paynes" (Perry, T. [director], originally aired March 30, 2011), one subplot involved a weight-loss contest between Ella and Curtis. Following the episode, the actress playing Ella Payne, Cassie Davis, revealed that she had lost seventy-five pounds while starring in the show. The issue of weight is tied to race, class, lifestyle, gender, age, and a myriad of structural relations well beyond individual control. Still, statistics suggest that obesity rates vary by race: according to the U.S. Center for Disease Control (2009), statistics for the period 2006–2008 indicate that 39.2 percent of non-Hispanic black women were obese, and blacks were 51 percent more likely to be obese than either Hispanics or whites (p. 740).

Despite these disparities, even when weight is highlighted in the sitcoms, body size and shape as well as issues of health and well-being are cast as apolitical and essentialized as gender differences significant largely for their bearing on heterosexual attractiveness.

74   In her overview of women characters on fifty years of television sitcoms, Spangler claims that this model of an egalitarian black marriage was exemplified by *The Cosby Show*'s Clair and Cliff Huxtable, whose relationship is characterized by what Clair in one episode described as reciprocal care and mutual respect (2003, p. 157). Another television scholar examining forty years of prime-time family representations argued that the Huxtable family is patriarchal: Cliff Huxtable's charm "overlays a subtle message: Father knows best, or else'" (Taylor, 1989; cited in Spangler, p. 158).

75   This depiction of marital solidarity underscores the postfeminist emphasis on marriage, yet this is a social injunction that defies the statistics for black women, given that between 1970 and 2007, the proportion of U.S.-born black women aged thirty to forty-four who were married fell from 62 percent to 33 percent, and, in 2009, only 42 percent of U.S. black women were married, less than any other racial/ethnic group (White House Council on Women and Girls, 2011; Cohn, Passell, Wang & Livingston, 2011; Toldson & Marks, 2011). Toldson and Marks rehearse several debates over why black marriage rates are lower than for other groups. Black marriage is a contested issue that calls forward arguments about the legacy of slavery, the effects of poverty, education, incarceration, and institutionalized racism on available partners, ongoing stigmas against interracial marriage, and more.

76   These younger, sexualized female characters are postfeminist caricatures: enlightened about their own sexual objectification and obsessed with status and consumption. Rose (1994; 1997; 2008), Thompson (2009), and others have argued that certain recent popular culture performances of young black women's sexuality are not necessarily objectified and exploited but can be seen as self-defined and empowering. The most proactive analysis is Shayne Lee's identification of a variety of contemporary black female performers as empowered "erotic revolutionaries." She explains, "I deem my subjects erotic revolutionaries because they effectively wage war against the politics of respectability" (2010, p. xiv).

77   Thompson, 2009, p. 3. Her comment bears repeating (see also n. 59): "No other group of African Americans find themselves responsible for setting professional, aesthetic, political, moral, ethical, historical, and cultural values" (2009, pp. 3–4).

78   Thompson argues that the black lady entails hiding or dissimulating sexual energies and desires: "The performance of middle-class black womanhood includes a particular set of precepts that determine how black women may construct or present themselves. This performance relies heavily upon aggressive shielding of the body; concealing sexuality; and foregrounding morality, intelligence, and civility as a way to counter negative stereotypes. Conservative sexual behavior is the foundation of the performance of middle-class black womanhood" (2009, pp. 2–3).

79   Intersectionality has become a critical concept in feminist studies, and we will
      have more to say about it in chapter 2. According to Brah and Phoenix, this con-
      cept signifies "the complex, irreducible, varied, and variable effects which ensue
      when multiple axis of differentiation—economic, political, cultural, psychic, sub-
      jective and experiential—intersect in historically specific contexts" (2004, p. 76).

80   The tenuousness of an ironic frame for racial comedy is explored in Haggins,
      2009.

81   For example, Ella Payne kicks Curtis out of their home after he tells her boss that
      she quit because he thought she was spending too much time at her job ("Mov-
      ing Out," and "Back Where We Belong" (Perry, T. [director]). Both episodes
      originally aired on May 27, 2009 IMDb). Their son Calvin was also living there
      after his wife kicked him out. The men are shown as childish (both wives drop
      off teddy bears along with other personal belongings) and weak in relation to the
      family matriarchs.

82   According to Davis-Sowers (2012), informal kin adoption is an "ongoing famil-
      ial practice" among black families. African American kinship care patterns draw
      on both an African heritage that emphasizes extended family and community
      over the nuclear family, egalitarian familial roles, and the inherent value of chil-
      dren (see Hill, 1999) along with a reliance on kin ("mutualism") as a resilient
      response to a heritage of slavery and ongoing institutionalized racism and day-
      to-day oppressions. Less sanguinely, Thompson (2009) points out that kinship
      care is often necessitated by public policies intended to safeguard children and
      communities and punish "bad" black mothers. For example, the high incarcera-
      tion rate among African American women leaves children without mothers. A
      Pew report in 2008 states that among African American women in their thirties,
      one in one hundred is behind bars; one in fifty-three adults in their twenties is
      incarcerated or imprisoned. The report states that these rates are not based on
      increasing crime rates but rather are "principally because of a wave of policy
      choices," a point Thompson's language-based analysis of policy decisions dem-
      onstrates is often premised in negative images of black women and men, moth-
      ers, and families.

83   Kinship care is defined as "the full-time nurturing and protection of children who
      must be separated from their parents by relatives, members of their tribe or clans,
      godparents, stepparents, or other adults who have a kinship bond with a child
      (Child Welfare League of America, 1994, p. 2; cited in Crumbley & Little, 1997,
      p. xiii).

84   According to the federal Adoption and Foster Care Analysis and Reporting Sys-
      tem, in 2009, there were an estimated 423,773 children in foster care. African
      American children made up 30 percent or 127,821 of that number, although they
      represented only 15 percent of the child population in 2009 (U.S. Department of
      Health and Human Services, 2011).

85   There is ethnographic and sociological evidence that such extended kin and com-
      munal care networks are decreasing among black families and in black com-
      munities (see, e.g., Roschelle, 1997). Such changes make the alternative familial
      arrangements in these sitcoms all the more significant.

86   Alice Walker (1983) offers a formative definition of womanism that conjoins the history, experiences, identities, and behaviors of black women and emphasizes the importance of black women's relationships with other black women. For further discussion of womanism, see chap. 2, n. 12.

87   Ella Payne's friends serve as markers for the show's insistent multiculturalism: her best friend is black, the eccentric Claretha; she is friends with her Hispanic neighbor and together they smooth relations between their husbands; and she maintains a friendship with her working-class white coworker Rosie and her crass and addled mother.

88   We draw on Lisa Beauboeuf-Lafontant's treatise, *Behind the Mask of the Strong Black Woman: Voice and the Embodiment of a Costly Performance* for this analysis.

89   Harris-Lacewell, 2001, p. 3; quoted in Beauboeuf-Lafontant, p. 26.

90   Radford-Hill, 2002, p. 1086.

91   Beauboeuf-Lafontant documents the psychic, physical, social, and cultural toll the strength discourse takes on black women. She explains the concept of strength as a social construction of "virtuous exceptionalism" through which black women are held to be exceptions to suffering and injury who "always rise above the socially orchestrated unfairness" of their material circumstances, internalizing the discourse of strength to repress their own vulnerabilities. In this way, strength casts black women as "less than human" (pp. 16–18). Harris-Perry affirms, "When black women are expected to be super-strong, they cannot be simply human" (2011, p. 185).

92   See Katrina Bell McDonald's study of black women's class/identity divergences (black "stepsisterhood") and the legacy and unity of shared sensibilities (black sisterhood). McDonald notes that "oppression is not uniformly realized across the population of black women," so collective empowerment and communication are difficult (2006, p. 176). Radford-Hill cautions that cultural norms and competition among middle-class black women make informal friendships unlikely sites for political sisterhood. She observes, "Competition for men, economic opportunity, and social status make it difficult to share our experiences openly" (2002, p. 1088).

93   Legal scholar Lani Guinier calls this the "miner's canary" warning. Coal miners were alerted to poisons in the mine when canaries, with their more sensitive respiratory systems, began to gasp for breath. The experiences of people of color or women or any marginalized group can be taken as a similar kind of warning system about the quality of societal conditions for all. In this sense, the plethora of denigrating images of black women can be taken as indicative of inadequacies in the dominant cultural imaginary and societal perceptions more generally. The problem is not just offering better images of black women but making changes to a society that has accepted reductive and derogatory images as adequate for understanding who such woman are and what their possibilities might be. "If we begin to examine the structure in which the canary is presently gasping for air," Guinier argues, "we can fix the atmosphere in the mine so that our democracy as a whole can not only survive, but thrive" (2005, ¶34).

94   Jordan-Zachery details the ways slavery enforced patterns that cast black women
      as outside the norms of femininity, ladyhood, and even humanness. As she notes,
      black slave women were denied the virtues of (white) womanhood, male protec-
      tion either by relatives or through state sanctions for the weaker sex and mothers,
      and even participation in institutions like marriage and homemaking. She argues
      that a myth of sexual promiscuity supported these patterns: "black women were
      portrayed as sexually loose (a) because they were participating in a historically
      designated work domain (work outside the home), (b) because they were not
      protected by men, and (c) because it allowed slaveholders to sexually exploit
      them without consequence" (2009, p. 33).

Chapter 2

1   See recent discussions of the relevance of the black mammy to late twentieth-
      century U.S. culture (McElya, 2007; Wallace-Sanders, 2011).
2   http://www.hstg.org.
3   E.g., Davis, 1990.
4   McElya, 2007.
5   Cooks, 1995.
6   Manring, 1998.
7   Goings, 1994.
8   In an online etymological blog, World Wide Words, freelance etymologist and
      curator Michael Quinion (2010) observes a racist element in the etymology of
      the popular expression "Aunt Sally." He explains, "An *Aunt Sally* in its popular
      sense today is a person or thing that's been set up as an easy target for criticism,
      abuse or blame, in political circles often to deflect attention from the real issues
      and waste opponents' time." A reference to the game Old Aunt Sally appeared in
      an 1866 news report posted from London in which the reporter observed, "Aunt
      Sally is a big black doll on a stick, with a pipe in her mouth, and an orange or
      some toy for a prize, which you win by hitting her with a stick if you are lucky."
      Quinion notes that the designation "aunt" could "refer to an old black woman, a
      term employed both by blacks and whites in the USA from the eighteenth cen-
      tury onwards but also known in London; aunt could also be applied familiarly to
      any elderly woman."
9   Black feminist theorist Patricia Hill Collins (2000) coined this term.
10   For example, E. Frances White articulates instances of black women's involve-
      ment that have been ignored by many historians of feminism, civil rights, and
      activism (White, 2001). Focus on antiracism united forces but it also gave us
      stories that leave out some people. White points out that African American expe-
      riences of racism intersect with sexism but suggests that black feminists tend to
      leave out complexities of the black community that are troubling, particularly
      silences about homophobia, classism, and sexism in order to fashion a compel-
      ling narrative against racism. See White (2001) for a nuanced history of black
      feminism in the U.S.; see also Combahee River Collective, 1982.
11   Coleman (2009) identifies as a black feminist theologian with theoretical and
      political links to womanism and womanist theology. However, she warns of the
      dangers of the academic commodification of the term womanist "by hierarchical

(often white and male) entities [who] co-opted it, as yet another way to brand and classify black women and our thoughts" (p. 122).

12   Some feminists of color identify with the term "womanist" rather than "black feminist." Activist and writer Alice Walker popularized the term "womanism" to describe black feminists and feminists of color, as well as women who love and appreciate other women and women's culture (Walker, 1983, p. xi). The term has been adopted within academic feminist writing not only as a designation for (some) African American feminists but also to indicate multicultural, intersectional perpsectives: "In placing the womanist sensibility outside rigid ethnic boundaries, a womanist is characterized as flexible, intercultural, and self-defined" (Carstarphen, 1999, p. 374).

13   See Bobo & Seiter, 1997; hooks, 1981; Hurtado, 1989; Joseph & Lewis, 1981. It is dangerous to speak for others, especially so given the limited cultural spaces where black women have been afforded space to speak for themselves. "The opportunities for Black women to carry out autonomously defined investigations of self in a society which through racial, sexual, and class oppression systematically denies our existence have been by definition limited" (Hull, Bell-Scott, & Smith, 1982, p. xviii).

14   Moore, 2008; Samuels, 2011

15   Bobo, 1991.

16   Gillespie, 1999, p. 90.

17   http://www.pagebypagebooks.com.

18   The propensity for white authors to use black characters to serve particular narrative functions upholds the existing cultural hierarchies and justifies their inevitability. Novelist and literary critic Toni Morrison suggests, "Africanism is the vehicle by which the American self knows itself as not enslaved, but free; not repulsive, but desirable; not helpless, but licensed and powerful; not a blind accident of evolution, but a progressive fulfillment of destiny . . . [it also serves] to signal modernity . . . being hip, sophisticated, ultra-urbane" (Morrison, 1992, p. 52).

19   Patton, 1993.

20   Carstarphen, 1999.

21   Gillespie, 1999, p. 82; (on the mammy stereotype in media), see also Bogle, 1994; Christian, 1980.

22   McElya (2007) argues persuasively that the mammy remains an important icon in contemporary culture, and that the longing to own one's own romanticized mammy is still prevalent among white audiences and reflected in advertising, television, and film. Further, the mammy image has exerted significant influence on black women entertainers as they define themselves and their art within a racist society (Dreher, 2012).

23   According to Amazon.com, the anniversary edition includes not only the digitally remastered film but also the following "collectibles": Commemorative fifty-two-page photo and production art book; ten 5' × 7' watercolor reproduction art prints; archival correspondence from producer David O. Selznick; reproduction of 1939 original program; bonus CD soundtrack sampler; Warner Bros. Home Entertainment Presents *1939: Hollywood's Greatest Year*, a

documentary narrated by Kenneth Branagh; *Gone with the Wind: The Legend Lives On* featurette; and Emmy-winning telefilm *Moviola: The Scarlett O'Hara War* (http://www.amazon.com/Gone-Anniversary-Ultimate-Collectors-Blu-ray/dp/B0013N7FZ6).

24   Published in 1991 by Alexandra Ripley, *Scarlett* tells the story of Scarlett's pursuit of and eventual reconciliation with Rhett; it sold millions of copies and remains in print.

25   Yet this old song of racism now plays alongside a rich countermelody. A historical parallel novel, published in 2001, written from the perspective of Scarlett's half sister—daughter of Scarlett's father and her slave mammy—offers a very different view of the period of the Civil War and Reconstruction, talking back to Mitchell's whitewashed utopia of slavery with a grittier, more realistic tale of the ravages of racism (Randall, 2001). While the alternative story offered in *The Wind Done Gone* cannot erase or even balance the racist ideology of Mitchell's novel and film, the bestselling counternarrative is a hopeful sign.

26   Goings (1994), in his study of racist collectibles, argues that it is impossible to enumerate precisely how many were produced, some as regional items, others as premiums for nationally distributed goods.

27   Goings, 1994.

28   Patton, 1993.

29   Kaplan (2002) explains her deeply mixed feelings about African Americans giving and receiving black collectibles. In her essay, "Thoroughly Modern Mammy," she discusses her inability to embrace the "redemptive quality" that some "politically enlightened and erudite black people" locate in black memorabilia (¶2). She explores the belief among some African Americans that "taking back" images such as the mammy is a powerful practice and that owning mammy figures can be part of owning their history and refusing to forget the racist history they represent.

30   Goings, 1994, pp. xxiii–xxiv.

31   Nyong'o, 2002, p. 371.

32   The fact that so many of the collectibles are ceramic figurines with glossy painted surfaces provides a troubling metaphor to the ways we understand black subjectivity as it is represented in culture: "the material form of the ceramic figurine seems . . . particularly apt for specifying blackness as a hardened form of subjectivity. In this racial simile, a black skin is as hard as stone; not skin at all, but a mask, with perhaps nothing behind it. This invulnerability provides an alibi for racist violence" (Nyong'o, 2002, p. 377).

33   Goings, 1994, p. 37.

34   Roberts, 1994; Turner, 1994.

35   Manring, 1998, p. 12.

36   http://www.rubyplaza.com/item/649946-27063-3/1954-Ad-AUNT-JEMIMA-PANCAKES.

37   http://www.yesterdaypaper.com. Domain is currently for sale.

38   http://www.auntjemima.com/tradition/index.htm. No longer accessible.

39   Manring, 1998, pp. 182–183; emphasis added.

40   The film featured several prominent actors, including Jon Voight, Don Cheadle,

Ving Rhames, and Esther Rolle (as Aunt Sarah)—well known for her work as both outspoken maid Florida Evans on the popular 70s sitcoms *Maude* and *Good Times*, a black sitcom in which she played the family matriarch, as well as a housekeeper in the critically acclaimed film *Driving Miss Daisy*.

41 As O'Grady eloquently puts it, Aunt Sarah needs "to be sprung from a historic script surrounding her with signification while at the same time, and not paradoxically, it erases her completely" (2009, p. 324).

42 Such manifestation of politics through art is necessary for protest and social change: "self-expression is not a stage that can be bypassed. It is a discrete moment that must precede or occur simultaneously with the deconstructive act" (O'Grady, 2009, p. 322).

43 Lazzari & Schlesier, 2007, p. 402.

44 Reid, 2001.

45 African American men also note the persistence of the aunt mammy and of Aunt Jemima in particular. Black poet Richard Jones (2003) published a collection of poems entitled *The Liberation of Aunt Jemima: A Poetic Tribute to the Spiritual Woman*, which features poems that affirm the strength of black women who have resisted racist stereotypes and constructed productive and fulfilling lives for themselves. See also *Collected Poems* by Robert Hayden (1997), including the poem "Aunt Jemima of the Ocean Waves," which portrays a conversation with a woman playing the role of the mammy aunt as "fat woman" in a Coney Island freak show, during which the character recounts her life and the narrator expresses admiration at her strength and remarkable resilience.

46 Poet Opal Palmer Adisa (2004). Used by permission of the artist.

47 Holladay, 2002.

48 Clifton, 1991, p. 13.

49 In her critical reading of the poem, Holladay contends, "Neither 'aunt' nor 'nanny' tells us anything about the slave woman's identity. Together, the labels are nonsensical, amounting to 'aunt grandmother,' an ironic gloss in itself on the thoughtless, racist habit of addressing older black women in familial—overly familiar—ways. The name 'aunt nanny' is a means of co-opting the unidentified woman's identity and subsuming her into the white family that owned her" (Holladay, 2002, p. 126).

50 Hollaway, 2002.

51 Dickerson & Clarke, 1993.

52 Clarke, 1996, pp. 33–34.

53 For a discussion of minstrelsy in *Bamboozled*, Spike Lee's film that updates and critiques the minstrel show traditions that persist in contemporary films, see Nyong'o, 2002.

54 Anderson, 2008, p. 35.

55 Anderson, 2008, p. 53. Further, she suggests:

> If we recover, or reinvent, the image of Aunt Jemima in the image of a black woman who is ill and resists the efforts of white society to ridicule, silence, or kill her, then what was once a racist image of the alleged support of black women for white society now changes. That image is transformed into one that represents the collective strength and resolve of black women, who

celebrates her larger body and nappy hair as beautiful, and who comes from a long line of "race women" who have struggled against racism and sexism. (p. 119)

56 Clarke, 1996, p. 34.
57 http://auntjemimasrevenge.blogspot.com/.
58 Lorde: "the master's tools will never dismantle the master's house. They may allow us temporarily to beat him at his own game, but they will never enable us to bring about genuine change" (1984, p. 112).
59 Catanese, 2005, p. 702.

Chapter 3

1   Nettlebeck, 2001.
2   Hicks, 2007.
3   Marshall, 2004.
4   Jean, 2010; original air date, May 7, 2011.
5   Hoecherl-Alden & Lindenfeld, 2010.
6   Novero, 2004.
7   This point is convincingly argued by Hoecherl-Alden & Lindenfeld (2010): "The film's rhetorical configuration suggests that it is only through Mario's culinary and erotic intervention that Martha (and thus, German culture and nationhood symbolized through Martha) can sustain herself and flourish: multicultural society and intercultural engagement appear not only as inevitable, but also as valuable to German identity" (p. 128).
8   This analysis is paraphrased from Cecilia Novero's (2004) insightful critique.
9   Novero's (2004) poignant visual analysis of this moment in the film is worth quoting at length:

> Her sense of inadequacy takes on a classical indexical form: a full length shot shows her sitting alone in the dark in the center of the frame, with her arms crossed around her white body and her gaze cast downward. The loneliness and exclusion indexed through her body contrast with the fullness provided by the "authenticity of motherhood" captured by the simple home video's images, the loud voices and laughter coming from the TV. (p. 42)

10 We draw here on Walters (1995).
11 As Walters (1995) puts it, the narrative in *Mostly Martha* depicts a punishment for the feminist attack on maternalism:

> We are being punished for wanting it all: the Superwoman syndrome and the Cinderella complex are the watchwords that construct a female identity in crisis, a subjectivity at war with its own history, a woman bereft. As popular wisdom would have it, contemporary women are now caught in the binds their foremothers unwittingly made for them: in renouncing traditional values of Mom and apple pie (especially Mom), today's woman is a lost soul, an ambitious career woman who has lost touch with that essential part of her femaleness—motherhood. (p. 121)

12 This is a point made convincingly by Negra (2004).
13 A movie critic at ReelzChannel.com who credited *Raising Helen* as the model

for *No Reservations* grumbled, "Even the idea behind *No Reservations* is really just *Raising Helen* in chef's toque: ill-equipped aunt inherits progeny of beloved sister, and the relationship with said progeny softens her up and somehow brings men into her life. Describing it this way makes it obvious how distinctly female a fantasy it is—that becoming a single mother makes you more appealing to men rather than vice versa."

14 The ongoing cachet of this romantic narrative was evident in a recent holiday feature on the Hallmark Channel: *A Princess for Christmas* (2011, Damien, M. [director]). In this made-for-television movie, the aunt has custodial care of her two nieces and a nephew. Not only does she move from a state of desperation and ineptness to good mothering but she ends up marrying a dashing European prince! Yet another example is the contemporary romance novel *Smooth Talking Stranger* (2009), in which a young independent woman comes to realize the ultimate fulfillment of motherhood and marriage. Author Lisa Kleypas' heroine Ella Varner must learn to manage her advice column, "Miss Independent," and other responsibilities when her sister suddenly leaves her newborn son Luke in Ella's care. Ella almost immediately loses her five-year relationship with her live-in boyfriend, an environmental crusader who wants nothing to do with babies. Soon Ella finds herself head over heels in love with an older, wealthy Texas man who is not only a great lover but welcomes the baby into his life and family.

15 Feminist cultural critic Angela McRobbie (2009) identifies "retreatism" as a prevalent postfeminist motif in popular media narratives.

16 As feminist scholar Diane Negra (2004) observes, "the particular target of such discourse is the well-educated professional white woman who, unencumbered by feminist dogma about her entitlement to non-familial personal rewards, abstains from paid work in a display of her 'family values'" [para. 3].

17 The *New York Times* published a well-cited article, "The Opt Out Revolution" (Belkin, 2003), claiming that college-educated white collar women were "opting out" of the workforce in favor of motherhood, a move that seemed to counter feminist arguments for women's place in the corporate world. Later reports argued that this phenomenon had been overstated ("The Truth behind Women Opting Out," Gardner, 2006). Stone (2007) maintained that it was the hard-driving demands of the professional workplace and not families that provoked the choice to opt out while Bennetts (2007) decried the "willfully retrograde choice" that some highly educated women continued to make to opt out and urged women to "have it all"—work and family.

18 Feminist scholar Diane Negra observes, "the popular culture landscape has seldom been as dominated as it is today by fantasies and fears about women's 'life choices'" (2009, p. 2). The postfeminist maternal aunt resolves those fears by making the right (conventional, neotraditional) choices.

19 Tasker & Negra, 2005.

20 Note, for example, that most proposals for balancing work and family do not alleviate the unrelenting sociocultural demands on mothers to rationally manage family life and children's development so as to maximize social achievements and cultural capital. See Warner, 2005; also Sotirin, Buzzanell, and Turner, 2009.

21 The Pew Research Center reports a drop in marriage among U.S. adults from 72 percent in 1960 to 51 percent in 2010 (Fry & Cohn, 2010). This ongoing decline suggests that the postfeminist emphasis on marriage and nuclear family arrangements in these films may be quite out of step with lived experience.

22 Among the classic analyses framing women's fiction as a site of resistance and pleasure as well as hegemonic incorporation and formulaic conventions, see Radway, 1984; Gledhill, 1987; Baym, 1978.

23 We draw in this chapter on Lauren Berlant's insightful treatise "The Female Complaint" (1988) and on her book, *The Female Complaint: The Unfinished Business of Sentimentality in American Culture* (2008). The "good life in love" is Berlant's phrase (2008, p. 4).

24 "The complaint genres of 'women's culture' . . . tend to foreground a view of power that blames flawed men and bad ideologies for women's intimate suffering, all the while maintaining some fidelity to the world of distinction and desire that produced such disappointment in the first place" (Berlant, 2008, p. 2).

25 According to Berlant, this dimension of complaint in women's culture is possible because within the "patriarchal social context," women's genres are trivialized and hystericized: "The a priori marking of female discourse as less serious is paradoxically the only condition under which the complaint mode can operate as an effective political tool: the female complaint allows the woman who wants to maintain her alignment with men to speak oppositionally but without fear for her position within the heterosexual economy—because the mode of her discourse concedes the intractability of the (phallocentric) conditions of the complaint's production" (1988, 243).

26 Hewlett, Forster, Sherbin, Shiller, & Sumberg, 2009. See also Caldwell, 2009; Kochhar, 2011; Lowrey, 2011; Ludden, 2011; Rake & Rotheroe, 2009.

27 Tasker and Negra (2006) assert that postfeminist fictions never resolve the dilemmas they pose: "Indeed, they require feminism to finish them, to truly wrestle with the problems of gender inequality and misogyny that they acknowledge but cannot resolve" (pp. 172–173).

28 Author J. K. Rowling wrote seven novels in the Harry Potter series, and there have been eight films based on these books. Dates for the British and U.S. releases are: *Harry Potter and the Philosopher's Stone* (1997) U.K. and *Harry Potter and the Sorcerer's Stone* (1998) U.S.; *Harry Potter and the Chamber of Secrets* (1998) U.K. and (1999) U.S.; *Harry Potter and the Prisoner of Azkaban* (1999) U.K. and U.S.; *Harry Potter and the Goblet of Fire* (2000) U.K. and U.S.; *Harry Potter and the Order of the Phoenix* (2003) U.K. and U.S.; *Harry Potter and the Half-Blood Prince* (2005) U.K. and U.S.; and *Harry Potter and the Deathly Hallows* (2007) U.K. and U.S. Films include *Harry Potter and the Philosopher's Stone* (2001; Columbus, C. [director]); *Harry Potter and the Chamber of Secrets* (2002; Columbus, C. [director]); *Harry Potter and the Prisoner of Azkaban* (2004; Columbus, C. [director]); *Harry Potter and the Goblet of Fire* (2005; Cuaron, A. [director]); *Harry Potter and the Order of the Phoenix* (2007; Newell, M. [director]); *Harry Potter and the Half-Blood Prince* (2009; Yates, D. [director]); *Harry Potter and the Deathly Hallows–Part I* (2010; Yates, D. [director]); and *Harry Potter and the Deathly Hallows–Part II* (2011; Yates, D. [director]).

29   The harsh treatment of an orphan child by relatives is a staple plot device rooted in the traditions of European and American novels of the eighteenth and nineteenth centuries, which in turn were influenced by fairy tale conventions (Clarke, 2000). Arguably the most famous such story in the literary canon is Charlotte Brontë's *Jane Eyre*, which begins with poor orphaned Jane being cruelly mistreated as a young child by her aunt, Mrs. Sarah Reed, who also encourages her children to treat Jane cruelly. This novel has deeply influenced many American novels featuring women protagonists (Seelye, 2005).

30   Dahl, 1961; Selick [director], 1996.

31   MacDonald, 1995, p. 152.

32   In contrast to the aunts we discuss here, a powerful Japanese anime set at the end of World War II, *Grave of the Fireflies* (1988), mollifies the cultural abhorrence of the aunt's cruelty by providing a psychosocial justification. The film features a malevolent aunt who initially takes in her young niece and nephew but grows increasingly resentful and cruel as food becomes scarce. The children flee and eventually starve to death. The film implies that the aunt is hardened by the devastations and despair of war; thus her malevolence is part of the film's message about the suffering and tragedy visited on everyday lives, especially children, during wartime.

33   Bad mothering "confessions" have become popular, exemplified by the media attention given to *Bad Mother* by Ayelet Waldman, a "momoir," that is, a memoir about her mothering experiences. When Waldman admitted in print that she preferred sex with her husband to time with her children, there was a public uproar. Another momoir, *Battle Hymn of the Tiger Mother*, was written by Amy Chua, a Chinese American mother, advocating unrelentingly strict mothering and criticizing the leniency of mainstream American mothering. This book provoked another uproar against "bad" mothers.

34   We draw on Hardwig's (1989) elaboration of an intimate ethics.

35   See Meyers, 2000, p. 166.

36   Autonomy, in feminist philosopher Marilyn Friedman's (2000) words, "involves choosing and living according to standards or values that are, in some plausible sense, one's 'own'" (p. 37). Against the masculinist, rational individualism that equates autonomous action with the unreflective goals of self-sufficiency, self-reliance, and the protection of rational self-interests (Code, 1991), feminist reconceptualizations of autonomy begin with the insight that the capacities and competencies of autonomy are not developed in isolation and through self-transparency but in the context of relational commitments and identifications and exercised in social contexts. Relational autonomy entails exercising the skills of introspection, imagination, and volition in the context of multiple relationships and shared commitments among particularized others (Friedman, 2000, p. 44).

37   This kind of reflection is not autonomous or isolated but is enabled in the context of alternative relationships and commitments that provide the emotional and cultural resources necessary for enacting an alternative moral perspective. As Friedman puts it, "in most cases in which autonomous reflection does lead people to reject the commitments that bound them to particular others, they are at the same

time taking up new commitments that link them through newly shared conviction to different particular others" (2000, p. 44).

38   It would take considerable speculation to suggest how each of these nephews was able to distance himself from his aunt's vicious psychological and physical abuse in order to critically reflect on his investments in the aunting relationship.

39   This point has been made eloquently by feminist scholars such as Rich, 1977; Martin and Mohanty, 1986; Pratt, 1988; and Coontz, 1992.

40   Martin & Mohanty, 1986, p. 193.

Chapter 4

1   *Bewitched* was a popular television show (Saks, 1964–1972) and a spin-off movie (Ephron, 2005).

2   The *Sabrina, the Teenage Witch* television series ran for seven seasons (Scovell, 1996–2003). *Sabrina, the Teenage Witch* was originally an Archie comic, then a made-for-TV movie (Takács, 1996), and was followed by a spin-off animated series, *Sabrina: The Animated Series*, featuring a slightly younger (12-year old) Sabrina (Holland, 1999–2000).

3   Written by well-known novelist Alice Hoffman (1995).

4   Dunne, 1998.

5   Harkness, 2011.

6   The lighthearted story *Island of the Aunts* (Ibbotson, 2000) was designated one of the best children's books of the year by School Library Journal (http://www .schoollibraryjournal.com/article/CA83190.html). An adult book that features an aunt with magical abilities is *Like Water for Chocolate* (Esquivel, 1995); see also the film by the same name. Although never labeled a witch, master chef Tita wields kitchen magic as her form of agency and expression in this romantic story. Further illustrating her magical abundance, Tita's body responds to the cry of her newborn nephew, producing milk and enabling her to nurse the baby while her sister is too ill following the birth. A TV show that is similarly magical but not labeled witchcraft was the short-lived, critically acclaimed *Pushing Daisies* (Fuller, 2007–2009), which ran on ABC from October 2009 to June 2009, garnering seventeen Emmy nominations and seven wins. The quirky show combined conventions of old-fashioned murder mysteries and private detective stories with fairy tale tropes, including magic. The primary female character, Charlotte (called Chuck) was raised by her eccentric, agoraphobic aunts Lily and Vivian, retired traveling performers. Although Chuck's aunts are not witches, they are eccentric, dramatic, and mysterious, and they clearly suspect Chuck and Ned's (the male lead character's) magical abilities.

7   Primavera, 1999. Another variation on the association between aunts, magic, and witchcraft occurs in the young adult novel *The Witch of Blackbird Pond*, set in 1687. Orphan Kit Tyler is sent from a plantation in Barbados to live with her aunt and uncle in a small, Puritan New England town. When Kit aids an elderly Quaker woman accused of witchcraft by the townspeople, she finds herself accused of witchcraft, and her life is in jeopardy. Kit's story is often used in schools as an accessible way of teaching about the Salem witch trials in

Massachusetts Bay Colony. Here the plot device of having Kit live with her aunt frames Kit as an outsider, as lacking the close ties and protection of a nuclear family, and hence being more vulnerable to accusations of witchcraft. The aunt tries to help her niece to fit in; she represents the restrictive, religious culture of the time, and her efforts to instruct Kit in the community's shared knowledge offer children who read the story an appreciation for what people accepted at that period of time and how their shared views gave rise to the hysteria of witch trials.

8   Consider Harry Potter's wild popularity—he is a labeled a wizard, not a witch, and studies at a school of witchcraft and wizardry (explicitly including both masculine and feminine forms of magic). While the spells are not divided, and indeed Hermione is more proficient than either Harry or Ron (the other two main characters), nonetheless they must be given gendered labels in order to be sensible to audiences. Boys and men are simply not witches.

9   De Blécourt, 2000, p. 298.

10   Barstow (1988) argues that "over 80 percent of the victims were women" (p. 7); although men 'qualified,' women were overwhelmingly singled out" (p. 9). Also see Briggs (1996).

11   Pearson (2010, p. 142) identifies six different types of violence surrounding the witch: physical violence, psychological violence, patriarchal violence (structural, institutional), violence of silence/ing (exclusion, indifference), invisible violence (magic, ill-wishing, cursing), and mimetic violence (scapegoating). Further she advocates a move away from focusing on how many women were tortured to what it meant that they were tortured:

> It is not numbers that matter—as if violence were dependent upon quantity for its existence; as if one woman raped, tortured, hanged, or burned could not be counted as a victim of violence. Whether it be one, one hundred, or one hundred thousand, the violence is inherent in the procedures used, sanctioned and legitimized by state and church, and in the extra-legal forms of violence found in mob-rule; and it is inscribed on the body of the witch. (pp. 143–144)

12   Purkiss, 1996.

13   Such as "The Green Woman" in *Don't Bet on the Prince: Contemporary Feminist Fairy Tales in North America and England*, by Jack Zipes.

14   Pearson, 2010. One popular feminist interpretation claimed, "Between 1400 and 1700, approximately half a million people, most of them women, were burned as witches" (Nelson, 1979, p. 452). Pearson (2010) acknowledges that the estimates of millions of women are unlikely to be true and yet claims that the tens of thousands of women murdered "is still, surely, horrific enough!" (p. 143).

15   E.g., Gordon, 1995; Purkiss, 1996; Rountree, 1997.

16   Such "questions concern the gender relations between accusers and accused as well as the gendered domains of bewitching and unwitching. . . . A witchcraft accusation, I would suggest, articulated the crossing of male-designated boundaries rather than being restricted to a specific female space . . . in principle it sufficed to cross a boundary at a wrong moment" (de Blécourt, 2000, pp. 297, 303–304).

17   Hutton, 2011.

18   Fully exploring the complexities of the history of witch hunts is beyond the scope
     of this book, and we do not wish to do a disservice to the historians who continue
     to glean more historical data about witchcraft and render ever more complex
     interpretations of gender and witchcraft. Nor do we wish to perpetuate a false
     dichotomy between heroic feminist (female) historians who attempt to uncover
     the truth about witch hunts and patriarchal (male) historians who arrogantly dis-
     tort that truth because of their inherent sexism. However, the debates are inher-
     ently political; they reveal much about the forging of a feminist approach to
     history and some of the quandaries as feminists sought to bring a gendered lens
     to the center of historical analysis from its marginalized place on the outskirts of
     the field. While our allegiance is firmly with feminist approaches to knowledge
     construction, we also freely acknowledge that such approaches are no more neu-
     tral or value-free than the patriarchal approaches they challenged.
        Some feminist historians advocated fiercely for sexism as the primary fac-
     tor in the witch hunting craze. A female historian, Larner (1981), thoroughly
     investigated gender and sex as categories in witchcraft persecution, arguing
     variously that witch hunting was gender- and sex-based persecution and yet ulti-
     mately concluding that it was not fundamentally based in sex and gender, that it
     was "sex-related but not sex-specific." Feminist historian Barstow (1988) refers
     to Larner's conclusion as "the most disappointing of all," clearly advocating
     for her desire to frame witch-hunting as inherently about sex and gender, rather
     than about Christianity, the increasing rich/poor gap, changes in the church and
     secular legal systems, economic issues, or other factors to which Larner gave
     more credence. Foltz (1995) affirms Barstow's (1994) conclusions on the sex-
     based nature of women's persecution as witches: "In my view, Barstow's femi-
     nist analysis of the witch hunts is indispensable in understanding *what really
     occurred.*" She laments that "so few historians are willing to commit to a femi-
     nist position" (p. 515). Another scholar applauds the feminist ire evident in one
     author's historical account of witchcraft because she argues that this account is
     not meant as neutral historical description but "is meant as a political statement
     perhaps even as provocation. . . . [The author's] anger is refreshing in a time of
     so much positioning, posturing, fashioning, and negotiating that masquerades as
     feminist while scripting egos and upholding a comfortable status quo. Isn't anger
     a first step toward change?" (Becker-Cantarino, 1994, p. 170).
        While early feminist zeal may have led to some unreliable interpreta-
     tions, the androcentric (i.e., male-centered) historians also offered up mislead-
     ing interpretations by de-emphasizing, or even flat-out denying, the centrality
     of gender to the witch hunting craze. Separating gender from the phenomenon
     of witchcraft ignores the reality of the witchcraft construct in local contexts
     and ignores large bodies of evidence that reveal sex- and gender-based motiva-
     tions and justifications for witch hunting. Barstow (1988) points out that such
     androcentric historians are reluctant to acknowledge that "women were accused
     primarily by men, tried by male juries, searched by male prickers, sentenced by
     male judges, tortured by male jailers, burned to death by male executioners—
     while being prayed over by male pastors" (p. 17).

We concur with de Blécourt (2000) who reviews the ongoing debates between feminist and androcentric historians. He makes two fundamental arguments that are relevant to our discussion. The first is that historians have invested too much in debating the specific numbers of victims. Counting aggregate numbers of victims and glossing over details to discern common threads across the witch hunts is not sufficient to arrive at coherent historical interpretations: "Counting women is misleading precisely because they were accused of behaving as non-women, of failing to adhere to the social norm of femininity" (de Blécourt, 2000, p. 293). Second, he points out that feminist historians, eager to reclaim the history of witch persecution, have often uncritically, or at least freely, relied on evidence, arguments, and constructs from the research of the very androcentric historians whom they criticized for ignoring gender as a key category. That is, many historical interpretations of witchcraft incorporate into their reasoning building blocks of historical evidence that reflect sexist assumptions, even when the final interpretation of witch hunting is intended to be feminist or at least nonsexist. While all research draws upon previously published research for context and justification, such an approach has weakened the veracity of historical claims. De Blécourt (2000) proposes shifting the research question in studies of the European witch craze from whether sexism and oppression of women was the underlying cause for and purpose behind the persecution of women as witches to asking instead how women were constructed as failing to conform to gender roles and hence accused of witchcraft: "When and how was a woman turned into her contrast, into a non-woman?" (p. 291). This question leads nicely into our own study of the representation of aunts as witches. Since motherhood is central to cultural definitions of womanhood, it is not surprising, then, that an aunt—as nonmother and hence suspect, marginal, even perhaps nonwoman—is often the witch in popular narratives.

19   "It is a religious myth, and the religion it defines is radical feminism" (Purkiss, 1996, p. 8).

20   *TV Guide* (2002) named *Bewitched* as one of the "50 Greatest TV Shows of All Time."

21   http://www.imdb.com/name/nm0521079/bio.

22   See Belkin, 2003; also Gardner, 2006; Stone, 2007; and Bennets, 2007, for arguments complicating the assumption that well-educated, married, economically secure women were choosing family over career.

23   According to Spangler, *Bewitched* featured two primary relationship tensions: husband/wife and mother/daughter. While both tensions portrayed cultural anxieties over women's changing place, the marriage relationship in particular caricatured women's marital subordination. She observes, "The couple struggles . . . to accept each other for who and what they are—she a powerful, talented, modern woman and he an egocentric, insecure, and traditional man" (2003, p. 81).

24   According to http://www.harpiesbizarre.com/nickname.htm, Endora called Darrin a startling array of nicknames, including Beady eyes, Charm Boy, Dagwood, Dalton, Dar-Dar, Darius, Darwick, Darwin, Darwood, David, Dawson, Dear Boy, Delbert, Dennis, Denton, Derek, Derwin, Dexter, Digby, Dino, Dobbin,

Dogwood, Donald, Dorian, Dumbo, Dum Dum, Dumpkin, Duncan, Durweed, Durwood, Featherhead, Glum-Dum, Tinker Bell, What's His Name, and Low-grade mortal.

25 U.S. Department of Housing and Urban Development, 2007.

26 This stereotype was explicitly challenged by the popular TV sitcom *The Golden Girls* (1985–1992).

27 See Featherstone & Hepworth, 2005; Hepworth, 2004.

28 Indeed, Marion Lorne, who portrayed Aunt Clara, was born in 1883, a time distant enough to render her a character who remembers the days of yore when women held very different social status.

29 As Douglas opines, "While they are the 'girl power' generation, the bill of goods they are repeatedly sold is that true power comes from shopping, having the right logos, and being 'hot'" (hence their hyper-feminine appearances; 2010, pp. 6–7).

30 Both girls want to win the all-city track meet—young women are strong and athletic in this postfeminist vision—and hence prove themselves worthy of his attention and a date to the upcoming school dance. When Sabrina does succeed in defeating Libby by unwisely using her magic and (temporarily) securing the football player's attention, he turns out to be a jerk. Sabrina manages to escape his forceful attentions and casts a spell on his car, while Harvey rides to the rescue, scooping Sabrina up on his bicycle. The lesson is that young women should be careful to pick the right man for the right reasons.

31 Cultural critic Susan Douglas argues that images like Sabrina mislead young women to mistake purchasing power for political and social power.

> Yet the images we see on television, in the movies, and in advertising also insist that purchasing power and sexual power are much more gratifying than political or economic power. Buying stuff—the right stuff, a lot of stuff—emerged as the dominant way to empower ourselves . . . the wheedling, seductive message to young women is that being decorative is the highest form of power—when of course, if it were, Dick Cheney would have gone to work everyday in a sequined tutu. (2010, p. 5)

32 Coontz, 2000b; Douglas, 2010.

33 However, the $150/month teens spend is down from over $200/month just two years ago, reflecting the worsening global recession (Carter, 2011, p. 1). Nonetheless, teens remain a lucrative market: collectively, teens' "spending power exceeds $200 billion, with an average of $30 spent per mall or online shopping visit," making these highly educated, savvy yet skeptical consumers a highly sought-after target audience for marketers (Carter, 2011, p. 1).

34 E.g., McRobbie, 2009.

35 McRobbie (2009) argues that young women have become the "privileged subjects" of sociocultural discourses that cast them as "subjects of capacity," those with the cultural capacity to do well and hence emblematic of change; thus, considerable energy and capital is expended to monitor educational disparities and opportunities for girls, advance nontraditional career opportunities, and train girls in self-management practices, especially regarding reproduction and well-being (see pp. 59–60). This scrutiny on girls to realize their capacities effects self-disciplined participation in the new, meritocratic labor market and public

sphere. At the same time, there is an intense restabilization of traditional gender relations so that, despite their capacities in the labor market, young women are still focused on finding a man. This means compromising those very career ambitions and capacities that make them "subjects of capacity" and emblematic of change.

36 A 2011 Gallup poll reported that when asked what sex they would prefer if they could have only one child, 40 percent of Americans chose boys while only 28 percent chose girls; this same preference for boys was found when the question was asked in 1941 (CNN editors, 2011). However, examination of the data shows that while men display a marked preference for boys, women were almost equally divided in their preference. Interestingly, this is not an artifact of an older generation. The article reported that "it is significant that 18- to 29-year-old Americans are the most likely of any age group to express a preference for a boy because most babies are born to younger adults" (CNN editors, 2011, ¶5).

37 Douglas, 2010; Kelley & Kelley, 2011.

38 A slightly more grown up version of *Sabrina,* also aimed squarely at the teen female viewing audience, was the long-running series *Charmed* (Burge), which aired on the WB network from 1998 to 2006. The show featured the three hereditary good witch Halliwell sisters—Phoebe, Piper, and Prue (whose character died and was later replaced by another sister, Paige), who lived together (without parents or aunts) in San Francisco. Piper had two sons, Wyatt in Season 5 and Chris in Season 6, making Phoebe and Paige their aunts (http://www.imdb.com).

39 One reason to focus on the film is because the discrepancy between reviewers' and audience members' responses indicates the popular appeal of the film. At the time of its release, film critics largely panned the movie, while popular audiences continue to respond positively according to reviews compiled on the website Rotten Tomatoes. Out of fifty-five film critics' reviews, forty-four of them criticized the film for its trite, predictable plot, uneven cinematic effects, and narrative incoherence. Of 262 audience reviews, 73 percent were favorable; most responded to the genre, staging, and special effects. See http://www .rottentomatoes.com/m/practical_magic/

40 "Lime in the Coconut," Harry Nilsson, from the album *Practical Magic Soundtrack* (1998). Lyrics can be found at http://www.lyricskeeper.com/harry_nilsson -lyrics/226113-lime_in_the_coconut-lyrics.htm.

41 Written by Deborah Harkness, professor of history at the University of Southern California.

42 Diana's back story includes a need to shut down her provocative sexuality that led in the past to young men obsessing about her. Diana has earned a PhD and accomplished what still too rarely happens—she wrote a book of great acclaim and earned tenure in the exclusive old-boys club of the Yale history department. She exercises compulsively for long hours in order to keep her magic from overcoming her will. Diana represses her sexuality, her heritage, and her feminine power. Like the neotraditional maternal aunts we discussed in chapter 3, she is alienated from her true self. Of course, it takes a powerful man to recognize and reignite Diana's sensual power, and luckily Matthew is just the vampire to accomplish this end. In true hero fashion, Diana eventually finds him irresistible,

demonstrating that women really do need and want a man to guide the way. Taking the daddy complex to an extreme, Matthew is 1,500 years old, making Diana seem almost infantile in comparison and necessitating her need for his protection and wisdom.

43   The narrative will take two more books to accomplish in the projected trilogy. *Shadow of Night*, the second book in the All Souls Trilogy, was released in July 2012 in the U.S. and the U.K. (Harkness, 2012). A Warner Brothers Pictures movie is under development (see deborahharkness.com).

44   Interestingly, the pursuit does not include consummating their relationship with sexual intercourse, although there are long descriptions of sexual intimacy without coitus. Critics of another very popular vampire romance, the Twilight series, have referred to this plot device as "abstinence porn." The message of these vampire romances in which the woman desires sex but the vampire resists in order to save her is familiar: "When it comes to a woman's virtue, sex, identity, or her existence itself, it's all in the man's hands. To be the object of desire, [*sic*] in abstinence porn is not really so far from being the object of desire in actual porn" (Seifert, 2008, ¶18).

45   Noted postmodern feminist theorist Donna Haraway (2007) explores interspecies interaction and connections in her book *When Species Meet*. She builds on the concept of "symbiogenesis," from biology, which explains how life forms continually intermingle, leading to "ever more intricate and multidirectional acts of association of and with other life forms" (p. 31).

46   The allusion is to the classic movie directed by Stanley Kramer, *Guess Who's Coming to Dinner?* (1967).

47   A similar initial resistance of Matthew's mother to Diana leads to a subsequent bond between them, as the mother fights to protect and defend her son's beloved and comes to care for her in the process.

48   Aimee Carrillo Rowe (2008) argues for alliances among feminists across racial (and other) differences grounded in emotional connections among women that may form the basis for powerful political connections. She proposes not a singular vision—or a strict feminist party line—but instead a "politics of relation," the establishment of multiracial coalitions or power lines. This approach harkens back to Bernice Johnson Reagon's (1983) foundational discussion of the benefits and challenges to building coalitions across black and white feminist groups to allow for the preservation of different agendas and priorities while fostering collaborations based in shared desires and goals (see also Anzaldua, 1990; Lorde, 1984; McIntosh, 1988; Mohanty, Russo & Torres, 1991; Moraga & Anzaldua, 1981; Thompson, 2002). As communication scholars, we embrace an antiracist feminist perspective that privileges intersectional, embodied differences around race, as well as those related to (dis)ability, sexuality, class, religion, and age. See theorist Brenda J. Allen's (2011) convincing elaboration.

49   Guran, 2012.

50   Faludi, 1991.

51   Ehrenreich & English, 1973.

52   As one historian put it, "To interpret witches purely as victims, as many historians (including feminist historians . . .) have done, is to ignore or deny the

challenge these women represented to dominant institutions within their societies" (Rountree, 1997, pp. 221–222).

53   Starhawk, 1990, p. 76.
54   In invoking the legacy of witchcraft, contemporary feminists can "symbolically
      lay claim to the independent female power which the symbols represent: they
      image themselves as strong and autonomous, as having the right to choose and
      direct their own lives" (Rountree, 1997, p. 213).

Chapter 5

1   Russo, 1986.
2   Classic feminist texts in this regard span the various traditions of feminist think-
     ing. See, for example, Cixous, 1976; Daly, 1978; de Lauretis, 1990; Russo, 1986.
3   The eccentric aunt emerged as a standard figure in domestic narratives during
     the nineteenth century and became a comedic stock character in plays and novels
     during the first half of the twentieth century. Given the growing visibility of
     women's demands for rights and recognition throughout that century, eccentric
     aunts in the literature of the time may have both embodied and served as the
     targets of social anxieties and animosities over women's status.
4   See Kathleen Rowe's study of the reproductive and transgressive dimensions of
     unruly women in comedy genres (1995).
5   Kaufman, 1991.
6   Patrick Dennis, *Auntie Mame: An Irreverent Escapade* (1955). The Rosalind
     Russell movie *Auntie Mame* was directed by Morton DaCosta in 1958, while the
     Lucille Ball remake, *Mame*, was directed by Gene Saks in 1974. In a behind-the-
     scenes book about the various versions of Mame, Richard Jordan documents the
     continuing appeal of the Mame character: *But Darling, I'm Your Auntie Mame!
     The Amazing History of the World's Favorite Madcap Aunt* (1998).
7   Barreca, 1992. Mizejewski makes the important point that the cinematic eccen-
     tric woman is a racialized figure framed by white ideals of femininity and het-
     eronormativity, subjecting a black female eccentric star such as Queen Latifah to
     "racialized and contradictory cultural desires, including fascination with a black,
     full-figure body" (2007, ¶57).
8   The eccentric feminist is celebrated as a cultural trope, the "wacky chick hag,"
     in Doonan's *Wacky Chicks* (2003). Doonan urges women to transform "from
     Nora Normal to B.R.U.N.C.H.-y broad" ("belligerent, resilient, uninhibited,
     naughty, creative and hilarious"; p. xvi). His interviews with eccentric women
     who self-identify as feminist and empowered includes aging hippies, creative
     entrepreneurs, Riot Grrl alumni, and Radical Cheerleaders. We make note of
     wacky chicks here as postfeminist eccentrics.
9   Eccentricity as a strategy of gender struggle has been advanced as excessive, per-
     verse, subversive, or inverse sexual identities (the "in/appropriated other") and
     practices transgressive of normative forces (de Lauretis, 1984, 1990). Normative
     gender identities can be thought of as anchored in a core set of psychic, material,
     and sociocultural attributes and resources, historically established and secured
     in stabilized, often reified, binaries like male/female, dominant/subordinate, and

heterosexual/homosexual. While gender, race, class, ethnicity, age, ableness, and any number of other differences affect the way any particular identity might enact these core attributes or mobilize material resources in a given context, there is a normative pull to stay in line with the expectations, meanings, and possibilities grounded in dominant binary relations. This discursive conception of subjectivity and agency emphasizes that the specificity of lived differences is thus discursively linked to a nucleus of common meaning through chains of equivalences (e.g., an aunt is like a mother links the identity of aunt to the core qualities of a mother). However, there is an inherent instability in these chains of equivalence—the analogy is never fixed but is based on differences (Laclau & Mouffe, 1988). It is such differences that eccentricity exacerbates; the eccentric subject is not consistently and coherently anchored to a normative core but is positioned equivocally in relation to it.

10   West & Zimmerman, 1987; Butler, 1990.

11   This double masquerade casts the performance of womanliness both as submission to a dominant (masculinist) cultural-sexual economy in which woman's value derives from her desirability as a sexual object/spectacle and as a renunciation of female desire in order to "remain on the market" within the "dominant economy of desire" (Irigaray, 1985, p. 133). As Riviere (1929) observed, women must mask their own agency in a display of womanliness to appease male desire and fear of the feminine; for Irigaray, feminine masquerade is a renunciation of female desire in order to be desired. The double masquerade is thus both an appeasement and an auto-renunciation.

12   Russo, 1986.

13   Dollimore asserts that "Camp thereby negotiates some of the lived contradictions of subordination, simultaneously refashioning as a weapon of attack an oppressive identity inherited as subordination, and hollowing out dominant formations responsible for that identity in the first instance. So it is misleading to say that camp is the gay sensibility; camp is an invasion and subversion of other sensibilities, and works via parody, pastiche, and exaggeration" (2002, pp. 224–225).

14   Helene A. Shugart and Catherine Egeley Waggoner, 2008, p. 1.

15   Dollimore contends that the camp aesthetic "comes to life" at that point "when and where the real collapses into artifice, nature into culture; camp restores vitality to artifice. . . . The reality is the pleasure of unreality" and the primacy of fantasy (2002, p. 225).

16   See Shugart and Waggoner, 2008, p. 42. In their extended analysis of transgressive feminine camp, Shugart and Waggoner argue that even "lite" or "pop" camp has resistive potential: "the mere fact that camp has been commodified as a sensibility does not necessarily entail a qualification of its critical rhetorical potential; indeed, the very features that make up camp may make it more resilient than other critical devices and sensibilities that have gone before it—hence, the possibility that one might indeed read a 'pop camp' text as subversive" (p. 42).

17   We follow the groundwork by Shugart and Waggoner (2008) in identifying these features of transgressive camp. Their analysis of four contemporary eccentric feminine characters in popular culture—Xena the Warrior Princess, Karen

Walker in the television show *Will & Grace* (1996–2004), and the popular sing-
ers Macy Gray and Gwen Stefani—establishes the work of this resistive logic.

18   The ubiquity of the "crazy aunt" image was on display in a jibe against musician
     and then-*American Idol* judge Steven Tyler appearing in the popular magazine
     Entertainment Weekly. The quip over a picture of Tyler read, "It's that time of
     year when America lets its crazy aunt out of the attic" (2012, p. 80).

19   Shugart and Waggoner contend that the relation of the camp performance to foils
     and anchors is of particular import in realizing the critical potential of camp:
     "That critical potential depends on a delicate balance of both congruence and
     contrast, as conventional order is being disrupted in the promotion of alternative
     perspectives" (2008, p. 156).

20   The uncertainty over whether Henry is Augusta's son is a key theme in the
     novel, though the film dispenses with this uncertainty and makes more use of
     the mother-son bond.

21   These aunt/mother, mother/son analogies resonate with feminist critiques of
     structuralist kinship and heterosexual familial structures and re-visions of radi-
     cally alternative configurations. See, for example, Butler's analysis of the chal-
     lenge to kinship posed by a rereading of the classic Greek figure Antigone. She
     observes, "Various utopian projects to revamp or eliminate family structure have
     become important components of the feminist movement and, to some extent,
     have survived in contemporary queer movements as well" (2000, pp. 72–73).

22   In a trenchant analysis of gay politics, Maddison observes that women and gays
     are subject to oppression as a condition of both patriarchal power and the repro-
     duction of manliness/maleness: "Maleness is established through the suppres-
     sion of any bonding (identification) with women—this is what misogyny and
     homophobia police. . . . The principal identification required for the maintenance
     of patriarchy is with other men, with the potency of phallic authority through the
     elaboration of homosocial bonds" (2000, p. 89).

23   Robertson, 2002, pp. 271–272.

24   Robertson rightly points out that such an alliance is not a forgone event: "gay
     camp might be misogynist and feminist camp may or may not be antihomo-
     phobic. Although both feminists and gay men engage in discourses that are at
     variance with the dominant culture, those discourses are not always identical"
     ([1996] 2002, p. 271). Also, despite his careful consideration of heterosocial
     sistership as a strategy of dissent, Maddison (2000) ultimately finds this strategy
     insufficient for gay struggle because such alliances are fragile: he argues that
     women are in danger of losing the cultural capital they wield on the basis of their
     value within patriarchy while gay men risk being pathologized as feminine and
     cast as stereotypically effeminate (leaving them vulnerable to social stigma and
     often to violent repression).

25   For classic statements of this theory-driven celebration casting women's mad-
     ness as gender rebellion see: in literary theory, Gilbert & Gubar, *Madwomen
     in the Attic* (1979); in psychology, Chesler, *Women and Madness* (1972); in *l
     écriture féminine*, *Laugh of the Medusa* (Cixous, 1976); in social history, Ussher,
     Women's Madness: Misogyny or Mental Illness? (1992).

26   These images were advanced in the classic literary theory study of nineteenth-century women writers by Sandra Gilbert and Susan Gubar, *Madwoman in the Attic* (1979), an allusion to Charlotte Brontë's famous characters Jane Eyre (the exemplary woman) and mad Bertha Mason (confined to the attic). According to one contemporary feminist scholar, "Gilbert and Gubar were the first to unite the angel and the madwoman in a single being, applaud her expressive transgressions, and identify her with the woman writer" (Gezari, 2006, p. 264).

27   Russo, 1986, p. 222.

28   Chesler, 1972, p. 56.

29   Lemony Snicket Wiki: http://snicket.wikia.com/wiki/The_Wide_Window.

30   McRobbie points out that postfeminist culture normalizes women's illnesses like anorexia and anxieties such as self-beratement over body image, compulsiveness, and other modes of harming the self (2009, pp. 59–72). For an alternative analysis of the normalization of hysteria in an advertising-saturated culture, see Schutzman, 1999.

31   McRobbie attributes this observation to Judith Butler in *The Psychic Life of Power* (1997).

32   Robinson received the Hemingway/PEN Award in 1982 for best first novel for *Housekeeping*. According to literary critic Elaine Showalter, "In 2006 the *New York Times* asked 200 writers and 'literary sages' to nominate the best single work of American fiction in the past 25 years. . . . While Toni Morrison's *Beloved* topped the list, Marilynne Robinson was the only other woman novelist to receive more than two votes" (2009).

33   Robinson, 2009.

34   See Aldrich, 1989; Kirkby, 1986; Ravits, 1989; Wilson, 2008; for additional commentary, see Burke, 1991; Cowles, 2008; Foster, 1988; McDermott, 2004; Ryan, 1991.

35   As one critic observed, "The gradual, graceful process of de-evolution, of de-civilizing, that the novel enacts is also a rejection of the patriarchal values that have dominated American culture and a return to values and modes of being that have been associated in myth and imagery with the province of the female" (Kirkby, 1986, p. 92).

36   Geyh, 1993, p. 107.

37   As Ruthie observes of the neighbors, "They were obliged to come by their notions of piety and good breeding, and by a desire, a determination, to keep me, so to speak, safely within doors. . . . They had reason to feel that my social graces were eroding away, and that soon I would feel ill at ease in a cleanly house with glass in its windows" (Robinson, 1980, p. 183).

38   Gilbert and Gubar note ruefully in the introduction to a reissue of their classic study, "We were being accused of sins that in those early days we knew not of—essentialism, racism, heterosexism, phallologocentrism—accused, sometimes shrilly, by sister feminists and, sometimes, patronizingly, by male quasi-feminists" (2000, p. xxv).

39   In arguing that representations structure reality, feminist disability scholar Rosalind Garland-Thomson observes, "The way we imagine disability through images and narratives determines the shape of the material world, the distribution

of resources, our relationships with one another, and our sense of ourselves" (2005a, p. 523).

40 Donaldson, 2002, p. 113.

41 We join Donaldson in urging "an agenda that fights discrimination, advocates for the rights of women, seeks to dismantle ideologies of oppression, critiques medical discourses of mental illness, and demands equal access to social services and medical treatment" (2002, p. 112).

42 "How would the public landscape change if the widest possible diversity of human forms, functions, and behaviors were fully accommodated?" asks Rosalind Garland-Thomson. Her agenda is more expansive than what we propose here, but her focus on an inclusive politics that expands the imaginative resources for change is important. She avows, "I argue for applying the vibrant logic of biodiversity to [differently abled] humans. Such a logic reimagines a public sphere that values and makes a tenable space for the kinds of bodies variously considered old, retarded, crippled, blind, deaf, abnormal, ugly, deformed, or excessive" (2005, p. 120).

43 We note that in the context of contemporary anxieties over threats to national security and the shoring up of U.S. nationalism, these aunt narratives are newly relevant as depictions of the madness within, identified, for example, as "home-grown terrorists," extremist nationalists, and overly zealous civil and state authorities.

44 See Wilson, 2008; Geyh, 1993.

45 See chapter 3 for an analysis of the malevolent aunt's subversion of home as a place of safety and comfort.

46 The allusion is to Jonathan Swift's satirical 1729 essay known as "A Modest Proposal," in which he advances a utilitarian argument for feeding the populace by harvesting human babies.

47 In a poignant essay that includes details of her own childhood with a mother unable to keep house well enough to keep the family together, feminist philosopher Iris Marion Young agrees with feminist critiques of the desire for home but argues that there are human values in the conception of home that cannot be dismissed. She argues for "preservation" as a critical housekeeping task. "Preservation makes and remakes home as a support for personal identity without accumulation, certainty, or fixity" (2002, pp. 315–316).

48 Young observes, "If house and home mean the confinement of women for the sake of nourishing male projects, then feminists have good reason to reject home as a value. . . . [But] we look forward to going home and invite others to make themselves at home. House and home are deeply ambivalent values" (Young, 2002, p. 314).

49 See Wyatt's (1990) psychoanalytic analysis of the dissolution of Ruth's subjectivity in *Housekeeping*; also Kaivola's (1993) analysis of Ruth's failure to develop an autonomous sense of self and her merger with Sylvie.

50 We follow feminist cultural scholar Angela McRobbie's (2009, pp. 59–72) arguments in *The Aftermath of Feminism*.

51 The lesbian continuum was advanced by feminist scholar and poet Adrienne Rich in a classic treatise arguing for the political force of woman-identified

experiences. She explained, "I mean the term *lesbian continuum* to include a range—through each woman's life and throughout history—of woman-identified experience. . . . (p. 648). For Rich, lesbianism was not only a sexual orientation and identity but a form of political engagement, particularly against compulsory heterosexuality. She urged expanding the lesbian continuum "to embrace many more forms of primary intensity between and among women, including the sharing of a rich inner life, the bonding against male tyranny, the giving and receiving of practical and political support. . . ." (pp. 648–649; emphasis in original).

Chapter 6

1   Traeder & Bennett, 1998.
2   Milardo, 2010.
3   As Barber observes, "In the new brand marketing, the product is always beside the point when compared with emotions, feelings, and connections" (2007, p. 181).
4   The idea of a brand as a "lovemark" is from Jenkins, 2006.
5   As Banet-Weiser and Gray warn, "To take brand culture seriously as a culture means to examine how the circulation, both nationally and transnationally, of certain brands factors into contemporary understandings of and conflicts about cultural, political, and national identity. In the unpredictable context of global branding, marketers are increasingly turning to campaigns that encourage consumers to have deeply emotional and affective relationships to brands" (2009, p. 17).
6   See Hall's work on critical examinations of the work of cultural representations (1996, 1997, 1999).
7   Our critique draws on the feminist case against the commodification of the family (see, in particular, Hochschild, 2003a; Folbre, 2001).
8   See Radin, 1987; Silbaugh, 1997.
9   Our analysis here follows sociologist Arlie Hochschild's arguments in *The Commercialization of Intimate Life* (2003a).
10 E.g., Aunt Lute is number 53 so we will use a [53] designation. While this search was subject to the protocols for the most popular search engines, we are confident that our sample offers a reasonable basis for interrogating the aunt as a marketing image.
11 The DataMonitor Group: http://www.datamonitor.com/.
12 According to one of the founders, Aunt Lute was her cofounder's aunt who lived to over one hundred (personal communication, November 11, 2011). This aunt is not identified on the website or the publisher information.
13 Hochschild, 2003a.
14 We draw on Hochschild, 2003a.
15 This is Hochschild's (2003a) phrase.
16 We draw on feminist economist Nancy Folbre's (2001) arguments.
17 Folbre, 2001, p. 27.
18 We paraphrase Folbre's (2001) argument here.
19 This is sociologist Barbara Ehrenreich's (2000) phrase.
20 Hochschild (2003a) advances this claim in her studies of contemporary middle-class families.

21 Ehrenreich (2000) warns about these increasing stratifications.

22 See Duffy (2007) for an historical analysis of the gender-race-ethnic intersectionalities marking the segregation of the reproductive labor market during the twentieth century. See the special issue of *Politics and Society* (Jacoby, 2006) on "caring labor" issues in both domestic and global markets. The blog "caring labor.wordpress.com" documents feminist and labor issues in the domestic care labor movement.

23 This phrase is Ehrenreich's (2000).

Conclusion

1 Tasker & Negra, 2007, p. 22.

2 Tasker & Negra, 2007, p. 9.

3 Bruess & Pearson (1997) discuss the importance of interpersonal rituals in marriage and adult friendships. They found friends and spouses developed a number of relational rituals over time that made them feel connected to their partner and affirmed the value of their relationships. Our point on transition riturals contributes to feminist perspectives on the politics of generational change. See Stevenson, Everingham, & Robinson (2011).

4 Berlant, 1988; 2008.

5 A sociobiological argument for the health benefits of women's friendships emphasizes women's so-called tend-and-befriend response to stress over the fight-and-flight response:

> We suggest that females respond to stress by nurturing offspring, exhibiting behaviors that protect them from harm and reduce neuroendocrine responses that may compromise offspring health (the tending pattern), and by befriending, namely, affiliating with social groups to reduce risk. (Taylor, Klein, Lewis, Gruenewald, Gurung & Updegraff, 2000, p. 411)

6 O'Dell (2006) articulates the continued need for women's studies programs. See also the National Women's Studies Association website's information on the field of women's studies: http://www.nwsa.org.

7 For more on intersectionality, see Collins, 2000; Crenshaw, 1991; Mann & Kelley, 1997.

8 Recent content analyses indicate that representations of non-white race/ethnic groups have increased on television over the past twenty years (Harwood & Anderson, 2002; Mastro & Greenberg, 2000), yet these identities continue to be caricatured and do not offset the normalization of whiteness. Race is often reduced to black and white as we found in our own search for aunt characters on mainstream television (see chap. 1). In representations of other racial/ethnic groups, aunt characters often serve as little more than ethnic caricatures. For example, in the Greek-American comedy *My Big Fat Greek Wedding* (2002), the supporting character Aunt Voula is not developed as a character in her own right; rather, she sets the well-meaning but intrusive aunt stereotype within a caricatured portrait of Greek American culture and extended family life. This stereotype is well depicted in a memorable scene when her thirty-year-old spinster niece, Toula, finally brings a non-Greek fiancé home to her extended family.

Aunt Voula exclaims, "What do you mean he don't eat no meat?" A moment later she reassures her niece, "Is OK. I make lamb."

9   McRobbie, 2004, p. 262; for an exemplary analysis of the feminist contributions and historical significance of American nuns that also makes a case for re-visioning cultural relations and gendered identities, see Sullivan, 2005.

10   We argued this as well in our recent study of interpersonal and family communication among aunts, nieces, and nephews within extended families, chosen families, and community networks (Ellingson & Sotirin, 2010).

11   Baxter et al., 2009; Holtzman, 2008; Jordan-Zachery, 2009; Suter, Reyes & Ballard, 2010.

12   Grossberg, 2005, p. 102.

13   Baxter et al., 2009, pp. 186–187. See also Oswald, Blume, & Marks, 2005.

14   See Coontz, 1999, 1992.

15   Coontz, 2000b, p. xxviii. Television historian Lynn Spigel asked her students what family life in the fifties was like and how they knew about it. All of them drew on their exposure to fifties sitcoms. See the note above on Spigel's class exercise (p. 169, n. 43).

16   Franklin & MacKinnon, 2002a.

17   According to the reports on genome sequencing,

> Many diverse sources of data have shown that any two individuals are more than 99.9 percent identical in sequence, which means that all the glorious differences among individuals in our species that can be attributed to genes falls in a mere 0.1 percent of the sequence. There are two fallacies to be avoided: determinism, the idea that all characteristics of the person are 'hard-wired' by the genome; and reductionism, the view that with complete knowledge of the human genome sequence, it is only a matter of time before our understanding of gene functions and interactions will provide a complete causal description of human variability. The real challenge of human biology, beyond the task of finding out how genes orchestrate the construction and maintenance of the miraculous mechanism of our bodies, will lie ahead as we seek to explain how our minds have come to organize thoughts sufficiently well to investigate our own existence." (Venter et al., 2001, p. 1348)

18   Bowen, 2006; Hertz, 2009.

19   In their collection *Relative Values: Reconfiguring Kinship Studies*, Franklin and MacKinnon champion a broad purview for kinship studies: "Cultural understandings of kinship are shaped by—and, in turn, contribute to the shaping of—the political dynamics of national and transnational identities, the economic movements of labor and capital, the cosmologies of religion, the cultural hierarchies of race, gender, and species taxonomies, and the epistemologies of science, medicine, and technology" (2002a, p. 9).

Such expansions of the commonsensical understanding of kinship in American society often invoke anxiety. For example, new reproductive technologies challenge taken-for-granted biological and cultural assumptions about genetic bonds as the basis for kinship, unsettling understandings of identity and family (Rose & Novas, 2004). Both scientific discoveries and lived experiences continue to challenge academic and cultural conceptions of kinship. As Hird observes, the self-evidence of biological facts is constantly undermined "and cultural notions of kinship are constantly challenged to keep up with both scientific 'discoveries' and lived experience" (2004, p. 227).

20　Jacobson, 2009, 2008; Smith, Surrey, & Watkins, 2006.

21　Spinsters came to outnumber married women and eligible men in Victorian England. The advantages and disadvantages for the labor market, the marriage market, immigration, literacy, morality, and women's rights inspired considerable discussion over "the marriage question" at the time (see Heilman, 1998). Whether a woman was in the working class or in the "servant-keeping" classes made a difference; for the former there was exploitative low-wage, often physically grueling work to be had; for the latter, there were often few wage-earning options. In addition, white, middle- and upper-class unmarried women were often economically disadvantaged by a patrilineal inheritance system and few legal property rights. Whether spinsters or widows, these unmarried women often moved in with kin as nannies or domestics. Despite legal measures like the New York Women's Property Act of 1848, such kinservice remained prevalent into the twentieth century.

22　See, e.g., Eng, 1998. Just as telling is linguist Paul Baker's (2008) analysis of the terms accompanying "bachelor" and "spinster" in the British National Corpus. His analysis reveals the persistence of dominant stereotypes but also patterns that suggest a "critical discourse of spinsterhood," that is, the rejection of denigrating stereotypes and positive associations in usage.

23　Given that the U.S. Census Bureau reports that women now outnumber men in the U.S., this unmarried aunt figure may become increasingly visible.

24　*Aunt Rose* (2005). Tucker, J. (director), Nelson, J. (writer). Aunt Rose is literally the "madwoman in the attic" in this B-grade horror film.

25　See the classic feminist case for the spinster, *The Spinster and Her Enemies* (Jeffreys, 1985), radical feminist Mary Daly's definition of a spinster as a woman weaving webs with words (Daly & Caputi, 1987), or well-known images of the spinster in feminist poetry like Sylvia Plath's "Spinster" (1981) and Judy Grahn's *The Common Woman Poems* (1982).

26　In her definitive classic *The Woman Alone* (1973), feminist Patricia O'Brien made it clear that denigrating women as spinsters and witches was a strategy of containment and intimidation that expressed deep-rooted anxieties over the structure of society:

> Underlying all the criticisms and attacks on women along through history has been the uneasy fear that women who seek alternatives to marriage and motherhood might very well find them satisfying. The images of themselves that women have been presented with (and helped perpetuate) are intended to discourage or intimidate. And even though as a nation we are committing ourselves to cutting back the birth rate, women who do not marry pose questions about the structure of society. Those questions are difficult to articulate, because they are so deeply rooted in our anxieties about

what we are. If women are allowed to flee on their broomsticks, couldn't they possibly destroy all that has been so carefully put together by men? (p. 74; cited in Mustard, 2000, ¶12)

27 The U.S. Census reported that only 52 percent of all adults were married in 2009 (UPI, 2010).

28 See Notkin, 2011c; Shaw, 2010; also http://www.childfree.net/.

29 We found this in our own study of aunting, including among gay and lesbian couples, as well as heterosexual women who were single or married without children (Ellingson & Sotirin, 2010).

30 "Mother's Day is the Super Bowl of flowers. . . . More flowers are sold for Mother's Day than any time of year" (Mitch Spolan, as quoted in Duryee, 2011).

31 Notkin, M., 2011b, savvyauntie.com/l/panks.

References

Alberts, J. K., Tracy, S. J., & Trethewey, A. (2011). An integrative theory of the division of domestic labor: Threshold level, social organizing and sensemaking. *Journal of Family Communication, 11*, 21–38.

Aldrich, M. (1989). The poetics of transience: Marilynne Robinson's *Housekeeping. Essays in Literature, 16*, 127–140.

Allen, B. J. (2011). *Difference matters: Communicating social identity* (2nd ed.). Long Grove, IL.: Waveland Press.

Als, H. (2010, April 26). Mama's gun: The world of Tyler Perry. *The New Yorker, 86*, 68. Retrieved from LexisNexis.

Amritraj, A. (Producer), Hoberman, D. (Producer), & Shankman, A. (Director). (2003). *Bringing down the house* [Motion picture]. Burbank, CA: Touchstone.

Anderson, B. R. (1991). *Imagined communities: Reflections on the origin and spread of nationalism.* London: Verso.

Anderson, L. M. (2008). *Black feminism in contemporary drama.* Urbana: University of Illinois Press.

Anzaldua, G. (Ed.) (1990). *Making face, making soul: Haciendo caras.* San Francisco: Aunt Lute.

Auter, P. J., & Davis, D. M. (1991). When characters speak directly to viewers: Breaking the fourth wall in television. *Journalism Quarterly, 68*, 165–171.

Banet-Weiser, S., & Gray, H. (2009). Our media studies. *Television and New Media, 10*, 13–19.

Banyard, K. (2010). *The equality illusion: The truth about women & men today*. London: Faber & Faber.

Barber, B. R. (2007). *Consumed: How markets corrupt children, infantilize adults, and swallow citizens whole*. New York: W.W. Norton.

Barreca, R. (1992). *They used to call me Snow White, but I drifted: Women's strategic use of humor*. New York: Penguin.

Barstow, A. L. (1988). On studying witchcrafts as women's history: A historiography of the European witch persecutions. *Journal of Feminist Studies in Religion, 4*, 7–19.

Barstow, A. L. (1994). *Witchcraze: A new history of the European witch hunts*. San Francisco, CA: Pandora.

Baxter, J., Hewitt, B., & Western, M. (2005). Post-familial families and the domestic division of labor. *Journal of Comparative Family Studies, 36*, 583–600.

Baxter, L. A., Henauw, C., Huisman, D., Livesay, C. B., Norwood, K., Su, H., Wolf, B., Young, B. (2009). Lay conceptions of "family": A replication and extension. *Journal of Family Communication, 9*, 170–189.

Beauboeuf-Lafontant, T. (2009). *Behind the mask of the strong black woman: Voice and the embodiment of a costly performance*. Philadelphia: Temple University Press.

Beck, K,. & Clark, J. (2000). *The Andy Griffith show book: From miracle salve to kerosene cucumbers, the complete guide to one of television's best-loved shows* (3rd ed.). New York: St. Martin's Griffin.

Becker-Cantarino, B. (1994). "Feminist consciousness" and "wicked witches": Recent studies on women in early modern Europe. *Journal of Women in Culture and Society, 20*, 152–175.

Belkin, L. (2003, October 26). The opt-out revolution. *New York Times Magazine*. Retrieved from http://www.nytimes.com/2003/10/26/magazine/26WOMEN.html.

Bengtson, V. L. (2001). The Burgess Award Lecture. Beyond the nuclear family: The increasing importance of multigenerational bonds. *Journal of Marriage and Family 63*, 1–16. doi: 10.1111/j.1741-3737.2001.00001.

Bennetts, L. (2007). *The feminine mistake: Are we giving up too much?* New York: Voice.

Berlant, L. (1988). The female complaint. *Social Text, 19*, 237–259.

Berlant, L. (2008). *The female complaint: The unfinished business of sentimentality in American culture.* Durham, NC: Duke University Press.

Bianchi, S., Robinson, J., & Milkie, M. (2006). *Changing rhythms of American family life.* New York: Russell Sage Foundation.

Bianco, R. (2007, June 5). "House of Payne": It hurts to watch. *USA-Today.* Retrieved from http://www.usatoday.com/life/television/reviews/2007-06-05-house-of-payne_N.htm.

Bobo, J. (1991). Black women in fiction and nonfiction: Images of power and powerlessness. *Wide Angle, 13*, 72–81.

Bobo, J., & Seiter, E. (1997). Black feminism and media criticism: *The Women of Brewster Place.* In C. Brunsdon, J. D'Acci, & L. Spigel (Eds.), *Feminist television criticism: A reader* (pp. 167–183). Oxford: Clarendon.

Bogle, D. (1994). *Toms, coons, mulattos, mammies, & bucks: An interpretive history of blacks in American films.* New York: Continuum.

Bowen, L. (2006). *Reconfigured bodies: Ownership, responsibility, and control relations in the biotechnology age.* (Unpublished dissertation.) Michigan Technological University, Houghton, Mich.

Boylorn, R. M. (2011). As seen on TV: An autoethnographic reflection on race and reality television. *Critical Studies in Media Communication, 25*, 413–433.

Brah, A. & Phoenix, A. (2004). Ain't I a woman? Revisiting intersectionality. *Journal of International Women's Studies, 5*(3), 75–86.

Briggs, R. (1996). *Witches and neighbors: The social and cultural contexts of European witchcraft.* London: HarperCollins.

Brooks, D. E., & Hébert, L. P. (2006). Gender, race and media representation. In B. J. Dow & J. T. Wood (Eds.), *The Sage handbook of gender and communication* (pp. 297–317). Thousand Oaks, CA: Sage.

Brown, S., Cohon, D., & Wheeler, R. (2002). African American extended families and kinship care: How relevant is the foster care model for kinship care? *Children and Youth Services Review, 24*, 53–77.

Bruess, C. J. S., & Pearson, J. C. (1997). Interpersonal rituals in marriage and adult friendship. *Communication Monographs, 64*, 25–46.

Brunsdon, C. (2005). Feminism, postfeminism, Martha, Martha, and Nigella. *Cinema Journal, 44*, 110–116.

Burke, W. M. (1991). Border crossings in Marilynne Robinson's

Housekeeping [Review of the book *Housekeeping* by Marilynne Robinson]. *Modern Fiction Studies, 37*, 716–724.

Butler, J. (1990). *Gender trouble: Feminism and the subversion of identity*. New York: Routledge.

Butler, J. (1997). *The psychic life of power: Theories in subjection*. Palo Alto: Stanford University Press.

Butler, J. (2000). *Antigone's claim: Kinship between life and death*. New York: Columbia University Press.

Butler, J. (2002). Is kinship always already heterosexual? *Differences: A Journal of Feminist Cultural Studies 13*, 14–44.

Butler, J. (2004). *Undoing gender*. New York: Routledge.

Caldwell, C. (2009, August 24). The pink recovery: Why women are doing better. *Time*. Retrieved from http://www.time.com/time/magazine/article/0,9171,1916299,00.html.

Carstarphen, M. G. (1999). Gettin' real love: *Waiting to Exhale* and film representations of womanist identity. In M. Meyers (Ed.), *Mediated women: Representations in popular culture* (pp. 369–382). Cresskill, NJ: Hampton.

Carter, B. (2011, August). Marketing to tweens and teens: Insights, strategies, and tactics. *Licensing Journal, 31*(7), 1–4.

Chesler, P. (1972). *Women and madness*. New York: Doubleday.

Child Welfare League of America. (1994). *Kinship care: A natural bridge*. Washington, DC: CWLA Press.

Christian, A. J. (2011, January 21). "The Game" broadcasts the black sitcom revival. *Blog.ajchistian.com*. Retrieved from http://blog.ajchristian.org/2011/01/21/the-game-broadcasts-the-black-sitcom-revival/.

Christian, B. (1980). *Black women novelists: The development of a tradition, 1892–1976*. Westport, CT: Greenwood.

Christiansen, R. (2006). *The complete book of aunts*. London: Faber & Faber.

Chua, A. (2011). *Battle hymn of the tiger mother*. New York: Penguin.

Cixous, H. (1976). The laugh of the medusa. Keith Cohen and Paula Cohen (Trans.). *Signs, 1*, 875–893.

Clark, J. (n.d.). The Andy Griffith Show *Rerun Watchers Club*. Retrieved from http://www.mayberry.com/tagsrwc/index.htm.

Clarke, B. (1996). Artist statement. In K. A. Perkins & R. Uno (Eds.), *Contemporary plays by women of color* (pp. 32–33). New York: Routledge.

Clarke, B., & Dickerson, G. (1999). Re/membering Aunt Jemima: A menstrual show. In B. Taumann (Ed.), *Strange orphans: Contemporary African American women playwrights* (pp. 208–224). Würzburg: Königshausen & Neumann.

Clarke, M. M. (2000). Brontë's Jane Eyre and the Grimms' Cinderella. *Studies in English Literature 1500–1900, 40,* 695–710.

Clifton, L. (1991). slave cabin, sotterly plantation, Maryland, 1989. In *Quilting: Poems 1987–1990* (p. 13). Brockport, NY: BOA Editions.

CNN Editors. (2011, June 23). Gallup: Americans prefer having boys to girls, just as they did in 1941. Retrieved from http://globalpublic square.blogs.cnn.com/2011/06/23gallup-americans-prefer-boys-to -girls-just-as-they-did-in-1941/.

Code, L. (1991). *What can she know? Feminist theory and the construction of knowledge.* Ithaca, NY: Cornell University Press.

Cohn, D., Passell, J., Wang, W., & Livingston, G. (2011, December 14). Barely half of U.S. adults are married—a record low. Pew Social and Demographic Trends online. Retrieved from http://www.pew socialtrends.org/2011/12/14/barely-half-of-u-s-adults-are-married-a -record-low/?src=prc-headline.

Collins, P. H. (1990). *Black feminist thought: Knowledge, consciousness, and the politics of empowerment.* New York: Routledge.

Collins, P. H. (1998). *Fighting words: Black women and the search for justice.* Minneapolis: University of Minnesota Press.

Collins, P. H. (2000). *Black feminist thought: Knowledge, consciousness, and the politics of empowerment* (2nd ed.). New York: Routledge.

Collins, P. H. (2004). *Black sexual politics: African Americans, gender, and the new racism.* New York: Routledge.

Combahee River Collective. (1982). A black feminist statement. In G. T. Hull, P. Bell-Scott, & B. Smith (Eds.), *All the women are white, all the Blacks are men, but some of us are brave: Black women's studies* (pp. 13–22). New York: Feminist Press.

Coogan-Gehr, K. (2011). The politics of race in U.S. feminist scholarship: An archaeology. *Signs, 37,* 83–107.

Cooks, B. R. (1995). See me now. *Camera obscura: Feminism, culture and media studies, 12,* 66–83.

Coontz, S. (1992). The way we never were: American families and the nostalgia trap. New York: Basic Books.

Coontz, S. (1999). Introduction. In S. Coontz (Ed.), *American families: A multicultural reader* (pp. ix–xxxiii). New York: Routledge.

Coontz, S. (2000a). Historical perspectives on family studies. *Journal of Marriage and the Family, 62*, 283–297.

Coontz, S. (2000b). *The way we never were: American families and the nostalgia trap* (rev. ed.). New York: Basic Books.

Coontz, S., with Parson, M., & Raley, G. (1999). *American families: A multicultural reader*. New York: Routledge.

Cowles, G. (2008, April 30). Reading room: Conversation about great books [blogs]. Retrieved from http://readingroom.blogs.nytimes .com/tag/housekeeping/page/2/.

Crenshaw, K. W. (1991). Mapping the margins: Intersectionality, identity politics, and violence against women of color. *Stanford Law Review, 43*, 1241–1299.

Crouch, S. (2011, April 25). Nation in love with minstrelsy: Spike Lee, Tyler Perry, Snoop Dogg and the struggle to define blackness. *Daily News*. Retrieved from http://articles.nydailynews .com/2011-04-25/news/29489041_1_malt-liquor-byron-hurt-hip -hop#ixzz1RAb771sL.

Crumbley, J., & Little, R. L. (Eds.). (1997). Introduction. *Relatives raising children: An overview of kinship care* (xiii–xvi). Washington, DC: CWLA Press.

Cunningham, A. S. (1997). *Aunts: A celebration of those special women in our lives*. Chicago: Contemporary.

Daly, M. (1978). *Gyn/ecology: The metaethics of radical feminism*. Boston: Beacon Press.

Daly, M., & Caputi, J. (1987). *Webster's first new intergalactic wickedary of the English language*. Boston: Beacon Press.

Damian, M. (2011). *A princess for Christmas*. [Made-for-TV movie]. Hollywood: Media Pro Pictures, Motion Picture Corporation of America, & Riviera Films.

Davis, A. Y. (1990). *Women, culture, and politics*. New York: Vintage Books.

Davis-Sowers, R. (2006). Salvaging children's lives: Understanding the experiences of black aunts who serve as kinship care providers within black families. (Unpublished doctoral dissertation.) Georgia State University, Atlanta, GA.

Davis-Sowers, R. (2012). It just kind of like falls in your hands: Factors that influence black aunts' decisions to parent their nieces and nephews. *Journal of Black Studies, 43*(3), 231–250. doi: 10.1177/0021934711415243.

de Blécourt, W. (2000). The making of the female witch: Reflections on witchcraft and gender in the early modern period. *Gender & History, 12*, 287–309.

de Lauretis, T. (1984). *Alice doesn't: Feminism, semiotics, cinema.* Indianapolis: Indiana University Press.

de Lauretis, T. (1990). Eccentric subjects: Feminist theory and historical consciousness. *Feminist Studies, 16*, 115–150.

Dickerson, G. & Clarke, B. (1993). Re/membering Aunt Jemima: A menstrual show. *Women & Performance: A Journal of Feminist Theory 6:1*, 95–130.

Dollimore, J. (2002/1991). Post/modern: On the gay sensibility, or the pervert's revenge on authenticity. In F. Cleto (Ed.), *Camp: Queer aesthetics and the performing subject: A reader* (pp. 221–236). Ann Arbor: University of Michigan Press.

Donaldson, E. J. (2002). The corpus of the madwoman: Towards a feminist disability studies theory of embodiment and mental illness. *NWSA Journal, 14*, 99–119.

Doonan, S. (2003). *Wacky chicks: Life lessons from fearlessly inappropriate and fabulously eccentric women.* New York: Simon & Schuster.

Douglas, C. (2008, February 13). House of Payne: Vol. 1. *DVD verdict.* Retrieved from http://www.dvdverdict.com/reviews/housepayne vol1.php.

Douglas, S. J. (2010). *Enlightened sexism: The seductive message that feminism's work is done.* New York: Times Books.

Dreher, K. L. (2012). *Dancing on the white page: Black women entertainers writing autobiography.* Albany: SUNY Press.

Duffy, M. (2007). Doing the dirty work: Gender, race, and reproductive labor in historical perspective. *Gender & Society, 21*, 313–336.

Duryee, T. (2011, May 2). FTD.com offers Mother's Day deal on LivingSocial (This time without the fine print). All Things Digital, Commerce section. Retrieved from http://allthingsd .com/?p=69875&ak_action=printable.

Edwards, G. N. (2011, February 13). Entertainment: Life lessons from our beloved black sitcom characters. *Madame Noire.* Retrieved from http://madamenoire.com/41424/life-lessons -from-our-beloved-black-sitcom-characters/.

Ehrenreich, B., & English, D. (1973). *Witches, midwives and nurses: A history of women healers.* New York: Feminist Press.

Ehrenreich, B. (2000, April 1). Maid to order: The politics of other women's work. *Harper's Magazine*. Retrieved from http://www.barbara ehrenreich.com/maidtoorder.htm.

Ehrenreich, B., & Hochschild, A. R. (2003). Introduction. In B. Ehrenreich & A. R. Hochschild (Eds.), *Global woman: Nannies, maids, and sex workers in the new economy* (pp. 1–14). New York: Metropolitan.

Ellingson, L., & Sotirin, P. (2006). Exploring young adults' perspectives on communication with aunts. *Journal of Social and Personal Relationships, 23*, 499–517.

Ellingson, L. L., & Sotirin, P. (2008). Academic aunting: Reimagining feminist (wo)mentoring, teaching, and relationships. *Women & Language, 30*(1), 35–42.

Ellingson, L. L., & Sotirin, P. (2010). *Aunting: Cultural practices that sustain family and community life*. Waco, TX: Baylor University Press.

Eng, D. L. (2010). *The feeling of kinship: Queer liberalism and the racialization of intimacy*. Durham, NC: Duke University Press.

Eng, R. (1998). *Leather spinsters and their degrees of asexuality*. [E-book]. Houston: St. Mary. Retrieved from http://leatherspinsters .com/preview.html.

England, P., Budig, M., & Folbre, N. (2002). Wages of virtue: The relative pay of care work. *Social Problems, 49*, 455–473.

Entertainment Weekly. (2012, January 27). The bullseye. *Entertainment Weekly*, 80.

EURweb.com. (2009, May 28). Spike Lee likens Perry show to buffoonery. *Blackamericanweb.com*. Retrieved from http://www.blackamerica web.com/?q=articles/entertainment/gossip/9662.

Faludi, S. (1991). *Backlash: The undeclared war against American women*. New York: Doubleday.

Fann, J. (1998). BarneyFife.com. Retrieved from http://www.barneyfife .com.

Fann, J., & Lindsey, G. (2001). *The way back to Mayberry: Lessons from simpler times*. Peabody, MA: Broadman & Holman..

Featherstone, M., & Hepworth, M. (2005). Images of aging: Cultural representations of later life. M. L. Johnson (ed.) with V. L. Bengtson, P. G. Coleman, & T. B. L. Kirkwood, *The Cambridge book of age and ageing* (pp. 354–362). Cambridge: Cambridge University Press.

Ferguson, K. E. (1993). *The man question: Visions of subjectivity in feminist theory*. Berkeley: University of California Press.

Folbre, N. (2001). *The invisible heart: Economics and family values.* New York: New Press.

Foltz, T. G. (1995). Book review of *Witch crazy: A new history of the European witch hunts. Gender and Society, 9,* 514–516.

Foster, T. (1988). History, critical theory, and women's social practices: "Women's time" and housekeeping [Review of the book *Housekeeping* by Marilynne Robinson]. *Signs, 14,* 73–99.

Frank, T. (2004). *What's the matter with Kansas? How conservatives won the heart of America.* New York: Metropolitan.

Franklin, S., & McKinnon, S. (2001a). Introduction. In S. Franklin & S. McKinnon (Eds.), *Relative values: Reconfiguring kinship studies* (pp. 1–28). Durham, NC: Duke University Press.

Franklin, S., & McKinnon, S. (Eds.). (2001b). *Relative values: Reconfiguring kinship studies.* Durham, NC: Duke University Press.

Friedman, M. (2000). Autonomy, social disruption, and women. In C. Mackenzie & N. Stoljar (Eds.), *Relational autonomy: Feminist perspectives on autonomy, agency, and the social self* (pp. 35–51). New York: Oxford University Press.

Fry, R. & Cohn, D. (2010, January 19). Women, men, and the new economics of marriage. Pew Research Center. Downloaded from http://www.pewsocialtrends.org.

Gardner, M. (2006, October 30). The truth behind women "opting out." *Christian Science Monitor.* Retrieved from http://www.csmonitor.com/2006/1030/p13s02-wmgn.html.

Garland-Thomson, R. (2005a). Disability and representation. *PMLA 120*(2), 522–527.

Garland-Thomson, R. (2005b). Feminist disability studies. *Signs 30*(2), 1557–1587.

Gates, H. L., Jr. (1989, November 12). TV's black world turns—but stays unreal. *New York Times.* Retrieved from http://www.nytimes.com/1989/11/12/arts/tv-s-black-world-turns-but-stays-unreal.html?pagewanted=all&src=pm.

Genz, S. & Brabon, B. A. (2009). *Postfeminism: Cultural texts and theories.* Edinburgh: Edinburgh University Press.

Gerson, K. (2010). *Unfinished revolution: How a new generation is reshaping family, work, and gender in America.* New York: Oxford University Press.

Geyh, P. E. (1993). Burning down the house? Domestic space and feminine subjectivity in Marilynne Robinson's "Housekeeping" [Review of the book *Housekeeping* by Marilynne Robinson]. *Contemporary Literature, 34*, 103–122.

Gezari, J. (2006). Sandra M. Gilbert and Susan Gubar's *Madwoman in the Attic. Essays in Criticism, 56*, 264–279. doi: 10.1093/escrit/cgl003.

Giddings, P. (1996). *When and where I enter: The impact of black women on race and sex in America.* New York: Perennial.

Gilbert, S., & Gubar, S. (1979). *The madwoman in the attic: The woman writer and the nineteenth-century imagination.* New Haven: Yale University Press.

Gilbert, S. M., & Gubar, S. (2000). Introduction to *The madwoman in the attic: The woman writer and the nineteenth century literary imagination* (2nd ed.; pp. xv–xlv). New Haven: Yale University Press.

Gillespie, C. R. (1999). Mammy goes to Las Vegas: *Showgirls* and the constancy of African-American female stereotypes. In M. Meyers (Ed.), *Mediated women: Representations in popular culture* (pp. 81–90). Cresskill, NJ: Hampton.

Glenn, E. N. (1994). Social constructions of mothering: A thematic overview. In E. N. Glenn, G. Chang, & L. R. Forcey (Eds.), *Mothering: Ideology, experience, and agency* (pp. 1–31). New York: Routledge.

Goings, K. W. (1994). *Mammy and Uncle Moss: Black collectibles and American stereotyping.* Bloomington: Indiana University Press.

Goody, J. (1983). *The development of family and marriage in Europe.* Cambridge: Cambridge University Press.

Gordon, R. (1995). Earthstar magic: A feminist theoretical perspective on the way of the witches and the path to the goddess. *Social Alternatives, 14*, 9–11.

Grahn, J. R. (1982). *The work of a common woman: Collected poetry (1964–1977).* New York: St. Martin's.

Gray, H. (1995a). A different dream of difference. *Critical Studies in Mass Communication, 16*, 484–488.

Gray, H. (1995b). *Watching race: Television and the struggle for "blackness."* Minneapolis: University of Minnesota Press.

Gray, H.S. (2005). *Cultural moves: African Americans and the politics of representation.* Berkeley: University of California Press.

Grossberg, L. (2005). *Caught in the crossfire: Kids, politics, and America's future.* Boulder, CO: Paradigm.

Guinier, L. (2005, Spring). The miner's canary: Enlisting race, resisting power, & transforming democracy. *Liberal Education* online,

Association of American Colleges and Universities. Retrieved from http://www.aacu.org/liberaleducation/le-sp05/le-sp05feature3.cfm.

Gunther, M. (1990, August 26). Black producers add a fresh nuance. *The New York Times*. Retrieved from http://www.nytimes.com/1990/08/26/arts/television-black-producers-add-a-fresh-nuance.html?src=pm.

Guran, P. (Ed.) (2012). *Witches: Wicked, wild & wonderful*. Gaithersburg, MD: Prime Books.

Haggins, B. L. (1999). There's no place like home: The American dream, African-American identity, and the situation comedy. *Velvet Light Trap, 43*, 23–36.

Haggins, B. (2009). In the wake of "the nigger pixie": Dave Chappelle and the politics of crossover comedy. In J. Gray, J. P. Jones, & E. Thompson (Eds.), *Satire TV: Politics and comedy in the post-network era* (pp. 233–251). New York: New York University Press.

Hall, S. (1992). Cultural studies and its theoretical legacies. In L. Grossberg, C. Nelson, & P. Treichler (Eds.), *Cultural Studies* (pp. 277–294). New York: Routledge.

Hall, S. (1996) New ethnicities. In H. A. Baker, M. Diawara, & R. H. Lindeborg (Eds.), *Black British cultural studies: A reader* (pp. 163–209). Chicago: University Chicago Press.

Hall., S. (1997). The work of representation. In S. Hall (Ed.), *Representation: Cultural representations and signifying practices* (pp. 13–74). London: Sage.

Hall, S. (1999). Introduction [to Part III: Looking and subjectivity]. In J. Evans & S. Hall (Eds.), *Visual culture: The reader* (pp. 309–314). London: Sage.

Hanks, R. S. & Ponzetti, J. J. (2004). Family studies and intergenerational studies: Intersections and opportunities. *Journal of Intergenerational Relationships 3–4*, 5–22. doi: 10.1300/J194v02n03_02.

Haraway, D. (2007). *When species meet*. Minneapolis: University of Minnesota Press.

Hardwig, J. (1989/1995). In search of an ethics of personal relationships. In J. Stewart (Ed.), *Bridges not walls: A book about interpersonal communication* (pp. 324–333). New York: McGraw-Hill; reprinted from G. Graham & H. Lafollette (Eds.), *Person to person*. Philadelphia: Temple University Press.

Harkins, A. (2005). *Hillbilly: A cultural history of an American icon*. New York: Oxford University Press.

Harris, A. (2004). *All about the girl: Culture, power, and identity*. New York: Routledge.

Harris, R. L. (2011, March 7). Tyler Perry wins big. *New York Times*, C2. Retrieved from LexisNexis.

Harris, T. (1995). This disease called strength: Some observations on the compensating construction of black female character. *Literature and Medicine*, *1*, 109–126.

Harris-Lacewell, M. (2001). No place to rest: African American political attitudes and the myth of black women's strength. *Women and Politics, 23*(3), 1–33.

Harris-Lacewell, M. V. (2007, Summer). Righteous politics: The role of the black church in contemporary politics. *Cross Currents, 57*, n.p. Retrieved from http://www.thefreelibrary.com/Righteous+politics percent3A+the+role+of+the+black+church+in+contemporary... -a0168215071.

Harris-Perry, M. V. (2011). *Sister Citizen: Shame, Stereotypes, and Black Women in America*. New Haven: Yale University Press.

Harvey, S. (2009). Entries for "grandfather" (July 22, 2009) and "avuncular" (July 24, 2009). *The Virtual Linguist*. Retrieved from http://www .virtuallinguist.typepad.com.

Harwood, J., & Anderson, K. (2002). The presence and portrayal of social groups on prime-time television. *Communication Reports, 15*, 81–97.

Hayden, R. (1997). *Collected poems*. F. Glaysher (Ed.). New York: Liveright.

Heilman, A. (Ed.). (1998). *The late-Victorian marriage question: A collection of key new woman texts*. Vol. 5. London: Routledge.

Hepworth, M. (2004). Images of old age. In J. F. Nussbaum & J. Coupland (Eds.), *Handbook of communication and aging research*. (2nd ed., pp. 3–30). Mahwah, NJ: Lawrence Erlbaum.

Hertz, R. (2009). Turning strangers into kin: Half siblings and anonymous donors. In M. K. Nelson & A. I. Garey (Eds.), *Who's watching? Daily practices of surveillance among contemporary families* (pp. 156–174). Nashville: Vanderbilt University Press.

Hewlett, S. A., Forster, D., Sherbin, L., Shiler, P., & Sumberg, K. (2009). *Off-ramps and on-ramps revisited*. Center for Workife Policy, New York, NY. Available at http://www.worklifepolicy.org.

Hill, R. B. (1999). *The strengths of Black families: Twenty-five years later*. New York: University Press of America.

Hird, M. J. (2004). Chimerism, mosaicism and the cultural construction of kinship. *Sexualities, 7,* 217–232.

Hochschild, A. R. (1989). *The second shift: Working parents and the revolution at home.* New York: Viking.

Hochschild, A. R. (2001). *The time bind: When work becomes home and home becomes work.* New York: Holt.

Hochschild, A. R. (2003a). *The commercialization of intimate life: Notes from home and work.* Berkeley: University of California Press.

Hochschild, A. R. (2003b). Love and gold. In B. Ehrenreich & A. R. Hochschild (Eds.), *Global woman: Nannies, maids, and sex workers in the new economy* (pp. 15–30). New York: Metropolitan.

Hoecherl-Alden, G., & Lindenfeld, L. (2010). Thawing the north: Mostly Martha as a German-Italian eatopia. *Journal of International and Intercultural Communication, 3,* 114–135.

Hoff Sommers, C. (1995). *Who stole feminism? How women have betrayed women.* New York: Touchstone.

Holladay, H. (2002). Black names in white space: Lucille Clifton's South. *Southern Literary Journal, 34,* 120–133.

hooks, b. (1981). *Ain't I a woman? Black women and feminism.* Boston: South End Press.

hooks, b. (1992). *Black looks: Race and representation.* Boston: South End Press.

Hoover, S. M., Clark, L. S., & Alters, D. F. (2004). *Media, home and family.* New York: Routledge.

Hubert, J. (2009) *Perfection is not a sitcom mom.* Oakland, CA: Palamino Productions.

Hull, G., Bell-Scott, P., & Smith, B. (1982). *All the women are white, all the blacks are men, but some of us are brave: Black women's studies.* New York: Feminist Press.

Hurtado, A. (1989). Relation to privilege: Seduction and rejection in the subordination of white women and women of color. *Signs, 14,* 833–855.

Hutcheon, L. (2006) *A theory of adaptation.* New York: Routledge.

Hutton, R. (2011). Witch-hunting in Celtic societies. *Past & Present 212*(1), 43–71.

Irigaray, L. (1985). *This sex which is not one.* Trans. C. Porter. Ithaca, NY: Cornell University Press.

Izrael, J. (2011, April 22). Tyler Perry vs. Spike Lee: A debate over class and "Coonery." Tell Me More [blog]. Retrieved from

http://www.npr.org/blogs/tellmemore/2011/04/22/135630682/
tyler-perry-vs-spike-lee-a-debate-over-class-and-coonery.

Jacobson, H. (2008). *Culture keeping: White mothers, international adoption, and the negotiation of family difference.* Nashville: Vanderbilt University Press.

Jacobson, H. (2009). Interracial surveillance and biological parenting: Adoptive families in the public eye. In M. K. Nelson & A. I. Garey (Eds.), *Who's watching? Daily practices of surveillance among contemporary families* (pp. 73–93). Nashville: Vanderbilt University Press.

Jacoby, D. (2006). Caring about caring labor: An introduction. *Politics & Society 34*(1), 5–10. doi: 10.1177/0032329205284753.

Jeffreys, S. (1985). *The spinster and her enemies: Feminism and sexuality, 1880–1930.* North Melbourne: Spinifex Press.

Jenkins, H. (2006). *Convergence culture: Where old and new media collide.* New York: New York University Press.

Jhally, S., & Lewis, J. (1992). *Enlightened racism:* The Cosby Show, *audiences and the myth of the American dream.* Boulder, CO: Westview Press.

Johnson, D. (2004). Selling Sarafem: Priestly and bardic discourses in the construction of premenstrual syndrome. *Women's Studies in Communication, 27,* 330–351.

Johnson, E. P. (2003). *Appropriating blackness: Performance and the politics of authenticity.* Durham, NC: Duke University Press.

Jones, R. (2003). *The liberation of Aunt Jemima: A poetic tribute to the spiritual woman.* Lincoln, NE: iUniverse.

Jordan, R. T. (1998). *But darling, I'm your Auntie Mame! The amazing history of the world's favorite madcap aunt.* New York: Kensington Books.

Jordan-Zachery, J. S. (2009). *Black women, cultural images, and social policy.* New York: Routledge.

Joseph, G. I., & Lewis, J. (Eds.). (1981). *Common differences: Conflict in black and white feminists' perspectives.* Garden City, NY: Anchor Books.

Kaivola, K. (1993). The pleasures and perils of merging: Female subjectivity in Marilynne Robinson's *Housekeeping. Contemporary Literature, 34,* 670–690.

Kaplan, E. A. (2002, December 23). Thoroughly modern mammy.

LA Weekly. Retrieved from http://www.alternet.org/story/14825/thoroughly_modern_mammy.

Kaufman, G. (1991). *In stitches: A patchwork of feminist humor and satire.* Bloomington: Indiana University Press.

Kelley, B., & Kelley, S. (2011). *Undecided: How to ditch the endless quest for perfect and find the career—and life—that's right for you.* Berkeley, CA: Seal Press.

Keyes, A. (2010, May 12). Hilton Als: Tyler Perry simplifies, commodifies black life. Tell Me More [blog]. Retrieved from http://www.npr.org/templates/story/story.php?storyId=126778639.

Kirby, E. L., Golden, A. A., Medved, C. E., Jorgenson, J., & Buzzanell, P. M. (2003). An organizational challenge to the discourse of work and family research: From problematics to empowerment. In P. Kalbfleish. (Ed.), *Communication Yearbook 27* (pp. 1–43). Mahwah, NJ: Lawrence Erlbaum.

Kirkby, J. (1986). Is there life after art? The metaphysics of Marilynne Robinson's *Housekeeping* [Review of the book *Housekeeping* by Marilynne Robinson]. *Tulsa Studies in Women's literature, 5,* 91–109.

Kochhar, R. (2011, July 6). Two years of economic recovery: Women lose jobs, men find them. *Pew Research Center.* Retrieved from http://www.pewsocialtrends.org/2011/07/06/two-years-of-economic-recovery-women-lose-jobs-men-find-them/.

Kompare, D. (2004). *Rerun nation: How repeats invented American television.* New York: Routledge.

Laclau, E., & Mouffe, C. (1988). *Hegemony & socialist strategy: Towards a radical democratic politics.* London: Verso.

Langer, N. & Ribarich, M. (2007). Aunts, uncles—nieces, nephews: Kinship relations over the lifespan. *Educational Gerontology 33*(1), 75–83. doi: 10.1080/03601270600894279.

Lapowsky, I. (2009, October 26). Tyler Perry responds to Spike Lee's claim that his work is comparable to "Amos 'n' Andy." *Daily News.* Retrieved from http://articles.nydailynews.com/2009-10-26/entertainment/17937154_1_spike-lee-madea-amos-n-andy.

Larner, C. (1981). *Enemies of God: The witch-hunt in Scotland.* Baltimore: John Hopkins University Press.

Lazzari, M., & Schlesier, D. (2007). *Exploring art: A global, thematic approach* (3rd ed.). Belmont, CA: Wadsworth.

Lee, S. (2010). *Erotic revolutionaries: Black women, sexuality, and popular culture*. Lanham, MD: Hamilton Books.

Leitch, T. (2007) *Film adaptation and its discontents from* Gone with the Wind *to* The Passion of the Christ. Baltimore: John Hopkins University Press.

Lentz, K. M. (2000). Quality versus relevance: Feminism, race, and the politics of the sign in 1970s television. *Camera Obscura, 43*, 44–93.

Lorde, A. (1984). The master's tools will never dismantle the master's house. In A. Lorde (Ed.), *Sister outsider: Essays and speeches* (pp. 110–113). Freedom, CA: Crossing Press.

Lotz, A. (2006). *Redesigning women: Television after the network era*. Urbana: University of Illinois Press.

Loury, L. D. (2006). All in the extended family: Effects of grandparents, aunts and uncles on educational attainment. *The American Economic Review 96*(2), 275–278.

Lowrey, A. (2011, July 11). Where's the shecovery? Why men are gaining jobs more quickly than women. *Slate*. Retrieved from http://www.slate.com/id/2298963/.

Ludden, J. (2009, November 6). Recession drives women into role of breadwinner. *NPR Morning Edition*. Retrieved from http://www.npr.org/templates/story/story.php?storyId=120146408.

MacDonald, M. (1995). *Representing women: Myths of femininity in the popular media*. London: Oxford University Press.

Maddison, S. (2000). *Fags, hags and queer sisters: Gender dissent and heterosocial bonds in gay culture*. New York: St. Martin's.

Mann, S. A., & Kelley, L. R. (1997). Standing at the crossroads of modernist thought: Collins, Smith, and the new feminist epistemologies. *Gender and Society, 11*, 391–408.

Manring, M. M. (1998). *Slave in a box: The strange career of Aunt Jemima*. Charlottesville: University Press of Virginia.

Martin, B., & Mohanty, C. (1986). Feminist politics: What's home got to do with it? In T. de Lauretis (Ed.), *Feminist studies/critical studies* (pp. 191–212). Bloomington: Indiana University Press.

Mastro, D. A., & Greenberg, B. S. (2000). The portrayal of racial minorities on prime time television. *Journal of Broadcasting & Electronic Media, 44*, 690–703.

Mauer, M., & King, R. S. (2007). Uneven justice: State rates of incarceration by race and ethnicity. *Washington, D.C.: The Sentencing Project*. Retrieved from http://www.sentencingproject.org.

McDermott, S. (2004). Future-perfect: Gender, nostalgia, and the not yet presented in Marilynne Robinson's *Housekeeping* [Review of the book *Housekeeping* by Marilynne Robinson]. *Journal of Gender Studies, 13*, 259–270.

McDonald, K. M. (2006). *Embracing Sisterhood: Class, Identity, and Contemporary Black Women*. Lanham, MD: Rowman & Littlefield.

McDonald, M., Phipps, S., & Lethbridge, L. (2005). Taking its toll: The influences of paid and unpaid work on women's well-being. *Feminist Economics, 11*, 63–94.

McElya, M. (2007). *Clinging to Mammy: The faithful slave in twentieth-century America*. Cambridge, MA: Harvard University Press.

McIntosh, P. (1988). *White privilege and male privilege: A personal account of coming to see correspondences through work in women's studies* (Working Paper No. 189). Needham, MA: Wellesley College.

McKee, A. (2003). *Textual analysis: A beginner's guide*. London: Sage.

McRobbie, A. (2004). Post feminism and pop culture. *Feminist Media Studies, 4*, 255–264.

McRobbie, A. (2009). *The aftermath of feminism: Gender, culture and social change*. London: Sage.

Means Coleman, R. (2000). *African American viewers and the black situation comedy: Situating racial humor*. New York: Garland Press.

Means Coleman, R. R. (2003). Elmo is black! Black popular communication and the marking and marketing of black identity. *Popular Communication, 1*, 51–64.

Means Coleman, R. R. (2006). The gentrification of "black" in black popular communication in the new millennium. *Popular Communication, 4*, 79–94.

Meyers, D. T. (2000). Intersectional identity and the authentic self? Opposites attract! In C. Mackenzie & N. Stoljar (Eds.), *Relational autonomy: Feminist perspectives on autonomy, agency, and the social self* (pp. 151–180). New York: Oxford University Press.

Milardo, R. A. (2010). *The forgotten kin: Aunts and uncles*. New York: Cambridge University Press.

Mills, B. (2004). Comedy verité: Contemporary sitcom form. *Screen, 45*, 63–78.

Mizejewski, L. (2007). Queen Latifah, unruly women, and the bodies of romantic comedy. *Genders, 46*, n.p. Retrieved from http://www.genders.org/g46/g46_mizejewski.html.

Mohanty, C. T., Russo, A., & Torres, L. (Eds.). (1991). *Third world women and the politics of feminism.* Bloomington: Indiana University Press.

Moody, S. (2011). " 'Convergence Culture': Exploring the Literacy Practices of Online Romance Fiction Communities." Presented at Popular Romance in the New Millennium: An International Conference. McDaniel College. Westminister, MD, November 10–11, 2011.

Moore, M. L. (2008, March 24). The image of black women in entertainment. *Starpulse.com.* Retrieved from http://www.starpulse.com/news/index.php/2008/03/24/the_image_of_black_women_in_entertainmen.

Moraga, C., & Anzaldua, G. (Eds.). (1981). *This bridge called my back:* Morrison, T. (1992). *Playing in the dark: Whiteness and the literary imagination.* New York: Vintage.

Mouffe, C. (1993). *The return of the political.* London: Verso.

Mustard, D. J. (2000). Spinster: An evolving stereotype revealed through film. *Journal of Media Psychology, 4.* Retrieved from http://www.calstatela.edu/faculty/sfischo/spinster.html.

Negra, D. (2004). Quality postfeminism? Sex and the single girl on HBO. *Genders, 39,* n.p. Retrieved from http://www.genders.org/g39/g39_negra.html.

Negra, D. (2009). *What a girl wants: Fantasizing the reclamation of self in postfeminism.* New York: Routledge.

Nelson, A. (2008). African American stereotypes in prime time television: An overview 1948–2007. In T. Boyd (Ed.), *African Americans and popular culture: Theater, film, and television* (pp. 185–217). Westport, CT: Praeger.

Nelson, M. (1979). Why witches were women. In J. Freeman, (Ed.), *Women: A feminist perspective* (pp. 451–468). Palo Alto, CA: Mayfield.

Nielsen Company. (2009). *Television Audience 2009.* Downloaded from blog.nielsen.com.

Nielsen Television Rating Report. (2009, July 20). More half the homes in US have three or more TVs. Retrieved from http://blog.nielsen.com/nielsenwire/media_entertainment/more-than-half-the-homes-in-us-have-three-or-more-tvs/.

Norris, C. (2002, May 12). Bernie Mac smacks a nerve. *New York Times.* Retrieved from http://www.nytimes.com/2002/05/12/magazine/bernie-mac-smacks-a-nerve.html?pagewanted=all&src=pm.

Notkin, M. (2011a). *Savvy auntie: The ultimate guide for cool aunts, great-aunts, godmothers and all women who love kids.* New York: HarperCollins.

Notkin, M. (2011b). Savvy auntie. Retrieved from http://www.savvy auntie.com.

Notkin, M. (2011c). Unnatural women: Childless in America. *Huffington Post.* Retrieved from http://www.huffingtonpost.com/melanie-notkin/ unnatural-women-childless_b_1159279.html.

Novero, C. (2004). Nouvelle cuisine meets the German cinema: Bella Martha's recipe for contemporary film. *Food & Foodways, 12,* 27–52.

Nyong'o, T. (2002). Racial kitsch and black performance. *Yale Journal of Criticism, 15,* 371–391.

O'Brien, P. (1973). *The woman alone.* New York: Quadrangle.

O'Dell, C. (2006). The relevance of Women's Studies to the South Shore. *Psychological Review, 107,* 411–429. Retrieved O'Dell Relevance. pdf, from http://www.southshorejournal.org/archive/documents/.

O'Grady, L. (2009). Olympia's maid: Reclaiming black female subjectivity. In S. M. James, F. S. Foster, & B. Guy-Sheftall (Eds.), *Still brave: The evolution of black women's studies* (pp. 318–335). New York: Feminist Press.

Oswald, R. F., Blume, L. B., & Marks, S. R. (2005). Decentering heteronormativity: A model for family studies. In V. L. Bengtson, A. C. Acock, K. R. Allen, P. Dilworth-Anderson, & D. M. Klein (Eds.), *Sourcebook of family theory and research* (pp. 143–154). Thousand Oaks, CA: Sage.

Pashos, A., & McBurney, D. H. (2008). Kin relationships and the caregiving biases of grandparents, aunts and uncles: A two-generational questionnaire study. *Human Nature 19*(3), 311–330. doi: 10.1007/ s12110-008-9046-0.

Patton, P. (1993). Mammy: Her life and times. *American Heritage, 44,* 78–87.

Pearson, J. (2010). Resisting rhetorics of violence: Women, witches, and Wicca. *Feminist Theology, 18,* 141–159.

Pecora, M., & Mazzarella, S. (2001). *Growing up girls: Popular culture and the construction of identity.* New York: Peter Lang.

Perkins, K. A., & Uno, R. (1996). Introduction. In K. A. Perkins & R. Uno (Eds.), *Contemporary plays by women of color* (pp. 1–12). New York: Routledge.

Perry, R. (2004). *Novel relations: The transformation of kinship in*

English literature and culture 1748–1818. Cambridge: Cambridge University Press.

PEW Center on the States. (2008, February 28). Pew report finds more than one in 100 adults are behind bars. States' public safety performance project. Retrieved from http://www.pewcenteronthestates .org/news_room_detail.aspx?id=35912.

Plath, S. (1981). Spinster. In T. Hughes (Ed.), *The collected poems* (p. 49). New York: Harper & Row.

Pratt, M. B. (1984). Identity: Skin blood heart. In E. Bulkin, M. B. Pratt, & B. Smith, *Yours in struggle: Three feminist perspectives on anti-Semitism and racism* (pp. 11–63). New York: Long Haul Press.

Probyn, E. (1990). New traditionalism and post-feminism: T.V. does the home. *Screen, 31,* 147–159.

Probyn, E. (2006). Critical attachment: At home in the in-between. *Criticism, 48,* 273–279.

Projansky, S. (2001). *Watching rape: Film and television in postfeminist culture.* New York: New York University Press.

Purkiss, D. (1996). *The witch in history: Early modern and twentieth-century representations.* New York: Routledge.

Quinion, M. (2010). World wide words. http://www.worldwidewords .org/.

Radford-Hill, S. (2002). Keepin it real: A generational commentary on Kimberly Springer's "third wave black feminism?" *Signs, 27,* 1083–1190.

Radin, M. J. (1987). Market-inalienability. *Harvard Law Review, 100,* 1849–1937.

Rake, K. & Rotheroe, A. (2009, March). *Are women bearing the burden of the recession?* London: Fawcett Society.

Ravits, M. (1989). Extending the American range: Marilynne Robinson's *Housekeeping* [Review of the book *Housekeeping* by Marilynne Robinson]. *American Literature, 61,* 644–666.

Reagon, B. J. (1983). Coalition politics: Turning the century. In B. Smith (Ed.), *Home girls: A black feminist anthology* (pp. 356–368). New York: Kitchen Table.

Reid, M. A. (2001). *Black protest poetry: Polemics from the Harlem Renaissance and the sixties.* New York: Peter Lang.

Rich, A. (1972). When we dead awaken: Writing as re-vision. *College English, 42,* 18–30.

Rich, A. (1977). *Of woman born: Motherhood as experience and institution*. New York: Bantam Books.

Rich, A. (1980). Compulsory heterosexuality and lesbian existence. *Signs* 5(4), 631–660.

Riviere, J. (1929). Womanliness as masquerade. *International Journal of Psychoanalysis 10*, 303–313.

Roberts, D. (1994). *The myth of Aunt Jemima: Representations of race and region*. London: Routledge.

Robertson, P. (2002/1996). What makes the feminist camp? In F. Cleto (Ed.), *Camp: Queer aesthetics and the performing subject: A reader* (pp. 266–282). Ann Arbor: University of Michigan Press.

Robinson, D., & Fernandes, D. (2004). *The definitive* Andy Griffith Show *reference: Episode-by-episode, with cast and production biographies and a guide to collectibles*. Jefferson, NC: McFarland.

Robinson, M. (1980). *Housekeeping: A novel*. New York: Picador.

Robinson, M. (1985, October 13). Writers and the nostalgic fallacy. *New York Times*, pp. BR1, BR14.

Roschelle, A. (1997). *No more kin: Exploring race, class, and gender in family networks*. Thousand Oaks, CA: Sage.

Rose, N., & Novas, C. (2004). Biological citizenship. In A. Ong & Collier (Eds.), *Global assemblages: Technology, politics and ethics as anthropological problems* (pp. 443–463). Malden, MA: Wiley-Blackwell.

Rose, N. (1999). *Governing the soul: The shaping of the private self* (2nd ed.). New York: Free Association Books.

Rose, T. (1994). *Black noise: Rap music and black culture in contemporary America*. Middletown, CT: Wesleyan University Press.

Rose, T. (1997). Never trust a big butt and smile. In C. Brunsdon, J. D'Acci, & L. Spigel (Eds.), *Feminist television criticism: A reader* (pp. 167–183). Oxford: Clarendon.

Rose, T. (2008). *The hip hop wars: What we talk about when we talk about hip-hop—and why it matters*. New York: Basic Civitas Books.

Rountree, K. (1997). The new witch of the west: Feminists reclaim the crone. *Journal of Popular Culture, 30*, 211–229.

Rowe, A. C. (2008). *Power lines: On the subject of feminist alliances*. Durham, NC: Duke University Press.

Rowe, K. (1995). *The unruly woman: Gender and the genres of laughter*. Austin: University of Texas Press.

Russo, M. (1986). Female grotesques: Carnival and theory. In T. de

Lauretis (Ed.), *Feminist studies/critical studies* (pp. 213–229). Bloomington: Indiana University Press.

Ryan, M. (1991). Marilynne Robinson's *Housekeeping*: The subversive nature and the new American eve [Review of the book *Housekeeping* by Marilynne Robinson]. *South Atlantic Review, 56,* 79–86.

Samuels, A. (2011, May 9). Reality TV trashes black women: An unsettling new formula: Eye rolling, finger-snapping stereotypes. *Newsweek Magazine*. Retrieved from http://www.thedailybeast.com/newsweek/2011/05/01/reality-tv-trashes-black-women.html.

Sanders, H. E. (2007). Living a *Charmed* life: The magic of postfeminist sisterhood. In Y. Tasker & D. Negra (Eds.), *Interrogating postfeminism: Gender and the politics of pop culture* (pp. 73–99). Durham, NC: Duke University Press.

Saval, M. (2009, July 21). Tyler Perry. *The Daily Variety*. Retrieved from LexisNexis.

Sayer, L. C. (2005). Gender, time, and inequality: Trends in women's and men's paid work, unpaid work and free time. *Social Forces, 84,* 285–303.

Schiappa, E. (2008). *Beyond representational correctness: Rethinking criticism of popular media.* Albany: SUNY Press.

Schott Foundation on Public Education. (2010). Y*es we can: The 2010 Schott 50 state report on black males in public education.* Retrieved from http://blackboysreport.org/.

Schutzman, M. (1999). *The real thing: Performance, hysteria, & advertising*. Hanover, NH: University Press of New England.

Seelye, J. D. (2005). *Jane Eyre*'s *American daughters: From* The Wide, Wide World *to* Anne of Green Gables*: A study of marginalized maidens and what they mean.* Newark: University of Delaware Press.

Seifert, C. (2008). Bite me! (Or don't). *Bitch* online. Retrieved from http://bitchmagazine.org/article/bite-me-or-don't.

Shaw, R. L. (2010). Women's experiential journey toward voluntary childlessness: An interpretative phenomenological analysis. *Journal of Community Applied Social Psychology, 163,* 151–163.

Shields, M. L. (1981). *Searun: Surviving my mother's madness.* West Lakes, South Australia: Seaview Books.

Showalter, E. (1985). *The female malady: Women, madness, and English culture 1830–1980.* New York: Penguin.

Showalter, E. (2009, May 8). The female frontier. *Guardian.*

Retrieved from http://www.guardian.co.uk/books/2009/may/09/female-novelists-usa.

Shugart, H. A., & Waggoner, C. E. (2008). *Making camp: Rhetorics of transgression in U.S. popular culture.* Tuscaloosa: University of Alabama Press.

Silbaugh, K. (1997). Commodification and women's household labor. *Yale Journal of Law and Feminism.* Retrieved from http://heinonline.org/HOL/LandingPage? collection=journals&handle=hein.journals/yjfem9&div=10&id=&page=.

Slack, J. D. (1996). The theory and method of articulation in cultural studies. In D. Morley & K. H. Chen (Eds.), *Critical dialogues in cultural studies* (pp. 112–127). New York: Routledge.

Smith, A. M. (1998). *Laclau and Mouffe: The radical democratic imaginary.* New York: Routledge.

Smith, B., Surrey, J. L., & Watkins, M. (2006). "Real" mothers: Adoptive mothers resisting marginalization and recreating motherhood. In K. Wegar (ed.), *Adoptive families in a diverse society* (pp. 146–161). New Brunswick, NJ: Rutgers University Press.

Smith, V. (1998). *Not just race, not just gender: Black feminist readings.* New York: Routledge.

Sotirin, P., Buzzanell, P.M., & Turner, L. (2007). Colonizing family: A feminist critique of family management texts. *Journal of Family Communication 7*(4), 245–263.

Sotirin, P. J., & Ellingson, L. L. (2005). The "other" women in family life: Aunt/niece/nephew communication. In K. Floyd & M. T. Morman (Eds.), *Widening the family circle: New research on family communication* (pp. 81–100). Thousand Oaks, CA: Sage.

Sotirin, P., & Ellingson, L. L. (2007). Rearticulating the aunt: Feminist alternatives of family, care, kinship, and agency in popular performances of aunting. *Cultural Studies <=> Critical Methodologies, 7,* 442–459.

Spangler, L. (2003). *Television women from Lucy to Friends: Fifty years of sitcoms and feminism.* Westport, CA: Praeger.

Spigel, L., & Curtin, M. (1997). Introduction. In L. Spigel & M. Curtin (Eds.), *The revolution wasn't televised: Sixties television and social conflict* (pp. 1–20). New York: Routledge.

Spigel, L. (1995). From the dark ages to the golden age: Women's memories and television reruns. *Screen 36*(1), 16–33.

Springer, K. (2003). Good times for Florida and black feminism. *Cercles, 8*, 122–135.

Stacey, J. (1999). Gay and lesbian families are here; All our families are queer; Let's get used to it! In S. Coontz, M. Parson, & G. Raley (Eds.), *American families: A multicultural reader* (pp. 372–405). New York: Routledge.

Stam, R., & Raengo, A. (2005). *Literature and film: A guide to the theory and practice of film adaptation*. Malden, MA: Blackwell.

Starhawk. (1997). *Dreaming the dark: Magic, sex, and politics*. Boston: Beacon Press.

Stephanie. (2010, October 24). An afternoon with reel women. *Shadow and Act*. Retrieved from http://www.shadowandact.com/?p=33202.

Stevenson, D., Everingham, C., & Robinson, P. (2011). Choices and life changes: Feminism and the politics of generational change. *Social Politics, 18*, 125–145.

Stone, P. (2007). *Opting out? Why women really quit careers and head home*. Berkeley: University of California Press.

Streeter, R. (Producer). (2010, July 26). Tyler Perry's amazing journey to the top. [Television broadcast.] *60 Minutes*. New York: CBS.

Sturgis, I. (2004). *Aunties: Thirty-five writers celebrate their other mother*. New York: Ballantine.

Sullivan, R. (2005). *Visual habits: Nuns, feminism, and American post-war popular culture*. Toronto: University of Toronto Press.

Suter, E. A., Reyes, K. L., & Ballard, R. L. (2010). Parental management of adoptive identities during challenging encounters: Adoptive parents as "protectors" and "educators." *Journal of Social and Personal Relationships, 28*, 242–261.

Tasker, Y., & Negra, D. (2005). In focus: Postfeminism and contemporary media studies. *Cinema Journal, 44*, 107–110.

Tasker, Y., & Negra, D. (2006). Postfeminism and the archive for the future. *Camera Obscura, 62*, 170–177.

Tasker, Y., & Negra, D. (2007). Introduction. In Y. Tasker & D. Negra (Eds.), *Interrogating post-feminism: Gender and the politics of popular culture* (pp. 1–26). Durham, NC: Duke University Press.

Taylor, E. (1989). *Prime-time families: Television culture in post-war America*. Berkeley: University of California Press.

Taylor, S. E., Klein, L. C., Lewis, B. P., Gruenewald, T. L., Gurung, R. A. R., & Updegraff, J. A. (2000). Biobehavioral responses to stress in females: Tend-and-befriend, not fight-or-flight. *Psychological Review, 107*, 411–429.

Tennant, R. (2011, November 4). With e-books, reading goes underground. Libraryjournal.com

Terwilliger, C. (2001, March 25). Mayberry a religious experience to some. *Denver Post*, 2D.

Thompson, B. (2002). Multiracial feminism: Recasting the chronology of second wave feminism. *Feminist Studies, 28*, 337–360.

Thompson, E. (2007). Comedy verité? The observational documentary meets the televisual sitcom. *Velvet Light Trap, 60*, 63–72.

Thompson, L. (2009). *Beyond the black lady: Sexuality and the new African American class.* Champaign: University of Illinois Press.

Toldson, I. A., & Marks, B. (2011, August 8). New research shatters myths and provides new hope for black love and marriage. Empower magazine online. Retrieved from http://www.empowernewsmag.com/listings.php?article=2051.

Traeder, T., & Bennett, J. (1998). *Aunties: Our older, cooler, wiser friends.* Berkeley, CA: Wildcat Canyon.

Tucker, L. R. (1997). Was the revolution televised? Professional criticism about "The Cosby Show" and the essentialization of black cultural expressions. *Journal of Broadcasting & Electronic Media, 41*, 90–108.

Turner, J. W. (1994). *Collectible Aunt Jemima: Handbook and value guide.* London: Schiffer.

TV Guide. (2002, May 4–10). 50 greatest TV shows of all time. Retrieved from http://www.cbsnews.com/stories/2002/04/26/entertainment/main507388.shtml.

UPI. (2010, September 20). U.S. marriage continues to decline. Retrieved from http://www.upi.com/Health_News/2010/09/29/US-marriage-rate-continues-to-decline/UPI-77271285810979/.

U.S. Bureau of Labor Statistics. (2011, September 2). *Economic news release: Employment situation summary.* Retrieved from http://www.bls.gov/news.release/empsit.nr0.htm.

U.S. Census Bureau. (2010, September 16). *Income, poverty, and health insurance coverage in the United States: 2009.* Retrieved from http://www.census.gov/newsroom/releases/archives/income_wealth/cb10-144.html.

U.S. Centers for Disease Control. (2009, July 17). Differences in prevalence of obesity among black, white, and Hispanic adults—United

States, 2006–2008. *Morbidity and Mortality Weekly Report, 58,* 740–744.

U.S. Department of Health and Human Services, Administration for Children and Families (2011, June). *The AFCARS report: Preliminary FY 2010 estimates as of June 2011.* Retrieved from http://www.acf.hhs.gov/programs/cb/stats_research/afcars/tar/report18.htm.

U.S. Department of Housing and Urban Development. (2007). *Title VIII: Fair housing and equal opportunity.* Retrieved from http://portal.hud.gov/hudportal/HUD?src=/program_offices/fair_housing_equal_opp/progdesc/title8.

U.S. Department of Labor. (1965, March). *The Negro family: The case for national action.* Washington, DC: Office of Policy Planning and Research. Retrieved from http://www.dol.gov/oasam/programs/history/webid-meynihan.htm.

Ussher, J. (1992). *Women's madness: Misogyny or mental illness.* Amherst: University of Massachusetts Press.

Vavrus, M. (2002). *Postfeminist news: Political women in media culture.* Albany: SUNY Press.

Venter, C., et al. (2001). The sequence of the human genome. *Science, 291,* 1304–1351.

Waldman, A. (2009). *Bad mother: A chronicle of maternal crimes, minor calamities, and occasional moments of grace.* New York: Doubleday.

Walker, A. (1983). *In search of our mother's gardens: Womanist prose.* New York: Harcourt Brace Jovanovich.

Wallace-Sanders, K. (2011). *Mammy: A century of race gender, and southern memory.* Ann Arbor: University of Michigan Press.

Walters, S. D. (1995). *Material girls: Making sense of feminist cultural theory.* Berkeley: University of California Press.

Walz, T. (2002). Crones, dirty old men, sexy seniors: Representations of the sexuality of older persons. *Journal of Aging and Identity, 7,* 99–112.

Warner, J. (2005). *Perfect madness: Motherhood in the age of anxiety.* New York: Riverhead Books.

Weedon, C. (1997). *Feminist practice and poststructuralist theory* (2nd ed.). Oxford: Blackwell.

Wenger, G. C., & Burholt, V. (2001). Differences over time in older people's relationships with children, grandchildren, nieces and nephews in rural North Wales. *Aging and Society, 21,* 567–590.

West, C. (2000). *The Cornel West reader.* New York: Basic Civitas Books.

West, C., & Zimmerman, D. H. (1987). Doing gender. *Gender and Society 1*(2), 125–151.

What is the best work of American fiction of the last 25 years? (2006, May 21). *New York Times*, Books section. Retrieved from http://www.nytimes.com/ref/books/fiction-25-years.html.

White, E. F. (2001). *Dark continent of our bodies: Black feminism and the politics of respectability.* Philadelphia: Temple University Press.

White House Council on Women and Girls (2011, March). *Women in America: Indicators of social and economic well-being.* Washington, DC: U.S. Department of Commerce and Executive Office of the President. Retrieved from http://www.whitehouse.gov/administration/eop/cwg/data-on-wome.

Wilkie, J. R., Ferree, M. M., & Ratcliff, K. S. (1998). Gender and fairness: Marital satisfaction in two-earner couples. *Journal of Marriage and the Family, 60*, 577–595.

Williams, P. (1994). Feeding off the past: The evolution of the television rerun. *Journal of Popular Film and Television, 21*, 162–176.

Wilson, C. (2008). Delinquent housekeeping: Transforming the regulations of keeping house. *Legacy, 25*, 299–310.

Witherspoon, C. (2011, May 7). Slideshow: theGrio's top 10 favorite fictional moms. thegrio.com. Retrieved from http://www.thegrio.com/entertainment/slideshow-thegrios-top-10-favorite-ficitonal-moms.php.

Wood, J. T. (2010a). The can-do discourse and young women's anticipations of future. *Women & Language, 33*, 103–107.

Wood, J. T. (2010b). *Gendered lives: Communication, gender and culture* (9th ed.). Belmont, CA: Wadsworth.

Wood, J. T., & Dow, B. J. (2010). The invisible politics of "choice" in the workplace: Naming the informal parenting support system. In S. Hayden & D. L. Obrien Hallstein (Eds.), *Contemplating maternity in an era of choice: Explorations into discourses of reproduction* (pp. 203–225). Lanham, MD: Lexington Press.

World Congress of Families. (1997–2005). *Doctrine for natural families.* Retrieved from http://www.worldcongress.org.

Wyatt, J. (1990). *Reconstructing desire: The role of the unconscious in women's reading and writing.* Chapel Hill: University of North Carolina Press.

Young, I. M. (2002). House and home: Feminist variations on a theme. C. L. Mui & J. S. Murphy (Eds.), *Gender struggles: Practical approaches to contemporary feminism* (314–346). Lanham, MD: Rowman & Littlefield.

Zille, D. (n.d.). *The* Andy Griffith Show *episode guide and FAQ.* Retrieved from http://www.zille.com/griffith/epguide.asp.

Zipes, J. (1989). Don't bet on the prince: Contemporary feminist fairy tales in North America and England. New York, NY: Routledge.

Index

237